610.71
FIE

Field, Shelly.

Ferguson career coach.

34630102005190

$39.95

DATE			

FERGUSON

CAREER COACH

MANAGING YOUR CAREER IN THE

Health Care
Industry

The Ferguson Career Coach Series

610.71
FIE

FERGUSON

CAREER COACH

MANAGING YOUR CAREER IN THE

Health Care Industry

Shelly Field

Ferguson
An imprint of Infobase Publishing

Ferguson Career Coach: Managing Your Career in the Health Care Industry

Ferguson
An imprint of Infobase Publishing, Inc.
132 West 31st Street
New York NY 10001

Library of Congress Cataloging-in-Publication Data

Field, Shelly.
  Ferguson career coach : managing your career in the health care industry / Shelly Field.
    p. ; cm. — (The Ferguson career coach series)
  Includes bibliographical references and index.
  ISBN-13: 978-0-8160-5364-3 (hardcover : alk. paper)
  ISBN-10: 0-8160-5364-2 (hardcover : alk. paper)
1. Medicine—Vocational guidance—United States. 2. Medical personnel—Vocational guidance—United States. I. Title. II. Title: Managing you career in the health care industry. III. Series.
  [DNLM: 1. Health Occupations—United States. 2. Vocational Guidance—United States. W 21 F456f 2008]
  R690.F55 2008
  610.71'173—dc22   2007036656

Ferguson books are available at special discounts when purchased in bulk quantities for businesses, associations, institutions, or sales promotions. Please call our Special Sales Department in New York at (212) 967-8800 or (800) 322-8755.

You can find Ferguson on the World Wide Web at http://www.fergpubco.com

Text design by Kerry Casey
Cover design by Takeshi Takahashi

Printed in the United States of America

VB Hermitage 10 9 8 7 6 5 4 3 2 1

This book is printed on acid-free paper and contains 30% post-consumer recycled content.

Disclaimer: The examples and practices described in this book are based on the author's experience as a professional career coach. No guarantee of success for individuals who follow them is stated or implied. Readers should bear in mind that techniques described might be inappropriate in some professional settings, and that changes in industry trends, practices, and technology may affect the activities discussed here. The author and publisher bear no responsibility for the outcome of any reader's use of the information and advice provided herein.

Contents

1

INTRODUCING YOUR CAREER COACH

Have you made the decision that you want to work in the health care industry? Great! You've just chosen to work in one of the fastest-growing industries in the world.

Do you have a strong desire to help others? A genuine concern for their health and welfare? Can you deal with people who may be in stressful situations? Do you want to make a difference?

If so, you've chosen the right field. Depending on the path you choose within the health care industry, your career can be financially rewarding, fun, and challenging. But most of all, working in the health care industry means that you will often be in a position to make a difference in people's lives.

Some parts of the industry are easier to enter. Some are more competitive. Can you make it?

I'm betting you can, and if you let me, I want to help you get where you want to be. Whether you've just decided that you want to be in the health care industry, it's been your dream for some time, or you're in the industry and you want to move up the career ladder, this book is for you. Whether you want to work in patient care, medicine, research, business, administration, teaching, or any other area of health care, this book can be your guide to success.

I have been where you are. I know what it's like to want to have the career of your dreams so badly you can taste it. I know what it's like to want to experience success. I know what it's like to have a dream.

It doesn't matter if your dream is exactly like my dream or my dream is like yours. It doesn't even really matter exactly what you want to do. What matters is that if you have a dream—whatever it is—you can find a way to attain it.

I grew up in a family surrounded by the health care industry. My grandfather was a doctor, one of the early homeopathic physicians. My cousin became a doctor and is now the dean of a medical school. My great grandfather and an uncle were both pharmacists.

But my real connection to the health care industry came from my immediate family. My parents were owners of a public relations and marketing firm that handled hospitals, health care facilities, and doctors, among other clients. Being the workaholics they were, conversations at every meal quite naturally were peppered with "at the hospital today" this or "at the hospital today" that. When that wasn't happening, conversations centered on campaign ideas for clients, fund-raising, new doctors, new medical tests, equipment at the hospital, and so on.

At a time when mothers stayed home to take care of their children, my parents decided to build a new office and attach it to our home so my mom could work full time yet always be there for us. It was a good solution. We never came home to an empty house and both my parents were always just an open door away.

The only problem with an office attached to a home is that the office never really closes. I grew up thinking everyone's parents went back to work after dinner and that "hospital talk" was the norm. (I also grew up thinking that extension 2105, one of the hospital's administration extensions, was a relative, but that's another story.)

Because there was so much "hospital talk," I grew up hearing about the way hospitals were marketed, publicized, and advertised; spin control; physician recruitment; new medical tests; and medical procedures. I learned about union negotiations, strikes, and dealing with the press. I learned about volunteers and different departments within hospitals. I saw the searches for new executive directors and learned about not-for-profits and boards of directors. I saw new doctors come and establish practices and older doctors retire. And I saw how capital campaigns were developed, implemented, and executed.

My parents worked together, and since their company handled five or six different health care facilities, I was surrounded. My parents, in addition, were founders of the American Foundation for Alternative Health, an organization that gathered information on alternative therapies.

My parents seemed to love what they did and always made it seem exciting. It wasn't surprising that with the office just a door away, growing up we naturally wanted to "help." I remember collating press kits, stapling press releases, and stuffing envelopes as a child. As I got older, I remember answering phones, helping with fund-raisers, proofing press releases, writing press releases, and laying out newsletters.

At some time during this period, my mom was put on staff at one of the hospitals as the director of marketing, public relations, fund-raising, and development. (My father, president of their jointly owned public relations company, continued handling health care clients on a consulting basis.)

Although corporate staff members usually employed by a hospital work out of an office in that facility, somehow it was decided that my mom would continue to work out of her office.

I remember thinking how lucky my parents were to have such exciting jobs and how lucky I was to be able to "help." I remember them getting ready for a visit by President Lyndon Johnson for a hospital dedication; meeting him, shaking his hand, and having him autograph a Texas-style hat. I remember them doing the publicity for a fund-raiser concert by David Cassidy, the hottest teen pop superstar at the time. I remember them coordinating and publicizing a hospital fund-raiser starring Bob Hope and going to the show. I even remember my parents hopping on a helicopter to go to the original Woodstock festival, where their hospital was coordinating the emergency care for the 500,000 people who came to our community of Woodstock, New York. (Being that I did *not* work for the hospital, I never got to the Woodstock festival, but that is another story too.)

Is the health care industry always glamorous? Is it always exciting? Of course not, but excitement, like beauty, is in the eye of the beholder.

Who wouldn't think that saving someone's life was exciting? Who wouldn't think it was exciting to bring a new life into the world? Who wouldn't think it was exciting to come up with the next cure for cancer?

It also is exciting to see someone's face change when they hear they have a clean bill of health or get a treatment that makes them feel better, or to hear them tell you that you've made their life easier with your compassion, touch, or smile.

It's exciting for a new doctor to build a successful practice, for a physical therapist to see a patient take a step, and for a human resources director to hire the best employees possible. Excitement, in reality, is living your dream.

Was working in the health care industry my dream? While I would love to tell you it was, at the time I had another dream. Although it wasn't in the health care industry, I'm going to share it with you for a number of reasons.

Why? To begin with, I want to illustrate that dreams can come true. I want to show you how perseverance in your career (or in anything else, for that matter) can help you achieve your dreams and goals.

Furthermore, you might find it interesting to see how sometimes things you do in your career are stepping-stones to the career of your dreams. I've done a lot of things in my life in pursuing *my* dreams. Some worked out and some didn't. What I can say, however, is that I will never have to look back and say, I wish I had done this or that, because when I wanted to try something I always did.

Do I work in health care now? While I do a lot of things, part of my career *is* in the periphery of the health care industry. As a stress management specialist, I teach people how to deal with stress, how to manage stress, and how to reduce stress. I teach people how to use humor to feel better and how to find ways to laugh. But keep in mind, this segment of my career came

after I had done a lot of other things and lived a lot of dreams.

It's important to remember that dreams can change, but as long as you keep moving toward your goals, you're on the right road.

With that in mind, here's my story. For as long as I can remember, I wanted to be in the music industry, probably more than anything else in the world. I struggled to get in. Could I find anyone to help? No. Did I know anyone in the business? No. Did I live in one of the music capitals? No. The only thing I had going for me was a burning desire to be in the industry and the knowledge that I wasn't going to quit until it happened.

At the time I was trying to enter the industry, I wished there was a book to give me advice on how to move ahead, guide me toward my goals, and give me insider tips. Unfortunately, there wasn't. I wished that I had a mentor or a coach or someone who really knew what I should be doing and could tell me what it was. Unfortunately, I didn't have that either.

Did anyone ever help me? It wasn't that no one wanted to help, but most of the people in my network just didn't have a clue about the music industry. Did they know that the music industry was a multibillion-dollar business? Did they know that it offered countless opportunities? It really didn't matter, because no one I knew could give me an edge on getting in anyway.

A couple of times I did run into some music industry professionals who tried to help. In one instance, a few months after I had started job hunting, I finally landed an interview at a large booking agency. I arrived for my appointment and sat waiting for the owner of the agency to meet me. I sat and sat and sat.

A recording artist who was a client of the agency walked over to me after his meeting with the agent and asked how long I had been there. "Close to three hours," I replied. My appointment was for 1 P.M. and it was almost 4 P.M. "What are you here for?" he asked. "I want to be in the music industry," was my answer. "I want to be a tour manager."

"Someday," he said, "you'll make it and this joker [the agency owner] will want something from you and you can make *him* wait. Mark my words, it will happen." He then stuck his head inside the agency owner's door and said, "This woman has been sitting out here for hours, bring her in already." As I walked into the office, I had a glimmer of hope. It was short lived, but it was hope just the same.

The agency owner was very nice. During our meeting he told me something to the effect of, "If I ever need someone with your skills and talents, I'll be glad to give you a call. Keep plugging away." In other words, thanks for coming in. I talked to you, now please leave. Don't call me, I'll call you.

He then explained in a hushed voice that "Anyway, you know how it is. Most managers don't want *girls* on the road with their acts." Not only was I being rejected because of my skills and talents, but now it was because I was a *girl*. (Because my name is Shelly, evidently many people incorrectly assumed I was male instead of female when their secretaries were setting up appointments. The good news is that this got me into a lot of places I probably wouldn't have had a chance to get into. The bad news is that once I got there, they realized I was not a man.)

I smiled, thanked the agent for meeting with me, and left wondering if I would ever get a job doing what I wanted. Was it sexual discrimination? Probably, but in reality the agent was just telling me the way it was at that time. He actual-

Tip from the Top

During that interview, I learned two important lessons. One, use what you have to get your foot in the door. If someone thought I was a man because of my name, well, my idea was not to correct them *until* I got in the door. At least that way I could have a chance at selling myself.

The second lesson is choose your battles wisely. Had I complained about sexual discrimination at the point, I might have won the battle, but I would have lost the war.

ly believed he was being nice. Was it worth complaining about? I didn't think so. I was new to the industry, and I wasn't about to make waves *before* I even got in. The problem was that I just couldn't find a way to get in.

On another occasion, I met a road manager at a concert and told him about how I wanted to be a tour manager. He told me he knew how hard it was to get into the industry, so he was going to help me. "Call me on Monday," he told me Saturday. I did. "I'm working on it," he said. "Call me Wednesday." On Wednesday he said, "Call me Friday." This went on for a couple of weeks before I realized that while he was trying to be nice, he really wasn't going to do anything for me.

I decided that if I were ever lucky enough to break into the music industry, I would help as many people as I possibly could who ever wanted a job doing *anything* to fulfill their dream. I wasn't sure when I'd make it, but I knew I would get there eventually.

While like many others I dreamed about standing on a stage in front of thousands of adoring fans singing my number-one song, in reality, I knew that was not where my real talent was. I knew, though, that I did have the talent to make it on the business end of the industry.

I did all the traditional things to try to get a job. I sent my resume, I searched out employment agencies that specialized in the music industry, I made cold calls, and I read the classifieds.

And guess what? I still couldn't land a job. Imagine that? A college degree and a burning desire still couldn't get me the job I wanted. I had some offers, but they weren't offers to work in the music industry. I had offers for jobs as a social worker, a teacher, a newspaper reporter, and a number of other positions I have since forgotten. Were any of these jobs I wanted? No! I wanted to work in the music business, period. End of story.

As many of you might experience when you share your dreams, I had people telling me I was pipe dreaming. "The music industry," I was told, "is for *the other people. You know, the lucky ones.*" I was also told consistently how difficult the music industry was to get into and, once in, how difficult it was to succeed. In essence, I was being told not to get my hopes up.

Want to hear the good news? I eventually did get into the industry. I had to "think outside of the box" to get there, but the important thing was I found a way to get in. Want to hear some more good news? If I could find a way to break into the industry of my dreams, you can find a way to break into the industry of your dreams too! As a matter of fact, not only can you get in, but you can succeed.

Remember when I said that if I got in to the music business, I'd help every single person who ever wanted a job doing anything? Well, you want to work in the health care industry and I want to help you get there. I want to help you succeed. And I want to help you live your dreams.

Tip from the Coach

As big as the world is, it really is small. Always leave a good impression. Remember what the recording artist at the booking agency told me? A number of years after I broke into the music industry, his words actually did come true. At the time, I was working on a project booking the talent for a big music festival overseas, and the booking agent heard about it. He put in a call to me to see if I'd consider using his talent for the show. "Hi, Shelly, it's Dave. It's been a long time," said the voice mail. "I heard you were booking a new show and wanted to talk to you about having some of my acts appearing on the show. Give me a call." As soon as I heard his name, the words of that recording artist came flooding back into my mind. This was a true "mark my words" moment.

I was busy, so I couldn't call him right away. He kept calling back. He really wanted his acts on the show. I finally took his call and told him we'd get back to him. He must have called 25 times in a two-day period to see if we'd made up our mind. He finally said, "How long do you expect me to wait?"

I then reminded him of the day I sat in his office and waited and waited for him to see me. He, of course, didn't even remember the moment, but to his credit, he apologized profusely and promised never to have me wait again. I accepted his apology and told him he'd only have to wait . . . a little bit longer.

I'm a career expert and have written numerous books on a wide array of different career-oriented subjects. I give seminars, presentations, and workshops around the country on entering and succeeding in the career of your dreams. I'm a personal coach and stress management specialist to people in various walks of life, including celebrities, corporate executives, and others in various industries. Unfortunately, much as I wish I could, I can't be there in person for each and every one of you. So, through the pages of this book, I'm going to be your personal coach, your cheerleader, and your inside source not only to finding your dream career but getting into and succeeding in the health care industry as well.

A Personal Coach—What's That?

The actual job title of "personal coach" is relatively new, but coaches are not. Athletes and others in the sports industry have always used coaches to help improve their game and performance. Over the past few years, coaches have sprung up in many other fields as well.

There are those who coach people toward better fitness or nutrition, vocal coaches to help people improve their voices, acting coaches to help people with acting skills, and etiquette coaches to help people learn how to act in every situation. There are parenting coaches to help people parent better, retirement coaches to help people be successful in retirement, and time management coaches to help people better manage their time.

There are stress management coaches to help people better manage their stress; executive business coaches to help catapult people to the top; life coaches to help people attain a happier, more satisfying life; and career coaches to help people create a great career. Personal coaches often help people become more successful and satisfied in a combination of areas.

"I don't understand," you might be saying. "Exactly what does a coach do and what can he or she do for me?" Well, there are a number of things.

A coach can help you find your way to success faster. He or she can help motivate you, help you find what really makes you happy,

get you on track, and help you focus your energies on what you really want to do. Unlike some family and friends, coaches aren't judgmental. You, therefore, have the ability to freely explore ideas with your coach without fear of being rejected. Instead of accepting your self-imposed limitations, coaches encourage you to reach to your full potential and improve your performance.

Coaches are objective, and one of the important things they can do for you is point out things that you might not see yourself. Most of all, a coach helps you find the best in you and then shows you ways to bring it out. This, in turn, will make you more successful.

As your coach, what do I hope to do for you? I want to help you find your passion and then help you go after it. If being in some area of the health care industry is what you want, I want you to get in and I want you to be successful.

If you want to be on the business or administrative end of the industry, I'm going to help you find ways to get in. If you're already in, we'll work on ways to help you climb the career ladder to your dream position. Is your career aspiration to be in patient care? Do you want to be a physician, nurse, dentist, or physician assistant? Do you want to be a technologist or technician? A researcher? A teacher or instructor? Then we'll work on finding ways to catapult you to the top there too.

Look at me as your personal cheerleader, and look at this book as your guide. I want you to succeed and will do as much as possible to make that happen. No matter what anyone tells you, it is possible not only to get the job of your dreams in the health care industry but to succeed at levels higher than you dare to dream. Thousands of people have done so and now you can be one of them.

Did you ever notice that some people just seem to attract success? They seem to get all the breaks, are always at the right place at the right time, and have what you want? It's not that you're jealous, but you just want to get a piece of the pie.

"They're so lucky," you say. Well, here's the deal: You can be that lucky too. Want to know why? While a little bit of luck is always helpful, it's not just chance. Some people work to attract success. They work to get what they want. They follow a plan, keep a positive attitude, and know that they're worthy of the prize. Others just wait for success to come, and when all you do is wait, success often just passes you by.

The good news here is that you can be one of the lucky ones who attract success if you take the right steps. This book will give you some of the keys to control your destiny; it will hand you the keys to success in your career and your life.

Through the pages of this book, you'll find the answers to many of your questions about a career in the health care industry. You'll get the inside scoop on how the industry works, key employment issues, and finding opportunities.

You'll find insider tips, tricks, and techniques that have worked for others who have succeeded in the industry. You'll discover secrets to help get you in the door and up the ladder of success, as well as the lowdown on things others wish they had known when they were first beginning their quest for success.

If you haven't attended any of my career seminars, my workshops on climbing the career ladder and succeeding in your dream career, my stress management seminars, or any of the other presentations I offer, you will get the benefit of being there. If you have attended one, here is the book you've been asking for!

Change Your Thinking, Change Your Life

Sometimes, the first step in getting what you want is just changing the way you think. Did you know that if you think you don't deserve something, you usually don't get it? Did you know that if you think you aren't good enough, neither will anyone else? Did you know that if you think you deserve something, you have a much better chance of getting it? Or that if you think you are good enough, your confidence will shine through?

When you have confidence in yourself, you start to find ways to get what you want, and guess what? You succeed!

And while changing your thinking can change your life, this book is not just about a positive attitude. It's a book of actions you can take.

While a positive attitude is always helpful in order to succeed in whatever part of the industry you're interested in pursuing, you need to take positive actions, too.

If all it took for you to be successful was for me to tell you what you needed to do or even do it for you, I would. I love what I do and truly want to help everyone live their dream too. Unfortunately, that's not the way it works.

Here's the reality of the situation: I can only offer advice, suggestions, and tell you what you need to do. You have to do the rest. Talking about what you can do or should do is fine, but without your taking action, it's difficult to get where you want to go.

This is your chance to finally get what you want. You've already taken one positive step toward getting your dream career simply by picking up this book. As you read through the various sections, you'll find other actions to take that will help get you closer to a great career, whether you choose medicine, patient care, pharmaceuticals, research, teaching, business, administration, or any other segment of the health care industry.

As you read through the book, we'll talk about creating your own personal action plan. This plan can help you focus on exactly what you want and then show you the actions needed to get it.

Your personal action plan is a checklist of sorts. Done correctly, it can be one of the main keys to your career success. It will put you in the driver's seat and give you an edge over others who haven't prepared a plan themselves.

We'll also discuss putting together a number of different kinds of journals to help you be more successful in your career and life. For example, one of the problems many people experience when they're trying to get a new job, move up the career ladder, or accomplish a goal is that they often start feeling as though they aren't accomplishing anything. A career journal is a handy tool to help you track exactly what you've done to accomplish your goals. Once that is in place, you know what else needs to be done.

Is This the Right Career for Me?

Unsure about exactly what you want to do in the health care industry? As you read through the book, you'll get some ideas.

"But what if I'm already working at a job in another industry?" you ask. "Is it too late? Am I stuck there forever? Is it too late to get into the health care industry?"

Here's the deal: It is never too late to change careers, and going after something you're passionate about can drastically improve your quality of life.

Thousands of people stay in jobs because it's easier than going after what they want. You don't have to be one of them.

> ### Tip from the Coach
> Don't procrastinate. Every day you wait to get the career you are passionate about is another day you're not living your dream. Start today!

We all know people who are in jobs or careers that they don't love. They get up every day waiting for the workweek to be over. They go through the day, waiting for it to be over. They waste their lives waiting and waiting. Is this the life you want to lead? Probably not.

You now have the opportunity to get what you want. Are you ready to go after it? I'm hoping you are.

If the health care industry is where you want to work, there are countless opportunities. In addition to the traditional ones most people think of, there is an array of others for you to explore. No matter what your skills or talents, you can almost always find a way to parlay them into your career in the health care industry.

"Really?" you ask. "What if I'm an artist?" "What if I work in a bank?" "What if I'm a writer? "What if I'm a musician?" What do any of those have to do with the health care industry?

Here's the good news. If you think in a creative manner, you probably can use any of your skills to get you into the health care industry.

Artists who want to work directly with patients, for example, may become art therapists. Former bankers may work as geriatric care managers. Writers may find positions as medical writers. Musicians might become music therapists.

Don't be afraid to put your dreams together.

"Like what?" you ask.

Let's say you're a nurse and you also like the music business. You might be able to create a job going on the road with touring artists.

"Really?" you ask.

Definitely. A number of years ago, I was on a radio call-in show talking about getting into the music industry. A woman called and said, "I really want to work in the music business."

"What do you do now?" I asked.

"I'm a nurse," she replied.

"Use your skills," I told her.

"No," she said. "You didn't hear me. I'm a nurse."

"I heard you," I said. "Here's an idea. Why don't you put a small ad in the trades? There might be some touring acts dealing with drug rehab or medical issues who need a nurse on the road with them."

Four months later, she called me again. She had placed an ad in the trade journals and didn't get a response. She had, however, won tickets from a local radio station to a concert and "meet and greet" event for a major recording act appearing in her area. She went and enjoyed the show and met the act. In a conversation with the group's road manager, she coincidentally told him how excited she was to meet the group and happened to mention that she had just placed an ad in the trades for going on the road but that it hadn't brought in a response. A couple of weeks later, she got a call from the group's management asking if she was interested in going on the road with the group to handle first aid and minor medical needs. They located her number by calling the local radio station that had sponsored the contest she had won. While being in the right place at the right time certainly helped, had she not "thought outside of the box," she might not have been living her dream.

While your dream might not be the same as that woman's, remember this: She is no different from you. If you get creative and think outside of the box, you can create a great career too!

Words from the Wise

Always carry business cards with your phone number and other contact information. Make it easy for people to find you when an opportunity presents itself.

How to Use This Book to Help You in the Health Care Industry

Ideally, I would love for you to read this book from beginning to end, but I know from experience that that's probably not the way it's going to happen. You might browse the contents and look for something that can help you *now*, you might see a subject that catches your eye, or you might be looking for an area of the book that solves a particular problem.

For this reason, as you read the book, you might see what appears to be some duplication of information. In this manner, I can be assured that when I suggest something that may be helpful to you in a certain area, you will get all the information you need, even if you haven't read a prior section.

You should be aware that even if you're interested in a career in medicine, knowing about the business end of health care will be helpful to succeeding in your career.

Conversely, if your career aspirations are in the business or administrative segment of the health care industry, understanding other parts of the industry will be useful as well.

You might have heard the saying, "Knowledge is power." This is true. The more you know about the health care industry and how it works, the better your chances are of succeeding. This book is full of information to help you learn everything you need to know about the industry and how it works. I'm betting that you will refer to information in this book long after you've attained success.

As you read through the various sections, you'll find a variety of ideas to help you succeed. Keep in mind that every idea might not work in every situation and for every person. The goal is to keep trying things until one of them works. Use the book as a springboard to get you started. Just because something is not written here doesn't mean that it's not a good idea. Brainstorm to find solutions to barriers you might encounter in your career.

My job is to lead you on your journey to success in the health care industry. Along the way, you'll find exercises, tasks, and assignments that will help get you where you want to be faster. No one is going to be standing over your shoulder to make you do these tasks. You alone can make the decision regarding the amount of time and work you want to put into your career. While no one can guarantee you success, what you should know is that the more you put into your career, the better your chances of having the success you probably are dreaming about.

Are you worth the time and effort? I think you are! Is a career in the health care industry worth it? It's a huge industry and growing every day. If you have the passion and desire to work in this industry, it can be one of the best industries in the world in which to work. Aside from the opportunity to make a great living and fulfill your dreams, you have the opportunity to influence the health and lives of others.

No matter what level you're currently at in your career in the health care industry and in whatever capacity, this book is for you. You might not need every section or every page, but I can guarantee that parts of this book can help you.

Whether you're just starting out in your career as an intern or administrative assistant, you're an up-and-coming health care executive, or you're just starting medical school, this book can help you experience more success in your career and help you have a more satisfying and stress-free life.

A Sampling of What This Book Covers

This informative guide to success in the health care industry is written in a friendly, easy-to-read style. Let it be your everyday guide to success. Want to know how a segment of the health care industry works? Want to learn how to focus on what you really want to do? Check out the book!

Want to learn how to plan and prepare for your dream career? Do you want to focus on search strategies especially for the health care industry? How about tips for making those important industry contacts? Need some ideas on how to network? How about how to create the ideal health care–oriented resume or cover letter? Check out the book!

Do you need to know how to develop your action plan? Do you want to get your portfolio together? Want to know what business cards can do for you and your career? Check out the book!

Want to learn how to get your foot in the door? How about checking out tried-and-true methods to get people to call you back? Do you want to learn the best way to market yourself and why it's so important? Do you want to learn how to succeed in the workplace, deal with workplace politics, keep an eye out for opportunities, and climb the career ladder? You know what to do: Check out the book!

Do you want some tips on getting into med school? Want to know how to succeed as a physician? You've got it. You need to read this book.

Do you need important contact information so you can move your career forward? Check out the listings of important organization, unions, and associations. Want some Web sites to get you started looking for a great career? Check out Appendix II of the book.

Although this book won't teach you how to perform an operation or medical procedure, run a hospital, or teach a student how to be a better nurse, it will help you find ways to garner success wherever your passion lies.

If you dream of not only working in the health care industry but having a successful career and don't know how to make that dream a reality, this book is for you. Have fun reading it. Know that if your heart is in it, you can achieve anything.

Now let's get started.

2

FOCUSING ON A GREAT CAREER IN HEALTH CARE

Focusing on What You Really Want to Do

Do you wake up every morning dreading going to work? Do you ask yourself, "What should I be?" How about, "What should I do for the rest of my life?"

Do you know what you want to do? Do you daydream about working in the health care industry? Do you wonder how you're going to get in? Do you wonder how you can succeed?

Unless you're independently wealthy or just won the megamillion-dollar lottery, you, like most people, have to work. Just in case you're wondering, life is not supposed to be miserable. Neither is your job.

Life is supposed to have a purpose. That purpose is not sleeping, getting up, going to a job that you don't particularly care about, coming home, cooking dinner, and watching TV, only to do it all over again the next day.

To be happy and fulfilled, you need to enjoy life. You need to do things that give you pleasure. As a good part of your life is spent working, the trick is to find a career that you love and that you're passionate about—the career of your dreams.

This is not something everyone does. Many people just fall into a career without thinking about what it will entail ahead of time. Someone may need a job, hear of an opening, answer an ad, and then go for it without thinking about the consequences of working at something for which he or she really has no passion. Once hired, either it's difficult to give up the money, or just too hard to start job hunting again, or they don't know what else to do, so they stay. They wind up with a career that is okay but one they're not really passionate about.

Then there are the other people. The ones who have jobs they love, the lucky people. You've seen them. They're the people who have the jobs and life you wish you had.

Have you noticed that people who love their jobs are usually successful not only in their ca-

---

> ### ⭐ Tip from the Coach
> Okay is just that: It's okay. Just so you know, you don't want just okay; you don't want to settle; you want *great*! That's what you deserve, and that's what you should go after.

18

reer but in other aspects of life as well? They almost seem to have an aura around them of success, happiness, and prosperity. Do you want to be one of them? You can!

Finding a career that you want and love is challenging but possible. You are in a better position than most people. If you're reading this book, you've probably at least zeroed in on a career path. You've likely decided that one of the segments of the health care industry is what you are passionate about. Now all you have to do is determine exactly what you want to do in the industry.

What's your dream career? What do you really want to do? This is an important question to ask yourself. Once you know the answer, you can work toward achieving your goal.

If someone asks you right now what you really want to do, can you answer the question? Okay, one, two, three: "What do you want to do with your life?"

If you're saying, "Uh, um, well . . . What I really want to do is . . . well, it's hard to explain," then it's time to focus on the subject. Sometimes the easiest way to figure out what you want to do is to focus on what you don't want to do.

Most people can easily answer what they don't want to do. "I don't want to be a teacher. I don't want to work in a factory. I don't want to work in a store. I don't want to sell. I don't want to work with numbers," and the list goes on. The problem is that just saying what you don't like or don't want to do doesn't necessarily get you what you want to do. You can, however, use this information to your advantage.

It may seem simple, but sometimes just looking at a list of what you don't like will help you see more clearly what you do like.

Sit down with a sheet of paper or fill in the "Things I Don't Want to Do" worksheet and make a list of work-related things you don't like

to do. Remember that this list is really just for you. While you can show it to someone if you want, no one else really has to see it, so try to be honest with yourself.

Here's an example to get you started. When you make your list, add your personal likes and dislikes.

- ◎ I hate the idea of being cooped up in an office all day.
- ◎ I hate the idea of having to work with numbers.
- ◎ I don't want to have to commute for an hour each way every day.
- ◎ I don't like working in sales.
- ◎ I don't like working directly in patient care.
- ◎ I'm afraid to work near sick people.
- ◎ I don't like just being one of the crowd.
- ◎ I don't like making decisions.
- ◎ I don't like getting up early in the morning to go to work.
- ◎ I don't want to work in retail sales.
- ◎ I don't want to have to travel for work.
- ◎ I don't like doing the same thing day after day.
- ◎ I don't like being in charge.
- ◎ I don't like living in a big city.
- ◎ I don't like taking risks.
- ◎ I don't like working under constant pressure.
- ◎ I don't like not knowing where my next paycheck is coming from.
- ◎ I don't like being under constant deadlines.
- ◎ I don't like having a boss working right on top of me.
- ◎ I don't like someone telling me what to do every minute of the day.
- ◎ I don't like working where I don't make a difference.

Things I Don't Want to Do

We now know what you don't like. Use this list as a starting point to see what you do like. If you look closely, you'll find that the things you enjoy are the opposite of the things you don't want to do.

Here are some examples to get you started. You might make another list as well as using the "Things I Enjoy Doing" worksheet on the next page. Remember that the reason you're writing everything down is so you can look at it, remember it, and focus on getting exactly what you want.

◎ I hate the idea of being cooped up in an office all day.
  ▫ But I'd really like to work where I could move around a facility or even on the road.
◎ I hate the idea of having to work with numbers.
  ▫ But I really like writing and creating with words. Perhaps I would enjoy a career as a publicist or maybe a medical writer.
◎ I don't want to have to commute to work for an hour each way every day.
  ▫ But if I find a job that I love, perhaps I can find an apartment close by.
◎ I don't like to be in the limelight.
  ▫ But I really like supporting others who are there. I think I would like helping others become successful.
◎ I don't like just being one of the crowd.
  ▫ But I love being the one to make a difference. I think I would love working with patients on a one-on-one basis.
◎ I don't like making decisions.
  ▫ I like working in a situation where I'm given direction.

◎ I don't like getting up early in the morning to go to work.
  ▫ Maybe I can find a job where I work the night shift.
◎ I don't want to work in retail sales.
  ▫ But I'm really good at selling. I think I might be interested in selling pharmaceuticals or even medical equipment.
◎ I don't like working directly in patient care.
  ▫ But I really want to work in the health care industry. Maybe I'll look for a job in health care administration.

As you begin thinking about things you might enjoy and like doing, you'll begin coming up with more and more.

◎ I really enjoy working directly with people and want to work in patient care in some way.
◎ Ever since a physical therapist helped me when I broke my leg, I've wanted a career in that field. I love seeing people make progress.
◎ I love nursing and would love to teach others nursing skills.
◎ I like knowing that every day will be different.
◎ I like learning new things.
◎ I like making a difference in other people's lives.
◎ I like traveling for work. It gives me the opportunity to meet new people and see new things.
◎ I like knowing that at the end of my shift, my day is over.
◎ I want a career where I know I can constantly grow in my career area.

Things I Enjoy Doing

_____

_____

_____

_____

_____

_____

_____

_____

_____

_____

_____

_____

_____

_____

_____

As you can see, once you've determined what you don't like doing, it's much easier to get ideas on what you'd like to do. It's kind of like brainstorming with yourself.

You probably know some people who don't like their job. There are tons of people in this world who don't like what they do or are dissatisfied with their career. The good news is you don't have to be one of them.

You and you alone are in charge of your career. Not your mother, father, sister, brother, girlfriend, boyfriend, spouse, or best friend. Others can care, others can help, and others can offer you advice, but in essence, you need to be in control. This means that the path you take for your career is largely determined by the choices you make.

The fastest way to get the career you want is by making the choice to take actions now and going after it! You can have a career you love and you can have it in the health care industry. And when you're doing something you love, you'll be on the road not only to a great career but a satisfied and fulfilled life.

The next chapter will discuss how to develop your career plan. This plan will be your road map to success. It will be full of actions you can do not only to get the career in the health care industry you want but succeed in it as well. Before you get too involved in the plan, however, you need to zero in on exactly what you want your career to be.

Tip from the Coach

If you want some specific ideas of careers in health care, you might want to check out another of my books, *Career Opportunities In Health Care*.

Words from the Wise

If you give up your dream because you think you are too old or it's too late to start, the success you are wishing for might never come your way.

At this point you might be in a number of different employment situations. You might still be in school planning your career, just out of school beginning your career, or in a job that you don't really care for. You might be in your late teens, 20s, 30s, 40s, 50s, or even older.

"Older? Did you say older?" you ask. "Can I start a career in the health care industry even if I'm older?"

Yes. If you have a dream, it is never too late not only to pursue it but to succeed. And it doesn't matter what segment of the health care industry you're interested in.

Many people decide to go into health care administration, nursing, and teaching as second careers. There are others who after working in research or teaching become doctors. The point I'm making is that it's never too late to go after your dreams.

Okay, you've done some research on the health care industry and you've decided that this industry is the one in which you want to work, but do you know what your dream career is?

There are hundreds of exciting career choices, whether you want to be in patient care, pharmaceuticals, technology, teaching, or in the business or administrative segments of the industry. It's up to you to decide which one you want to pursue.

So let's focus for a bit on exactly what you want to do.

What's Your Dream?

I bet that you have an idea of what your dream job is, and I bet that you have an idea of what it should be like. I'm also betting that you don't have that job yet, or if you do, you're not at the level you want to be. So what can we do to make that dream a reality?

One of the challenges many people often have in getting their dream job is that they just don't think they deserve it. They feel that dream jobs are something many people talk about and wish they had but just don't. Many people think that dream jobs are for the lucky ones.

Well, I'm here to tell you that you are the lucky one. You can get your dream job, a job you'll love, and it can be in the health care industry!

If I had a magic wand and could get you any job you wanted, what would it be? Do you want to be a doctor? A nurse? A physician assistant? What about a nurse-midwife helping women deliver their children?

Do you want to work in research? Do you want to be the one who finds the cure for cancer, muscular dystrophy, or the common cold? Do you want to be a pharmacist? What about a technician or a technologist?

Do you want to help treat patients with cancer? Prepare them for treatment? Help calm their fears?

Is it your dream to work with the elderly? Or is your dream to work with children? The choice is yours.

Do you want to be the administrator of a large, prestigious hospital? What about the director of marketing or public relations at a hospital? Is it your dream to work in fund-raising and development, perhaps helping to raise enough funds to build a brand new health care facility? What about becoming the executive director of a health care association? The possibilities are endless.

Do you want to be a patient advocate? Have a career in medical records? Work in pharmaceutical sales? What about medical equipment sales? It's all up to you.

Have you always dreamed of teaching elementary or secondary school students about health care? Maybe your dream is to teach students how to be great nurses. Is it your dream to teach doctors how to be great doctors? Is your goal to be the dean of a medical school? It can all happen if you get the education and experience you need for the job.

Do you want to be a television medical correspondent? A medical illustrator? A medical writer? Your dream job can be a reality if you prepare.

Not sure what you want to do? Then read on!

Determining what you really want to do is not always easy. Take some time to think about it. Throughout this process, try to be as honest with yourself as possible. Otherwise, you stand the chance of not going after the career you really want.

Let's get started with another writing exercise. While you might think these are a pain now, if you follow through, you will find it easier to attain your dream.

Get a pad of paper and a pen and find a place where you can get comfortable. Maybe it's your living room chair. Perhaps it's your couch or even your bed. Now all you have to do is sit down and

---

⭐ Tip from the Coach

What are your dreams? Are you ready to turn them into reality? You increase your chances of success if you have a deep belief in yourself, your vision, and your ideas.

Words from the Wise

The only thing we have to fear is fear itself.

—Franklin Delano Roosevelt

daydream for a bit about what you wish you could be and what you wish you were doing.

"Why daydream?" you ask.

When you daydream, your thinking becomes freer. You stop thinking about what you *can't* do and start thinking about what you *can* do. What is your dream? What is your passion? What do you really want to do? Admit it now or forever hold your peace!

Many people are embarrassed to admit when they want something, because if they don't get it, they fear looking stupid. They worry that people are going to talk badly about them or call them a failure. Is this what you worry about? Do you really want to be a doctor, but you're afraid you'll fail? Is your dream to be a pharmacist, but you don't think you'll make it? Have you always wanted to be a medical correspondent, but you're worried nobody will want your opinion?

First of all, don't ever let fear of failure stop you from going after something you want. While no one can guarantee you success, know that the more you put into your career, the better your chances of having the success you are dreaming of.

One thing you never want to do is get to the end of your life and say with regret, "I wish I had done this" or "I wish I had done that." Will you get each and every thing you want? I'd like to say a definitive "yes," but that probably wouldn't be true.

The truth of the matter is you might not succeed at everything. But, and this is a major *but*, even if you fail, when you try to do something, it usually is a stepping-stone to something

else. And that something else can be the turning point in your career.

"How so?" you ask. "What do you mean?"

Later in the book, I'll share my story of doing stand-up comedy. The reason I bring it up here is to illustrate that while I certainly didn't turn into a megastar stand-up comedian, performing comedy was certainly a major stepping-stone for me to do other things I wanted to accomplish in my career. Had I not done stand-up, I probably would never have ended up doing stress management or even come up with the idea that I wanted to do something in that area.

Had I been too scared to try it or not wanted to take the risk for fear I would fail, I would have missed out on important opportunities that helped shape my career. I also would have always looked back and said, "I wish I had."

Your dreams are probably totally different from mine. That's okay. What you need to learn from the story is that taking risks and pursuing your dreams can lead to wonderful things.

Think about things that make you happy. Think about things that make you smile. Continue to indulge your passions as you daydream. As ideas come to you, jot them down on your pad. Remember, nothing is foolish, so write down all the ideas you have for what you want to do. You're going to fine-tune them later.

Tip from the Coach

If there is something that you want to do or something that you want to try in your career or your life, my advice is go for it—no matter what the risk and no matter how scared you are. Your life and career will benefit more than you can imagine and you'll never look back with regrets. Even if it doesn't work out, you'll feel successful because you tried.

Here's an example to get you started.

◎ I want to be a doctor. As a matter of fact, I want to be neurosurgeon.

◎ I want to be a television medical correspondent. I want to be more recognized than Sanjay Gupta from CNN.

◎ I want to be a nurse-midwife. I want to help hundreds of women deliver their children.

◎ I want to teach people how to become great doctors. Not only do I want to teach at a medical school; I want to teach at the most prestigious medical school in the country.

◎ I want a career in medical research. I want to discover a new cure for disease.

◎ I want to be a nutritionist for celebrities.

◎ I want to work in a hospital lab.

◎ I really want to be a patient advocate. I want to make everyone's hospital experience as good as it can be.

◎ I want to be a substance abuse counselor. I know I could make a difference to people doing that.

◎ I want to work in public relations in the health care industry. I can't wait to put together a public relations campaign for the hospital I work for!

◎ When I get my law degree, I really want to be a labor relations attorney. My favorite uncle always made the job sound so exciting when he was negotiating labor contracts for health care employees.

◎ I want to be a doctor and I want to work in television and film. You know what I really want to do? I want to be the person that helps the producers and directors make sure all the medical information is technically correct.

◎ I want to go on the road and travel around the country.

◎ I want to work in a high school and teach young people about health education.

◎ I want to be a nurse. As a matter of fact, I want to be a traveling nurse, going from location to location so I can have a great career and see different parts of the country.

◎ I want to become a family doctor and work in a less-populated part of the country where they don't have a lot of medical care.

◎ I want to be an architect for health care facilities. I want to design an award-winning building.

◎ I want to be on a team that turns around hospitals in trouble.

◎ I want to design advertising campaigns for doctors and health care facilities.

◎ I love inspiring and motivating people. I think it would be great to work with hospital volunteers.

Do you need some help focusing on what you really want to do in the health care industry? To choose just the right career, you should pinpoint your interests and what you really love doing. What are your skills? What are your personality traits? What are your interests? Fill in the following worksheet to help you zero in even more.

★ The Inside Scoop

When you write down your ideas, you are giving them power. You now have them down on paper, making it easier to go over them, look at them rationally, and fine-tune them.

Focusing on the Job of Your Dreams

Finish the following sentences to help pinpoint your interests and find the job of your dreams.

In my free time I enjoy

_____

In my free time I enjoy going

_____

My hobbies are

_____

Activities I enjoy include

_____

When I volunteer the types of projects I do are

_____

When I was younger I always dreamed of being a

_____

My skills are

_____

My talents are

_____

My best personality traits include

_____

My current job is

_____

Prior types of jobs have been

_____

The subjects I liked best in school were

_____

If I didn't have to worry about any obstacles, the three jobs I would want would be

_____

What steps can I take to get one of those jobs?

_____

What's Stopping You from Getting What You Want?

Now that you have some ideas written down about what you want to do, go down the list. What has stopped you from attaining your goals?

Is it that you told people what you wanted to do and they told you that you couldn't do it? Did they tell you it was too difficult and your chances of making it were slim? Do you not have the confidence in yourself to get what you want? Or is it that you need more education or training? Perhaps it's because you aren't in the location most conducive to your dream career? If you can identify the obstacle, you usually can find a way to overcome it, but you need to identify the problem first.

Do you know exactly what you want to do but can't find an opening? For example, do you want to work as the marketing director of a hospital but can't find a job? If this is the case, don't just keep looking, but look outside the box. Try to find ways to get your foot in the door, and once it is in, don't take it out until you get what you want.

Have you found the perfect job and interviewed for it, but then the job wasn't offered to you? While at the time you probably felt awful about this, there is some good news. Generally, when one door closes, another one opens. Hard to believe? It may be, but if you think about it, you'll see that it's true. Things work out for the best. If you lost what you thought was the job of your dreams, a better one is out there waiting for you. You just have to find it.

Sometimes when you know exactly what type of job you want, you just can't find a job like that available. Don't give up. Keep looking.

Remember, you may have to think outside the box to get what you want, but if you're creative, you can succeed.

Perhaps you're just missing the skills necessary for the type of job you're seeking. This is a relatively easy thing to fix. Once you know the skills necessary for a specific type of job, take steps to get them. Take classes, go to workshops, attend seminars, or become an apprentice or intern.

"But I'm missing the education necessary for the job I want," you say. "The ad I read said I needed a bachelor's degree and I don't have one."

Here's the deal. While you're not going to become a doctor unless you have gone through medical school, and you can't get a job as an accountant without the required education, educational requirements may be negotiable in many cases.

Just because an ad states that a job has a specific educational requirement doesn't mean you should just pass it by if your education doesn't meet that requirement. First of all, advertisements for jobs generally contain the highest hopes of the people placing the ads, not necessarily the reality of what they will settle for. Secondly, many companies will accept experience in lieu of education. Third, if you're a good candidate in other respects, many companies will hire you while you're finishing the required education.

Is a lack of experience stopping you from entering your dream career? This is easily fixed. If

---

★ Tip from the Coach

Start training yourself to find ways to turn *can'ts* in your life into *cans*.

you can't get experience in the workplace, volunteer. For example, do you need experience doing publicity for a career in the public relations department of a hospital? See if you can find an internship. What if that doesn't pan out? Volunteer to do publicity for the hospital's auxiliary. Can't do that? Volunteer to do publicity for another not-for-profit group. Experience is transferable.

How do you get this experience? Take every opportunity that presents itself to get the experience you need. Depending on what you want to do and where you live, you might need to get creative.

Is one of the obstacles you're facing that you just aren't in the geographic location of the opportunities you're looking for? There's no question that living in an area that doesn't have the opportunities you're looking for makes your job more difficult. If this obstacle is holding you back, put some time into developing a solution and find a way to move forward. If you're not prepared to move, you might want to start your career working in some capacity where you live.

Is what's holding you back that you don't have any contacts? Here's the deal: You have to find ways to make contacts. Take classes, seminars, and workshops in subject areas related to the portion of the health care industry in which you're interested.

Volunteer. Make cold calls. Network, network, and network some more. Put yourself in situations where you can meet people in the industry, and sooner or later, you will meet them.

What else is standing between you and success? "The only thing between me and success," you say, "is a big break." Getting your big break may take time. Keep plugging away. Most of all, don't give up. Your break will come when you least expect it.

⭐ Tip from the Coach

While you're working on your daydreaming exercise, don't get caught up in thinking any of your ideas are foolish or stupid. Let your imagination run freely. If these negative ideas come into your head, consciously push them way.

Are you just scared about going after what you want? Are you not sure you have the talent or the skills? Are you not sure you can make it? If you start doubting yourself, other people might do the same. Don't let fear stop you from doing what you want.

Don't let anyone chip away at your dream, and whatever you do, don't let anyone burst your bubble. What does that mean? You know how it is when you get excited about doing something and you're so excited that you just can't keep it to yourself. You might share your ideas of what you want to do with your family and friends. If they start trying to destroy your dream by pointing out all the possible problems you might encounter, don't let them undermine you. It's not that they're trying *not* to be supportive. For some people, it seems to be their nature to try shoot other people's dreams down.

Why? There are a number of reasons. Let's look at a few scenarios.

Scenario 1—Sometimes people are just negative. "Oh," they might say to you, "the health care industry is horrible. You don't want to get involved."

"Well," you tell them. "I do. I think it's a good industry to get into. I want to work in it because I want to help people."

Their response?

"It's hard work. You don't really want to do that. You'll hate it. Find some other way to help people."

Scenario 2—Sometimes people are jealous. They might hate their job and be jealous that you are working toward finding a great career. They might have similar dreams to yours and be jealous that you have a plan and they don't. Some might just be jealous that you might make it before they do.

Scenario 3—Sometimes people are scared of change. In many cases, friends or family are concerned about your well-being and are just scared of change. "You have a job," your girlfriend may say. "Why do you want to go back to school? It's going to take years to become a doctor. Why don't you think about it for a while?"

Scenario 4—Sometimes people just think you're pipe dreaming. "You're a pipe dreamer," your family may say. "What you need is a dose of reality. Do you know how long it takes to become a doctor? Do you know how hard it is to get into school? Thousands of people want to go to medical school. You're just one in a million. The odds are not good."

Scenario 5—Sometimes people really believe it's not realistic to think you should make a living doing something you love. "Nobody likes their job," your family may say. "It's just something you have to do."

Whatever the scenario, there you sit, starting to question yourself. Well, stop! Do not let anyone burst your bubble. No matter what anyone says, at least *you* are trying to get the career you want. At least *you* are following your dream.

While I can't promise you that you will definitely achieve every one of your dreams, I can promise you that if you don't go after your

---

Tip from the Coach

Almost everything you can wish for in life—including your career—starts with a dream. Go after yours!

---

dreams, they will be very difficult to achieve. So don't listen to anyone, and keep working toward what you want.

What Gives You Joy? What Makes You Happy?

Let's zero in further on what you want to do. Let's talk about what gives you joy. Let's talk about what makes you happy. Have you ever noticed that when you're doing something that you love, you smile? It's probably subconscious, but you're smiling. You're happy inside. And it's not only that you're happy; you make those around you happy.

So let's think about it. What makes you happy? What gives you joy? Is it helping others? Is it making someone feel better? Is it teaching? Is it writing? Is it putting together events? Is it a combination of things?

Does the thought of helping a patient recover make you smile? When you close your eyes, can you see yourself as the administrator of a prestigious hospital? Can you almost hear yourself giving a lecture to nursing students? Can you see yourself getting a standing ovation at a medical conference where you just delivered a paper on the way to cure not one but two diseases?

Are you smiling as you think about seeing your name on a sign outside of your new dental office? Can you hear the conversation in which a patient's husband calls to thank you for saving his wife's life? Are you smiling as you imagine yourself graduating from nursing school? Maybe that's your dream, what would make you happy.

Keep dreaming. Keep asking yourself what makes you happy. What gives you joy? Are you having a hard time figuring it out? Many of us do. Here's an idea to help get your juices flowing.

Take out your pad and a pen again. Make a list of any jobs or volunteer activities you've done, things you do in your off time, and hobbies. If you're still in school, you might add extracurricular activities in which you've participated.

Note what aspects of each you like and what you don't like. This will help you see what type of job you're going to enjoy.

What are your special talents, skills, and personality traits? What gives you joy and makes you happy?

Do you truly enjoy making others feel better? Are you compassionate? A career where you are working hands-on with patients in some capacity might be just what you should look for.

Have you always been good at motivating others? Are you inspiring? Are you good at organizing?

Is your special talent singing? What about playing an instrument? How about dancing? Do you want to use these talents working in the health care industry? Perhaps you might want to use those talents to develop a career as a music or dance therapist.

Is your special talent writing? What about taking photographs? Can you see the pictures that most people wish they could envision? There are dozens of ways you can parlay these talents into a wonderful career in the health care industry.

Are you always volunteering to do the publicity for a charity or not-for-profit? If you love doing that, you might really love doing publicity for a hospital, health care facility, medical group, or pharmaceutical company. You most likely would also really enjoy a career as a publicist for an association related to the health care industry.

Do you thrive on the excitement of putting together events? You probably would love a job as a special events coordinator, coordinating fund-raising galas and special events for hospitals and health care facilities. You might also like putting together press conferences and other types of events.

A few years ago, after one of the books I wrote on careers in casinos came out, I was doing some radio interviews. During one of those shows, a woman called to ask some questions regarding entering that industry.

"I just spent a week on vacation at a casino and I love the atmosphere. How difficult is it to get a job in a casino?" she asked.

"That depends on what you want to do," I told her. "What area of the industry are you considering?"

"I'm not sure," she replied. "I really don't have any experience working in gaming, but I always wished I could work in a casino. It's one of those pipe dreams, I guess. I don't really want to work as a dealer, but the whole casino atmosphere is exciting. I was thinking about some area of administration."

"What kinds of skills do you have?" I questioned. "What are your talents?"

"Hmm," she said. "I'm good with people, I have good communications skills, I have a good sense of humor...I don't know what else."

"What do you do now?" I asked her.

"I'm a nurse," she said. "I really like nursing. As a matter of fact, I love it, but I'm looking for a new challenge."

"Have you considered a job in a casino as a nurse?" I asked.

"I didn't even know they had nurses in casinos," she said.

"They don't all, but a lot of them do," I told her. "If you really like nursing and you want to work in a casino, it might be a good match. Why don't you call a few of them and give it a try."

About a year later, I was giving a stress management seminar at a casino. After my presentation, a woman walked up.

"I wanted to introduce myself," she said. "You probably don't remember this, but about a year ago, I called in when you were doing a radio show about jobs in casinos. I was the nurse who wanted to work in a casino."

"I do remember," I said. "What happened?"

"You were right. I called a number of casinos and asked about a job. I finally hit it lucky. I'm working here now as a nurse. This is the greatest. I just wanted to thank you."

"I'm glad it worked out," I told her. "Thanks for letting me know. Keep me posted on your career."

⭐ **Words from the Wise**

The first requisite for success is the ability to apply your physical and mental energies to one problem incessantly without growing weary.

–Thomas Edison

What Are Your Talents?

It's important to define what your talents are. Sometimes we're so good at something that we just don't even think twice about it. The problem with this is that often we don't see the value in our talent. What does this mean? It means that we may overlook the possibilities associated with our talents.

It is also important to know that you can have more than one talent. Just because you are a compassionate doctor doesn't mean you can't be a talented musician. Just because you're a talented writer doesn't mean you can't sing. Just because you are great working with numbers doesn't mean you're not good at organizing. Just because you're creative doesn't mean you can't make people laugh. Most of us have more than one talent. The trick is making sure you know what *your* talents are and using them to your advantage.

Do you know your talents? Can you identify them? This is another time you're going to have to sit down and start writing. Write down everything you're good at. Write down all of your talents, not just the ones you think are related to the area of the health care industry in which you're interested.

This is not the time to be modest. Remember that this list is for you, so be honest with yourself.

Can you finish this sentence? "I am a talented _____." You might be a talented doctor, nurse, administrator, lab technician, technologist, publicist, teacher, care giver, writer, photographer, salesperson, and so on.

Now finish the sentence, "I am talented in _____." You might be talented in organizing, supervising, cooking, or baking. You might be talented at negotiating, writing, persuasion, painting, drawing, decorating, or public speaking. Whatever your talents, there is usually a way you can use them to help your career.

How? Let's say you want to be a hospital public relations director. Your talents among others are creativity and writing. You also are very persuasive and a great negotiator. While creativity and writing are the talents that can help you become a successful public relations director, having the talent to persuade the media to give stories a certain spin or the talent to negotiate to get your press release in the paper or reporters to your press conference can be priceless.

I know a very talented doctor who is also a very successful singer and musician. He often sings and plays at area clubs and functions. Does he *need* to do this? Not really, but he *enjoys* doing it.

I also know a physician who is an amateur gourmet chef. He frequently gives cooking classes to illustrate that you can cook gourmet meals that are still healthy. Generally, when he gives the classes, there is media coverage. The result is he gets a ton of publicity, keeping his medical specialty in the public eye.

Use every talent you have to catapult you to the top. Don't discount those you feel are not "job related." Whether your extra talents get you in the door, help you stand out, or launch you up the career ladder, they will be a useful tool in your career.

Getting What You Want

You hear opportunity knocking. How do you get what you want? How do you turn your dream into reality? One of the most important things you need to do is have faith in yourself and your dreams. It is essential that you believe that you can make dreams happen in order for them to happen.

As we've discussed, focus on exactly what you really want. Otherwise, you'll be going in a million different directions. Remember that things may not always come as quickly as you want. No matter how it appears, most people are not overnight successes.

You will probably have to "pay your dues." What does that mean? On the most basic level, it means you probably have to start small to get to the big time. Before you get to ride in the limo, you're going to have to drive a lot of Chevys. (There's nothing wrong with a Chevy; it's just not the same as having a chauffeured limo.)

Depending on your situation, it might mean working in smaller hospitals before getting a job in larger, more prestigious facilities. It might mean working the "graveyard" shift instead of the more desirable daytime shifts. It might mean working as a coordinator before you become a director. It might mean working long hours as an intern and resident.

Paying your dues means you may have to pound on a lot of doors before the right one opens. It means you may have to take jobs that are not your ideal to get experience so you can move up the career ladder and get the job of your dreams. You may have to do a lot of the grunt work and stay in the background while others get the credit. While all this is going on, you have to be patient with the knowledge that everything you do is getting you closer to your goal.

If you look at every experience as a stepping-stone to get you to the next level of your career, it's a lot easier to get through the difficult things or trying times you may have to go through.

Setting Goals

Throughout this process, it's essential to set goals. Why? If you don't have goals, it's hard to know where you want to end up. It's hard to know where you're going. If you don't know where you're going, it's very difficult to get there.

It sometimes is easier to look at goals as the place you arrive at the end of a trip. You can also look at actions as the trips you take to get to your destinations.

What's the best way to set goals? To start with, be as specific as you can. Instead of your goal being, "I want to be a nurse," your goal might be, "I want a career as a nurse working in the pediatrics department of a hospital." Instead of your goal being, "I want to be a hospital marketing director," your goal might be, "I want to be a successful marketing director working in a prestigious health care facility." Instead of your goal being, "I want to be a doctor," it might be, "I want to be a successful cardiologist helping patients live healthy lives." Or it might be, "I want to be a successful cardiologist working as the head of the cardiology department at a prestigious hospital."

Instead of your goal being, "I want to teach at a school," it might be, "I want to be a health education educator teaching young people in a large high school." Instead of your goal being, "I want to be a chiropractor," your goal might be, "I want to be a chiropractor and develop a large, successful practice. Instead of "I want to be an oncologist," your goal might be, "I want to be a successful, compassionate oncologist working at Sloan Kettering in New York City.

Tip from the Top

Successful people continue setting goals throughout their career. That ensures their career doesn't get stagnant and they always feel passion for what they do.

Tip from the Coach

Goals are not written in stone. Just because you have something written down does not mean you can't change it. As you change, your goals might change as well. This is normal.

I want to specialize in pediatric oncology and help children."

Notice that the specific goals have actions attached to them. For example, in the goal "I want to be a hospital marketing director," the action is *becoming a successful marketing director in a prestigious health care facility*.

You should also try to make sure your goals are clear and concise. You'll find it easier to focus on your goals if you write them down. Writing down your goals will help you see them more clearly. Writing down your goals will also give them power, and power is what can make it happen.

So take out your pad or notebook and get started. As you think of new ideas and goals, jot them down. Some people find it easier to work toward one main goal. Others find it easier to develop a series of goals leading up to their main goal.

To help you do this exercise, first develop a number of long-term goals. Where do you think you want to be in your career in the next year? How about the next two years, three years, five years, and even 10 years?

Need some help? Here is an example of the goals for someone who is still in school and interested in becoming a director of marketing for a health care facility.

First-year goals:

◎ I want to get an internship with a large, prestigious hospital and learn as much as I can.

◎ I want to finish my bachelor's degree and graduate with a degree in marketing and communications.

Second-year goals:

◎ I want get a job as publicist in a hospital or health care facility.

◎ I want to continue my education and work toward a master's in marketing.

◎ I want to network and start getting known in my field.

◎ I want to get a promotion to assistant director of public relations at the hospital.

◎ I want to join and get involved in some trade associations.

Third-year goals:

◎ I want to complete my master's.

◎ I want to become the director of public relations at the same hospital or find a similar job at another facility.

◎ I want to continue networking and get involved in some volunteer projects that will help hone my skills and get me noticed in the health care industry.

◎ I want to be approached by a headhunter for a position as an assistant director of marketing at a large teaching hospital. (Okay, I really want to be approached by a headhunter for a position as the director of marketing; I think I'll have to work on that.)

Long-term goals:

◎ I want to be the director of marketing for a large, prestigious health care facility.

◎ I want to be recognized as a skilled and talented professional by my peers.

Once you've zeroed in on your main goals, you can develop short-range goals you might want or need to accomplish to reach your long-range goals. Feel free to add details. Don't con-

cern yourself with situations changing. You can always adjust your goals.

When focusing on your goals, remember that there are general work-related goals and specific work-related goals. What's the difference? Specific goals are just that. See the following examples:

◎ General Goal: I want to get a promotion.
  ▫ Specific Goal: I want to be promoted to the director of the department by the end of the year.

◎ General Goal: I want to work in the health care industry.
  ▫ Specific Goal: I want a career as a radiologist.

◎ General Goal: I want to work in medicine.
  ▫ Specific Goal: I want to be a family practitioner working in a rural area helping families get better health care.

◎ General Goal: I want to be a dentist.
  ▫ Specific Goal: I want a career as an oral surgeon with my own practice.

Visualization Can Help Make It Happen

Visualization is a powerful tool for success in all aspects of your life. Visualization is "seeing" or "visualizing" a situation the way you want it. It's setting up a picture in your mind of the way you would like a situation to unfold.

How do you do it? Simple. Close your eyes and visualize what you want. Visualize the situation that you desire. Think about each step you need to take to get where you want to go in your career, and then see the result in your mind. Want to see how it's done?

What do you want to be? How do you want your career to unfold? Want to be a doctor? A nurse? How about a pharmacist? Perhaps you want to be the next surgeon general? Want to be a dean of a medical school? A nursing school instructor? A hospital marketing director? The head of the radiology department? A dietician? A health and wellness coordinator? Whatever your dream career is, visualization can help you get there! How so?

Visualize driving up to the hospital and parking in the space that says "*Reserved for* [*insert your name here*]." You walk into the hospital and hear your name being paged. As you're walking down the hall to your office, people are saying, "Good morning, doctor."

You get to a door and see a sign outside your office. Do you see your name? "Doctor James Jones." Wow! You can hardly believe you are living your dream.

Now visualize yourself going on rounds. Imagine stopping in your patient's rooms. Visualize looking at their charts, making notations, and performing examinations. Can you hear the patients asking you questions? How about their families?

Visualize talking to the nurses. Can you see yourself giving orders for tests, procedures, and medications?

Now visualize yourself getting ready to go into surgery. You go through the door that says "Surgical Personnel Only." You put on your scrubs. You prepare for surgery.

Can you feel the energy in the air? Your heart is pounding in a good way. You're doing what you were trained to do! What a feeling.

Surgery was a success. You go out into the waiting room to talk to the family and give them the good news. You can just feel their relief. It's a good day, and it's only one of many. You're a physician and a surgeon. Got the picture? That's visualization!

Are you getting the idea? You need to visualize your life and your career the way you want it to be. Visualize yourself as you would like others to see you.

No matter what you want to do, you can visualize it to help make it happen. Visualize your career working as a doctor, a nurse, social worker, lab technician, technologist, dentist, pharmacist, or optometrist. Visualize yourself getting a job as an administrator of a hospital, an activities director, a marketing director, or health and wellness coordinator. See yourself going for the interview, getting the job, and then sitting at your desk. Visualize speaking to coworkers, going to meetings, and doing your work.

The more details you can put into your visualizations, the better. Add the colors of things around you; the fragrance of the flowers on your desk; the aroma of the coffee in your mug; the color of the suit your wearing; even the bright blue sky outside. Details will help bring your visualization to life.

Whatever your dreams, concentrate on them, think about them, and then visualize them. Here's the great news. If you can visualize it, you can make it happen! No one really knows why, but it does seem to work and it works well. Perhaps it's positive energy. Perhaps you're just concentrating more on what you want.

One of the tricks of visualizing to get what you want is actually visualizing all the actions you need to take to achieve your goal. If you don't know what these actions are or should be,

---

The Inside Scoop

Visualization works for more than your career. Use it to help make your dreams come true in all facets of life.

> ### ⭐ Tip from the Coach
> Make a commitment to your dream and stick to it. Without this commitment, your dream will turn into a bubble that will fly away and burst in mid air.

an easy exercise that might help you is called reverse visualization. In essence, you're going to play the scenes in reverse.

Start by visualizing at the point in your life where you want to be and then go back to the point where you are currently. If your dream is to be the head of cardiology at a large, prestigious hospital, that's where you're going to start. If you're currently in medical school, that's where you're going to end up.

If your dream is to be a hospital administrator, that's where you're going to start. If you have just graduated from college and you're looking for a job, that's where you're going to end up.

If your dream is to be a nurse, that's where you're going to start. As a matter of fact, as long as we are visualizing a scenario, let's visualize that you want to be the head of the nursing department for a large, prestigious hospital. If you're currently thinking about going to nursing school, that is where you're going to end up. As we did just a moment ago, start visualizing that you have what you want. Remember to visualize everything— your office, your uniform, your boss. Now, take one step back. Right before you got to that point in your career, what did you do? There were probably a number of things. Let's make a list of how events might have unfolded in reverse.

◎ You just became head of the nursing department of a large, prestigious hospital.

◎ You just got a promotion.

◎ You continued teaching while still being a nursing supervisor at the hospital.

◎ You were asked to be help develop the curriculum to improve the nursing program.

◎ You won nurse of the year! What an honor.

◎ You were nominated nurse of the year at your hospital.

◎ You were asked to teach a few classes in the nursing program at the hospital.

◎ You moved and got a new job as a nursing supervisor in a larger hospital.

◎ You got your master's degree!

◎ You got a promotion. You became a nursing supervisor.

◎ You decided that you wanted to continue your education and started taking classes toward your master's degree.

◎ You went to events to network and meet others interested in nursing.

◎ You love every day. It's like an adventure.

◎ You got the job!

◎ You interviewed for your first nursing job at a hospital.

◎ You graduated with a BSN.

◎ You absolutely loved every minute of the training.

◎ You got supervised clinical experience.

◎ You went through classroom instruction.

◎ You went to college to go through the nursing program.

◎ You graduated from high school.

◎ You were accepted.

◎ You applied to college because you wanted to end up with a bachelor's of science in nursing (BSN).

◎ You volunteered at the local hospital.

◎ You decided that you wanted to fulfill your dream of becoming a nurse. (This is where you are now.)

Here's a different example of the reverse visualization exercise you might do if you were interested in a career on the business end of the industry. It's the same concept, just a slightly different way of doing it.

Let's say you want a career in fund-raising and development for a hospital or health care facility. Think about where you'd like to work. Think about your job title. Visualize that you are the director of fund-raising and development for the facility of your choice.

Add your office environment, the office décor. Now add your coworkers. Next put yourself in the picture. Remember to visualize what you're wearing, your accessories, and even the color of your suit.

Visualize yourself speaking to colleagues, supervisors, and the board of directors. Create a picture in your mind of major fund-raising events. Visualize speaking to donors. Visualize getting a million-dollar donation. Feel the excitement of the day.

Now go backwards. Visualize yourself driving to work your first day. Keep visualizing. Now you're thinking about getting dressed that morning. Keep going. Remember hearing the alarm buzzing and how you just couldn't wait to get up to go to work.

Keep visualizing in reverse. Hear your cell phone ringing and remember the feeling you had when the voice at the other end told you that you got the job. Go back and visualize the feeling that you had waiting for that call. Visualize the thank-you note you wrote to the human

> ## Words from the Wise
> I have learned this at least by my experiment: that if one advances confidently in the direction of his dreams, and endeavors to live the life which he has imagined, he will meet with a success unexpected in common hours.
> –Henry David Thoreau

resources director. See the letter in your mind. Now remember leaving the interview. Visualize in detail what you wore, what the experience was like, the questions you were asked, and the feelings you had at that moment. Remember how much you hoped you would be hired.

Visualize filling out the application and developing and sending in your resume with your perfectly tailored cover letter. Now visualize seeing the job advertised and the excited feeling you had.

Recall all the preparation you did to find that job; the skills you updated; the people you spoke to; the networking. Visualize the internship you went through.

You are now back at the position in the visualization process where you currently are in your career. You have an idea of the steps needed to get where you want to go. This might not be the exact way your situation goes down, but it can get you started in the visualization process.

Paint a picture in your mind of what you want to achieve detail by detail. Whether you're using a reverse visualization or a traditional visualization technique, this powerful tool can help you get what you want. Give it a try. You'll be glad you did.

3

PLAN FOR SUCCESS IN THE
HEALTH CARE INDUSTRY

Take Control and Be Your Own Career Manager

There's an old saying that if you want something done right, you need to do it yourself. While this might not always hold true, as far as your career goes, there is a shred of accuracy to it.

It's important to realize that no one cares about your career as much as you do. Not your mother, your father, your sister, or your brother. Not your best friend, girlfriend, boyfriend, or spouse. Not your colleagues, your supervisors, or your business partner. It's not that these people don't care at all. They probably all want you to be successful, but no one really cares as much as you do.

If you want more control over success in your career, a key strategy to incorporate is becoming your own career manager. What does this mean? It means that you won't be leaving your career to chance. You won't be leaving your career in someone else's hands. You will be in the driver's seat! *You* will have control and *you* can make your dream career happen!

Will it take a lot of work? Yes, being your own career manager can be a job in itself. The payoff, however, will be worth it.

If you look at many successful people working in the health care industry or any other industry, for that matter, you will notice that most have a tremendous dedication to their career. Of course, they may have friends, colleagues, professionals, and others who advise them, but when it comes to the final decision making, they are the ones who take the ultimate responsibility for their career.

Now that you've decided to be your own career manager, you have some work to do. Next on the list is putting together an action plan. Let's get started!

What Is an Action Plan?

Let's look at success a little closer. What's the one thing successful people, successful businesses, and successful events all have in common? Is it money? Luck? Talent? While money, luck, and talent all certainly are part of the mix, generally the common thread most share is a well-developed plan for success. Whatever your goal, be it short-range or long-range, if you have a plan to achieve it, you have a better chance of succeeding. With that in mind, let's discuss how you can create your own plan for success.

What can you do with your plan? The possibilities are endless.

People utilize all types of plans to help ensure success. Everyone has his or her own version of what is best. To some, just imagining what they're going to do and how they're going to do it is plan enough. Some, especially those working on a new business, create formal business plans. Some people develop action plans. That's what we're going to talk about now.

What exactly is an action plan? In a nutshell, an action plan is a written plan detailing all the actions you need and want to take to successfully accomplish your ultimate goal: success in your chosen career.

How an Action Plan Can Help You Succeed

Success is never easy, but you can stack the deck in your favor by creating your own personal action plan. Why is this so critical? To begin with, there are many different things you might want to accomplish to succeed in your career. If you

go about them in a haphazard manner, however, your efforts might not be as effective as they could be. An action plan helps define the direction to go and the steps needed to get the job done. It helps increase your efficiency in your quest for success.

Another reason to develop an action plan is that actually seeing a plan in writing sometimes helps you see a major shortcoming or simply makes you notice something minor that may be missing. At that point, you can add the actions you need to take, and the situation will be easily rectified.

With an action plan, you know exactly what you're going to be doing to reach your goals. It helps you focus so that everything you need to do is more organized.

Many of us have had the experience of looking in a closet where everything is just jumbled up. If you need a jacket or a pair of pants from the closet, you can probably find them, but it may be frustrating and take you a long time. On the other hand, if you organize your closet, when you need that jacket or pair of pants, you can reach for them and find them in a second with no problem.

One of the main reasons you develop a plan is to have something organized to follow, and when you have something to follow, things are easier to accomplish and far less frustrating. In essence, what you're creating with your action plan is a method of finding and succeeding in your dream career no matter what area of the health care industry you are interested in pursuing. When you put that plan into writing, you're going to have something to follow and something to refer to, making it easier to track your progress.

"Okay," you say. "How do I know what goes into the plan? How do I do this?"

That depends a lot on what you want to do and what type of action plan you're putting together. Your action plan is going to be composed

---

Tip from the Coach

When you break large projects up into smaller tasks, they seem more manageable. It's kind of like spring-cleaning. If you look at cleaning the whole house at one time, it can seem impossible. Yet if you break the job up into cleaning one or two rooms at a time, it seems easier to accomplish. When you look at the ultimate task of finding the perfect career and then becoming successful, it too, can seem like a huge undertaking. Breaking up the tasks you need to accomplish will help you reach your goal.

---

of a lot of the little, detailed steps you're going to have to accomplish to obtain your goal.

Some people make very specific and lengthy action plans. Others develop general ones. You might create a separate action plan for each job you pursue, a plan for your next goal, or even a plan that details everything you're going to need to do from the point where you find yourself now up to the career of your dreams. As long as you have some type of plan to follow, the choice is yours.

Your Personal Action Plan for Success in the Health Care Industry

So you've decided to be your own career manager. It's now up to *you* to develop your personal action plan or plans for success in your career in the health care industry. Are you ready to get started?

A great deal of your action plan will depend on what area of the industry you're interested in and exactly what you want to do. We're going to go over specialized actions for plans later, but right now, let's look at some basics.

Take a notebook and pen, sit down, and start thinking about your career and the direction you want it to go. Start by doing some research.

What do you want to find out? Almost any information can be useful in your career. Let's look at some of the things that might help you.

Your Market

One of the first things to research is your market. What does that mean? For the most part, it means you need to determine what jobs and employment situations are available and where they are located. Who will your potential employers or clients be? Where will they be located?

While many jobs in health care can be located throughout the country, be aware that in some situations you might have to relocate to find the perfect job. Where are the best opportunities for the area you're interested in pursuing? With a bit of research, you can easily find the answer.

Remember that the clearer you are in defining your goals, the easier it will be to reach them. If, for example, you're seeking a career as a nurse, you want to know not only where you can find jobs but also which jobs appeal to you.

Although jobs for nurses can be located throughout the country and many nursing jobs are in hospitals, these are not the only places to work. If you do some research, you'll find that you can work in a variety of other situations. You might work in a private physician's office, for a medical group, or at a school. You might work at a large hotel or resort, an insurance company, a camp, or a casino. You might work at a large corporation, go on tour with a rock and roll group, sign up as the nurse for a boxing camp, or work in an array of other situations in almost every geographical area.

If you want to be a dietician, you might want to look into traditional opportunities such as hospitals, health care facilities, extended care facilities, nursing homes, schools, colleges, convalescent homes, and prisons. What about community agencies, medical clinics, private weight-loss

---

companies, and health spas? What about sports teams, prizefighters, and celebrities? What about corporations trying to help employees eat better? The choice is yours.

Want to work in some segment of health care administration? Do you want to work in a small, midsized, or large facility? Do you want to work in a hospital, or would you rather work in a long-term health care facility? Do you want to work in the nonprofit sector or work in a for-profit facility?

Let's say you're career choice is to be a physician. What area of medicine do you want to go into? Do you want to specialize? In what area of the country do you want to work? Do you want to be on staff at a hospital or other facility or in private practice? Do you want to be part of a medical group? Do you want to work in a clinic? Do you want to work in a teaching hospital? Explore all the opportunities.

Do you want to be a pharmacist? You might work in a pharmacy in a retail chain, a local pharmacy, a hospital, or even own your own pharmacy. What would be your dream?

Do you want a career in sales? Do you think you would like to sell medical equipment? What about medical supplies? How about pharmaceuticals? If you love sales, your options are unlimited.

Do you love writing and want to work in some aspect of the health care industry? You have

so many options! You can become a publications director for a health care facility or do public relations, publicity, or marketing. You might be a copywriter or a health care writer for a Web site, newspaper, or periodical. You could be a technical writer for medical books or the one who writes the instructions for taking medication. Would any of these be possibilities for you?

Is your dream to have your own marketing or public relations firm specializing in clients in the health care industry? If so, you'll want to research what your best location is to obtain and service clients. While larger areas offer more opportunities, you may find it easier to break into the industry in smaller, less metropolitan areas.

Is it your dream to have your own practice? If so, you might want to research the best geographic location. Would it be better for you to start a practice in a smaller rural area where there might be less competition or a larger area where there may be more patients? You will have to weigh the pros and cons of each.

Why do you have to research your market now? Why do you need this information at all? Because information is power. The more you think about your potential options and markets now, the more opportunities you may find.

What Do You Need to Do to Get What You Want?

Next, research what you need to do to get the career you want. Do you need additional skills? Training? Education? Experience? Do you need to move to a different location? Make new contacts? Get an internship? Do you need to get certified? Licensed? What do you need?

Would it help to take some writing classes? How about taking a class in a new computer software program? Do you need to take a seminar on grant writing? What about attending a workshop on publicity? Do you need additional continuing education? Do you need to join a union? Would a public speaking workshop help? Determine what is standing between you and the career you want.

If you are already working in the health care industry, you need to determine what stands between you and success. How can you climb the ladder of success and perhaps even skip a few rungs to get where you want to go?

Take some time thinking about this. If you can determine exactly what skills, qualifications, training, education, licensing, certification, or experience you're missing or what you need to do, you're halfway there.

It often helps to view on paper exactly what is standing between you and what you want. Here's a sample to give you an idea. Use the

What Stands Between Me and What I Want?	Possible Solution
I need more experience.	I'm going to look into an internship.
I need to get into medical school.	I'm going to make sure I keep my GPA up, study to do well on my MCAT, find volunteer activities where I can work with people who are ill to get experience, and get involved in extracurricular activities to make sure I have a well rounded background.
I need to get my degree.	I'm going to finish college.
I don't live near a large, prestigious hospital and I don't want to move without a job.	I'm going to go on the Web and check out the Web sites of hospitals I'm interested in working at to see what types of opportunities are available.
I want to work for a marketing or public relations company that specializes in the health care industry.	I'm going to cold call and send out letters to see if there are jobs available or I can create my own job. I also might see if I can get some experience working in the public relations or marketing department of a hospital or health care facility.
I need to be bilingual.	I'm going to look into an immersion course to see if I can learn another language quickly.
I want to open up my own practice.	I'm going to see if I can speak at civic and not-for-profit group meetings to get better known in the community.
I need a master's to succeed.	I'm going to start by taking a couple of classes. I can afford both the time and money to do this.
I need to find a way to advance my career and can't get a promotion because my supervisor isn't going anyplace.	I'm going to start to actively search for a better job.

What Stands Between Me and What I Want?	Possible Solution

blank form on page 44 to help you clarify each situation and the solution to what you feel is standing between you and the career you want.

How Can You Differentiate Yourself?

No matter what area of the health care industry you want to pursue, I can almost guarantee you that other people want the same type of job.

Thousands of people want to be doctors. Thousands want to be physician assistants, nurses, therapists, technologists, technicians, or dentists or work in some other segment of patient care, and thousands want to work in the social work or mental health counseling areas.

There are also thousands of people who want to work in health care administration or in health care marketing, public relations, wellness, fund-raising, and development. Many want to work in other areas of the business end of the health care industry.

And don't forget all the people who want to work in the health care industry in education, journalism, communications, retail, wholesale, and all the segments in between.

I can almost hear you say, "That is a lot of competition. Can I make it? Can I succeed?"

To that I answer a definitive, "Yes!" Lots of people succeed in all aspects of the health care industry. Why shouldn't one of them be you?

Here's the challenge. How can you stand out in a positive way? What attributes do you have or what can you do so people choose you over others?

"I don't like to draw attention to myself," you say. "I just kind of like to blend into the crowd."

Well, you're going to have to find a way to get rid of that attitude if you want to make it. Why? Because the people who get the jobs, the ones who succeed, the ones who make it, are the

The Inside Scoop

Successful people usually have something special about them, something that sets them apart from others. Sometimes it is related to their career; sometimes it isn't. Noted psychologist Dr. Joyce Brothers first gained fame in the 1950s when she went on the popular game show *The $64,000 Question*. Brothers' specialty was boxing. She answered the questions and not only won *The $64,000 Question* but then followed with a win on the *$64,000 Challenge*. She parlayed her experience into a position as a cohost of a show on NBC called *Sports Showcase* before snagging appearances in a series of syndicated television programs as a psychologist, the field in which she had trained. Today, Dr. Joyce Brothers still appears on radio and television as well as writing columns and articles for leading magazines. Had she not originally taken advantage of her expertise in boxing, she might never have gained the fame and recognition she has enjoyed over the years.

ones who have found a way to set themselves apart from others.

How? Perhaps it's your personality or the energy you exude. Maybe it's your sense of humor or the way you organize things. Perhaps it's your calm demeanor in the eye of a storm. Maybe it's your smile or the twinkle in your eye. Some people just have a presence about them.

It might be the special way you have of dealing with patients. Perhaps you have a way of calming ill children down, making them feel better. Maybe it's your bedside manner.

It might be the way you write press releases, the way you craft fund-raising letters, or the way you write grants that bring in huge sums of money. It might be the way you can look at an accounting ledger and *see* the error while everyone else has been trying to find it.

Maybe it's the way you motivate people or inspire them. Maybe it's the way you can take a complicated project and just make it easier to understand. Perhaps it is that you are not only a visionary but have the ability to bring your visions to fruition.

Everyone is special in some way. Everyone has a special something they do or say that makes them stand out in some manner. Most people have more than one unique trait. Spend some time determining what makes you special in a positive way so that you can use it to your advantage in your career.

How to Get Noticed

Catching the eye of people important to your career is another challenge. How are you going to bring your special talents and skills to the attention of people who can make a difference to your career? This is the time to brainstorm.

First of all, instead of waiting for opportunities to perform to present themselves, I want you to seek them out. You are also going to want to market yourself. We're going to discuss different ways to market yourself later, but at this point you need to take some time to try to figure out how to make yourself and your accomplishments known to others.

Consider joining a not-for-profit or civic organization whose mission you believe in. And don't just join—get involved. How? That depends what your passion is and where your talents lie. If, for example, your career aspiration is to work in health care marketing or public relations, you might offer to do the marketing, publicity, or public relations for a not-for-profit or one of their events. You might even want to volunteer to handle the publicity for a hospital auxiliary.

If you're interested in a career in fund-raising and development, you might volunteer to do fund-raising for a not-for-profit or even suggest a fund-raising idea and then chair the project.

If you are an aspiring doctor, you might want to volunteer in a health care facility or clinic in some capacity. This will be helpful when applying to med school. It not only helps illustrate that you know what working with ill patients is all about; it helps you make important contacts.

Why volunteer when you're trying to get a job? What's the point? Aside from doing something for someone else, it can help you get noticed.

"But I want to work in the health care industry," you say. "I can see volunteering in a health care oriented area, but what will volunteering for an unrelated industry and not even getting paid for it do for my career?"

It will give you experience. It will give you exposure. And maybe someone else involved in that not-for-profit or civic group for which you're volunteering will have some contacts in the health care industry.

Need some other ideas? Think creatively. Are you a nutritionist? Think about giving a class in preparing healthy snacks or meal planning at a local school or civic group meeting. Don't forget to call the media and send out a press release on your activities. Similarly, if you're a nurse, you might give a class in basic first aid.

What about coordinating a fund-raiser for your local hospital? How about offering to develop a newsletter for the hospital auxiliary? What about volunteering to put together a community cookbook for a not-for-profit organization?

Just keep coming up with ideas and writing them down as you go. You can fine-tune them later.

Why are you doing this? You want to get your name out there. You want to call attention to yourself in a positive manner. You want to set yourself apart from others. You want people in the health care industry not only to know you exist but to remember you when opportunities arise.

Have you won any awards? Honors and awards always set you apart from others and help you get noticed.

What can you do to set yourself apart?

Think about these questions. Can you come up with more? Once you determine the answers, it's easier to move on to the next step of writing your plan.

What Should Your Basic Action Plan Include?

Now that you've done some research and brainstormed some great ideas, you're on your way. What should your basic action plan include?

Career Goals

One of the most important parts of your action plan will be defining your career goals. Are you just starting your career? Are you looking for a new job or career? Are you already in the industry and want to climb the career ladder? Are you interested in exploring a different career in health care from the one you're in now?

Do you want to be a doctor, chiropractor, dentist, optometrist, or physician assistant? Do you want to be a patient advocate, administrator of a health care facility, public relations director, marketing director, or fund-raising and development director? Do you want to be a technician, technologist, or researcher? Do you want a career in social work, counseling, or stress management? Do you want to be a psychiatrist or psychologist? Do you want to be a medical photographer? A medical writer? A television medical correspondent? Do you want to work in the human resources department of a major hospital? How about a career as the labor attorney for a health care institution? Do you want to design health care facilities? How about doing the interior design for hospitals?

Would you like to be in charge of the food service department of a large hospital? Handle patient admissions? Work as a medical advisor to films or television shows?

The sky is the limit if you know what your goals are.

When defining your goals, try to make them as specific as possible. For example, instead of writing in your action plan that your goal is to be a doctor, refine your goal to be a successful, respected cardiologist working in a large, prestigious teaching hospital in New York City (if that's what you want to do). Instead of writing that your goal is to be a nurse, refine your goal to be a nurse in a regional hospital working on the pediatric floor. Instead of defining your goal to be a dentist, you might define your goal to be an oral surgeon or perhaps even a prosthodontist. Instead of defining your goal to work in wellness, you might define it as becoming a health and wellness director for a major hospital or whatever your career goal or aspiration might be.

It's important when thinking about goals to include your short-range goals as well as your long-range ones. You might even want to include mid-range plans. That way, you'll be able to track your progress, which gives you inspiration to slowly but surely meet your goals. For example, let's say you're interested in pursuing a career as a pharmacist. Your short-range goals might be to graduate from an accredited college resulting in a pharmacy degree. Your mid-range goals might then be to land a position as a pharmacist at a small hospital, then a similar position at a larger hospital. Your long-range goal might be to become the pharmacy director at a large, prestigious hospital or health care facility.

Keep in mind that goals are not written in stone, and it's okay to be flexible and change them along the way. The idea is that no matter what you want, moving forward is the best way to get somewhere.

What You Need to Reach Your Goals

The next step in your action plan is to put in writing exactly what you need to reach your goals? Do you need some sort of training or more education? Do you need to learn new skills or brush up on old ones? Do you need to move to a different geographic location? Do you need to network more? Do you need to make more contacts?

Your Actions

This is the crux of your action plan. What actions do you need to attain your goals?

- ◎ Do you need to get a degree or attend some industry related workshops?
  - ▫ Your actions would be to identify colleges and universities that offer such

a degree, apply, and go through and graduate with the degree you need.
- ◎ Do you need to take some classes or attend some workshops?
  - ▫ Your actions would be to identify, locate, and take classes and workshops.
- ◎ Do you need to find seminars and attend them?
  - ▫ Your actions would be to investigate potential seminars to see if they will assist in accomplishing your goals and, if so, attend them.
- ◎ Do you need to go to college, get a bachelor's degree, or even a law degree?
  - ▫ Your actions would be to go to college, get a degree, and so on.
- ◎ Do you need to go to med school?
  - ▫ Your actions would be to apply to med school, get in, go to med school, and graduate with either an MD or DO degree.
- ◎ Do you need to learn how to write better? Do you need better written communications skills?
  - ▫ Your actions would be to find classes to help you hone your skills.
- ◎ Do you need to find a way to feel more comfortable speaking in public?
  - ▫ Your actions would be to find and take a course in public speaking.
- ◎ Do you need to move to another geographic location?
  - ▫ Your actions would be to find a way to relocate.
- ◎ Do you need to attend industry events, conferences, and conventions?
  - ▫ Your actions would be to locate and investigate events, conferences, and conventions, and then attend them.

◎ Do you need to find more ways to network or just network more?

    ▫ Your actions would be to develop opportunities and activities to network and follow through with those activities and opportunities.

◎ Do you need more experience?

    ▫ Your actions might include becoming an intern, volunteering, or finding other ways to get experience. Talk to people who might be able to help you find opportunities to volunteer.

◎ Do you need to join a union?

    ▫ Your actions would be to call the specific union you need to join and check out the requirements.

◎ Do you need to find a headhunter to help you locate the perfect job?

    ▫ Your actions would be to talk to people in the industry, get suggestions, and then contact a number of headhunters.

Your Timetable

Your timetable is essential to your action plan. In this section, you're going to include what you're going to do (your actions) and when you're going to do them. The idea is to make sure you have a deadline for getting things done so your actions don't fall through the cracks. Just saying

---

Tip from the Coach

Try to be realistic when setting your timetable. Unrealistic time requirements often set the groundwork for making you feel as though you've failed.

"I have to do this" or "I have to do that" isn't effective.

Remember there is no right or wrong way to assemble your action plan. It's what you are comfortable with. You might want yours to look different in some manner, have different items, or even have things in a different order. That's okay. The whole purpose of action plans is to help you achieve your career goals. Choose the one that works for you.

Let's look first at an example of a basic action plan, and then look at the same plan partly filled in by someone whose career goal is to be a cardiologist and heart surgeon. After that are exmples of alternative action plans for someone interested in nursing and one for someone interested in a career in hospital or health care marketing.

After reviewing these samples, use the blank plan provided on page 57 to help you create your own personal action plan. Feel free to change it or add sections to better suit your needs.

The Inside Scoop

Don't start panicking when you think you are never going to reach your career goals. Just because you estimate that you want to reach your long-range goals within the next five years, seven years, or whatever you choose does not mean that is the way it will actually turn out. It might take you longer or you might get there faster. Your timetable is really just an estimate of when you want to reach a specific goal.

Example 1

My Basic Action Plan

Career Goals

Long-range goals:
Mid-range goals:
Short-range goals:

My market:

What do I need to reach my goals?

How can I differentiate myself from others?

How can I catch the eye of people important to my career?

What actions can I take to reach my goals?

What actions do I absolutely need to take now?

What's my timetable?
   Short-range goals:
   Mid-range goals:
   Long-range goals:

Actions I've taken: Date completed:

Example 2

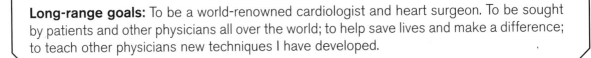

My Basic Action Plan

Career Goals

Long-range goals: To be a world-renowned cardiologist and heart surgeon. To be sought by patients and other physicians all over the world; to help save lives and make a difference; to teach other physicians new techniques I have developed.

Example 2, continued

Mid-range goals: To go through and finish medical school; to go through my residency and get board certified in cardiology and surgery; to be on staff at a prestigious teaching hospital.

Short-range goals: To be accepted into med school.

My market (short-term): Medical schools

My market (long-term): Patients with heart disease; hospitals, medical groups.

Possibilities for employment (after getting my MD): Hospitals, medical groups, private practice.

Possibilities for employment long-range: Major teaching hospitals; private practice.

What do I need to reach my goals?
Graduate from college. (Maybe I should have gone into a pre-med program . . . Oh, well.)
Volunteer in hospitals, clinics, or other health-related facilities.
Get involved in extracurricular activities and volunteer projects.
Prepare for the MCAT.
Take the MCAT.
Apply to med schools (and get in).
Finish med school.
Go through internship, residency, and fellowship.
Get board certified.
Search out opportunities.
Learn as much as I can; continue education.
Network in the industry.
Market myself.
Keep myself healthy and in shape.

How can I differentiate myself from others? I have a 4.0 GPA, have a scientific aptitude, and have taken a lot of science and biology coursework. I volunteer in a clinic and have been involved with a number of not-for-profit projects. I am very well rounded in my activities. I've networked and have a number of good contacts. I interview well. I also test well, so I should be able to do well on the MCAT.

How can I catch the eye of people important to my career? Get involved in some not-for-profit project. (I'm thinking of working on the van in the community that brings health care to those who can't afford health care.)

(continues)

Example 2, continued

What actions can I take to reach my goals? Explore different MCAT test-prep courses. Take MCAT test-prep course; volunteer on health care van; talk to a number of cardiologists to make sure this is the path I want to follow.

What actions do I absolutely need to take now? Graduate college and get my undergraduate degree. Look into med schools. Take MCAT test-prep course; volunteer on health care van or other health-related project; network; develop resume.

What's my timetable?
Short-range goals: Within the next 18 months
Mid-range goals: Within the next seven years I want to be on staff at a hospital
Long-range goals: Within the next 15 years

Actions I've Taken
Volunteered on health van.
Talked to Dr. Reyes about cardiology.
Worked with "Healthy Kids" program.
Talked to Dr. Johnston regarding his career.
Started developing my resume.
Looked into MCAT prep class.
Found class and took it.
Took MCAT.
Looked into med schools.
Visited med schools.
Filled in med school applications.
Graduated college.
Continue on with actions.

★ The Inside Scoop

If you want to go to medical school, you will need to take the MCAT—Medical College Admission Test. This is the examination you must take before you apply to med school. The score you receive on the MCAT can play a big part in which program accepts you.

The MCAT is a five-and-a-half-hour examination that tests your knowledge of physical and biological sciences, verbal reasoning, and writing skills. It is composed of multiple-choice questions as well as an essay portion.

While the MCAT had traditionally been given with paper and pencils, that changed in 2007. The MCAT is now given at specific computer-based testing sites and administered and taken totally on computers.

Example 3

My Basic Action Plan

Career Goals

Long-range goals: To become director of nursing at a large, prestigious hospital; teaching in nursing program.

Mid-range goals: Continue my education; get my master's degree in nursing; work in large hospital on oncology floor.

Short-range goals: To become an RN with a BSN degree.

Possible employers: Hospitals, private physician's office, medical groups, schools, large hotel, resort, insurance companies, camps, casinos, large corporations. (I really want to work in a hospital, specializing in oncology or at least on the oncology floor.)

What do I need to reach my goals? Apply and get accepted to a nursing program. Go through and graduate from nursing program.

How can I differentiate myself from others? I have a great sense of humor; I'm empathetic and compassionate and people always tell me they feel better around me.

How can I catch the eye of people important to my career? I've been volunteering in the local hospital since I was a teenager. I am also a volunteer with the American Cancer Society and helped run one of their biggest fund-raisers here.

What actions can I take to reach my goals? Contact my supervisor in the volunteer program at the hospital. Tell her my goals and ask if she can point me in the right direction. Contact the American Nurses Association and the National League for Nursing. Check out various colleges and see which offer accredited nursing programs.

What actions do I absolutely need to take now? Contact my supervisor in the volunteer program at hospital. Ask for letter of recommendation. Contact my supervisor at the American Cancer Society. Fill in application for college and nursing program.

What's my timetable?
 Short-range goals: I want to get accepted into a nursing program within the next six months. It will take me four years to get a BSN.
 Mid-range goals: Within the next year and a half to two years
 Long-range goals: Within the next 10 years, I want to be the director of nursing at a large hospital. (I really want to be the director of nursing in seven years, but I'll be realistic.)

(continues)

Example 3, continued

Actions I've taken (short-term):
1. Spoke to my supervisor at hospital volunteer program. Asked for letter of recommendation.
2. Spoke to director of our chapter of the American Cancer Society. Asked for letter of recommendation.
3. Checked out colleges in guidance center. Looked online. Went to visit some schools.
4. Filled in applications for college.
5. Continue on with actions.

Example 4

My Personal Action Plan

CAREER GOALS (Long-range): Marketing director at large, prestigious hospital

CAREER GOALS (Short-range): Obtain internship at hospital in marketing or public relations department

Action To Be Taken	Comments	Timetable/ Deadline	Date Accomplished
Short Range			
Look into internship possibilities at hospitals and health care facilities.	Contact college advisor to see if school has internship programs in health care facilities; contact hospital human resources departments regarding internships; check out hospital Web sites.	ASAP	October
Fill in internship application.	Get references from former employers and college advisor.	ASAP	November
Go through internship program.	Get letters of recommendation.	This semester	May

Action To Be Taken	Comments	Timetable/ Deadline	Date Accomplished
Look for seminars, workshops, etc. related to health care marketing, publicity, fund-raising, etc.	Contact American Hospital Association, Public Relations Society of America (PRSA), American Marketing Association, colleges, other industry associations. Look on Internet.	Find by January	
Find listing of names, addresses and Web sites of hospitals and health care facilities.	Check directories and Internet.	This month	
Find listing of names, addresses, and phone numbers of health care–oriented recruiters, headhunters, etc.	Check directories, Internet, newspapers.	This month	
Read industry periodicals and visit Web sites to get familiar with trends in health care, marketing, and not-for-profits.	See if library subscribes to any hospital or health care periodicals; call up marketing director at local hospital and ask for suggestions.	This week and continually	
Get letters of recommendation from Internship Coordinator and directors of departments in which I interned.		Before internship ends	
Make appointment with HR director of hospital in which I interned.	Check into possibility of getting job after graduation.		
Look into industry conferences and conventions to network.	Try to attend one or two. Call up in advance to see if they have career fairs.		
Read books about health care marketing, marketing in general, publicity, etc.	Do search on Amazon, then go to library to borrow books.	Browse through at least one a week.	

(continues)

Example 4, continued

Action To Be Taken	Comments	Timetable/ Deadline	Date Accomplished
Take classes in marketing, publicity and fund-raising.		This semester	
Volunteer to do marketing or publicity for a not-for-profit.	Call Janine Reynolds, president of General Hospital auxiliary, to see if I can be of assistance in some manner. Talk to Mark Summer to see if I can help with the publicity or in any other capacity for the college's annual fund-raising gala.	Call this week.	
Start working on resume.		Finish first draft by end of next week.	
Start building career portfolio.		Start now and keep going.	
Find networking events.	Call chamber of commerce.	Start now and continue.	
Make up business cards.	Find printer; check out other people's business cards for ideas.		
Develop marketing package and brochure.		Finish by mid-March.	
Send out marketing package and brochures to hospitals and health care facilities.		ASAP after marketing package and brochures are completed.	
Contact hospitals and health care facilities. Start with hospital I did internship with.	Send letters and resumes asking about openings.	Start in March.	
Contact industry associations.	Check to see if there are any networking events or career fairs.	Start in April.	
Check out trade publications for job openings.			
Continue on with actions.			

My Personal Action Plan

CAREER GOALS (Long-range):

CAREER GOALS (Short-range):

ACTION TO BE TAKEN	COMMENTS	TIMETABLE/ DEADLINE	DATE ACCOMPLISHED
SHORT RANGE			
LONG RANGE			

Specialized Action Plans

What things might be in your specialized action plan? That depends on the area in which you're interested in working and the level you currently are in your career. Let's first look at some actions you might take. Remember, these are just to get you started. When you sit down and think about it, you'll find tons of actions you're going to need to take.

- Identify your skills.
- Identify your talents.
- Identify your passions.
- Look for internships.
- Develop different forms of your resume.
- Develop cover letters.
- Network.
- Go to industry events.
- Make contacts.
- Volunteer to get experience.
- Obtain reference letters.
- Get permission to use people's names as references.
- Develop your career portfolio.
- Attend career fairs.
- Look for seminars and workshops in your area of interest.
- Take seminars, workshops, and classes.
- Get a college degree.
- Make business cards.
- Perform research online.
- Learn about industry trends.
- Make cold calls to obtain job interviews.
- Read books about the health care industry.

Now look at some actions you might have if your career aspiration is to become a doctor or work in another area of medicine. Specific actions will, of course, be dependent on the particular area of medicine you are targeting. Remember, this list is just to get you started thinking. It is by no means complete.

- Explore MCAT prep courses.
- Take MCAT prep course.
- Take MCAT.
- Look into steps needed for certification.
- Get certification.
- Go through internships.
- Go through refresher courses.
- Take continuing education courses.
- Subscribe to trade journals.
- Join trade associations.
- Join appropriate unions.
- Search out headhunters, recruiting agencies, and executive recruiters.

Now let's say you're interested in a career in medical equipment or pharmaceutical sales. What other actions might you add?

- Take courses, seminars and workshops in sales training and techniques.
- Make up business cards.
- Research pharmaceutical companies I would be interested in representing.
- Send out cover letters and resumes to those companies asking about openings.
- Place cold calls to human resources directors of pharmaceutical companies.
- Find relevant trade magazines and read them on a regular basis.
- Get experience selling.

Using Action Plans for Specific Jobs

Action plans can be useful in a number of ways. In addition to developing a plan for your career, you might utilize action plans to look for specific jobs. Let's look at an example.

Action Plan Looking for Specific Job

Job title: Health and Wellness Coordinator

Job description: Develop and implement health education and wellness activities in facility and surrounding community.

Company name: Station Community Hospital

Contact name: Jack Johnson

Secondary contact name: Janet Roper

Company address: 342 Briarcliff Road, Some City, NY 11111

Company phone number: (123) 222-2222

Company fax number: (123) 222-3333

Company Web site address: http://www.stationhospital.org

Company e-mail: stationhospital@stationhsopital.org

Secondary e-mail:

Where I heard about job: Saw ad in the *Record*

Actions taken: Tailored resume and cover letter to job; spoke to references to tell them I was applying for job and make sure I could still use them as references; faxed resume and cover letter.

Actions needed to follow up: Make sure suit and other clothing needed for interview is clean and pressed; review portfolio; make extra copies of my resume; browse company Web site; do research on hospital and community; call if I don't hear back within a week.

Interview time, date, and location: Received call on 3/10; they want me to come in for interview; interview set for 2:00 p.m. on 3/12 with Jack Johnson, HR director at hospital.

More actions to follow up on: Get directions to hospital; pick out clothes for interview; try everything on to make sure it looks good; rehearse giving answers to questions most likely to be asked during interview.

(continues)

(continued)

Comments: Went to interview; nice office and very nice people working there. I would like the job. Mr. Johnson seemed interested in my career portfolio; he said he was conducting interviews for the next week and would get back to me one way or another in a couple of weeks.

Extra actions: Write note thanking Mr. Johnson for interview.

Results: 3/19—Mr. Johnson called and asked me to come back for another interview to meet with the director of marketing. During the interview they told me that they had reviewed my career portfolio and wanted to put the health promotion and wellness coordinator job together with a job handling health and wellness publications. (They just received a grant.) They asked if I would be interested in the job!!! It would be more money and my job title would be Assistant Director of Health Promotion and Wellness. They told me to think about it for a couple of days and get back to them. I'm going to call them tomorrow to accept the job and discuss salary and benefits!

Use the blank plan provided on page 61 when you find specific jobs you're interested in to keep track of your actions. Fill in this worksheet for any of the jobs you apply to. Feel free to change the it or add sections to better suit your needs.

How to Use Your Action Plan

Creating your dream career takes time, patience, and a lot of work. For your action plan to be useful, you're going to have to use it. It's important to set aside some time every day to work on your career. During this time, you're going to be *taking actions.* The number of actions you take, of course, will depend on your situation. If you are currently employed and looking for a new job, you may not be able to tackle as many actions as someone who is unemployed and has more time available. Keep in mind that some actions may take longer than others.

For example, putting together your career portfolio will take longer than making a phone call. So if you're working on your portfolio, you might not accomplish more than one action in a day.

Try to make a commitment to yourself to take at least one positive action each day toward getting your dream career or becoming more successful in the one you currently have. Do more if you can. Whatever your situation, just make sure you take *some* action every single day.

Keeping a Daily Action Journal

In addition to creating an action plan, you'll find it helpful to keep an action journal recording all the career-related activities and actions you take on a daily basis. Use the journal to write down all the things you do on a daily basis to help you attain your career goals. You then have a record

Action Plan for Specific Job

Job title:

Job description:

Company name:

Contact name:

Secondary contact name:

Company address:

Company phone number:

Company fax number:

Company Web site address:

Company e-mail:

Secondary e-mail:

Where I heard about job:

Actions taken:

Actions needed to follow up:

Interview time, date and location:

Comments:

Results:

of all the actions you have taken in one place. Like your action plan, your action journal can help you track your progress.

How do you do this? Here's a sample to get you started. Names and phone numbers are fabricated for this sample.

With your daily action journal, you can look back and see exactly what you've done, whom you've called, whom you've written to, and what the result was. Additionally, you have names, phone numbers, times, dates, and other information at your fingertips. As a bonus, as you review

your daily action journal, instead of feeling like you're not doing enough, you are often motivated to do more.

The next step is to discuss your personal career success book.

★ The Inside Scoop

Once you start writing in your daily action journal, you'll be even more motivated to fulfill your career goals.

Daily Action Journal

Monday, March 8

Read daily papers.

Called Cindy Warren, human resources director of Hunter Memorial Hospital. I saw her doing an interview on local news (212-212-2121). Cold call, not in. Her secretary, Mary, said she would be in on Wednesday.

Surfed Internet looking for stories about health care marketing.

Worked on revamping my professional resume.

Tuesday, March 9

Read daily paper and scanned classified section.

Read health care/medicine section of a couple of Sunday papers online.

Got a "Thank you for coming in for an interview, but we've decided to promote from within" letter. Called and thanked Ms. Hart for letting me know and asked if she could make any suggestions on how I could interview better or other places I could look for a job. She told me no one had ever called her and asked and suggested I revamp my resume to highlight my education and volunteer experience. She suggested I call a medical group that she heard was looking for a publicist.

Wednesday, March 10

Called Cindy Warren, told her how much I enjoyed her interview on TV news, and asked if I could set up an appointment to come see her. She suggested I go in and fill in an application and asked what area I was interested in. I told her I just got my BA in marketing and communications and did an internship in Wayne County Hospital. Interestingly enough, she knew the PR director there. She told me to fax or e-mail my resume and she would look at it and call me back after she reviewed it.

Faxed and e-mailed my resume (just to be sure). Also sent a letter thanking her for taking the time to speak to me.

Worked on career portfolio.

Called Hilo Medical Group 434-9999 to ask about the publicist position. It turns out it is more a job as a receptionist. I thanked them but declined an interview.

Thursday, March 11

Received a call from Cindy Warren. She told me she was impressed with my resume and asked me to come in for an interview tomorrow!

Printed clean copies of my resume.

Checked on clothing to wear to interview.

My Daily Action Journal

Date:

Date:

Date:

Date:

Date:

Your Personal Career Success Book

What is your personal career success book? It's a folder, scrapbook, notebook, binder, or group of notebooks where you keep all your career information. Eventually, you might have so much that you'll need to put everything in a file drawer or cabinet, and that's okay. It means your career is progressing.

You will find your personal career success book useful no matter what part of the health care industry you are pursuing, whether your passion is the business or administrative segment of the industry, patient care, teaching, sales, research, or anything else.

What can go in your personal success career book? You can keep your action plans, your daily action journals, and all of the information you need to get your career to the level you want to reach.

What else can go into your personal success career book? What about career-related correspondence? It's always a good idea to keep copies of all the letters you send out for your career, as well as career-related correspondence you receive. Don't forget copies of e-mail.

Why do you want to keep correspondence? First of all, it gives you a record of people you wrote to as well as people who wrote to you. You might also find ways to make use of letters people send you. For example, instead of getting a rejection letter, reading it, crumpling it up and throwing it in the trash, take the name of the person who signed it, wait for a period of time, and see if you can pitch another idea, another job possibility, or anything that might further your career or get you closer to where

you want to be. Call that person and ask if he or she can point you in another direction. Ask what you could have done better or differently. Take the advice constructively (whatever it is) and then use it for next time.

Will the person at the other end always help? Probably not, but they might and all you need is one good idea or suggestion to get you where you want to go. It's definitely worth the call or the letter.

What else can go in your book? Keep copies of advertisements for jobs that you might want or be interested in now and even in the future. Keep copies of information on potential companies you might want to work for or who may offer employment opportunities.

"I don't need to write it down," you say. "I'll remember it when I need it."

Maybe you will and maybe you won't. Haven't you ever been in a situation where you do something and then say to yourself, "Oh, I forgot about that. If I had only remembered whatever it was, I wouldn't have done it like that." Or, "It slipped my mind." Writing things down means you're not leaving things to chance.

Keep lists in this book of potential support staff or people who might be helpful in your career. Keep names and addresses of recruiters and headhunters. You might not need an attorney now, but if you needed one quickly who would you call? If you need an accountant, who would you use? How about a publicist, printer, or banker? As you hear of professionals who others think are good, write down their names. That way you'll have information when you need it.

If everything is in one place, you won't have to search for things when you need them.

What else? You might keep lists of media possibilities, names, addresses, phone and fax numbers, and e-mail addresses. Let's say you're watching television and see an interview about something in the area of the health care industry in which you're interested. It might be an interview with a doctor, nurse, therapist, marketing director, producer, or director. At the time, you think you're going to remember exactly what you saw, when you saw it, and who the reporter or producer was. Unfortunately, you will probably forget some of the details. You now have a place to jot down the information in a section of your book. When you need it, you know where to look!

Don't forget to clip out interesting interviews, articles, and feature stories. Instead of having them floating all over your house or office, file them in this book. Want to network a bit? Write the reporter a note saying you enjoyed his or her piece and mentioning why you found it so interesting. Everyone likes to be recognized, especially people in the media. You can never tell when you might make a contact or even a friend.

It goes without saying that you should also clip and make copies of all articles, stories, and features that appear in the print media about you. Having all this information together will make it easier later to put together your career portfolio.

What else is going into your personal career success book? Copies of letters of recommendation; notes from supervisors and colleagues; and even letters from patients thanking you for doing such a good job.

As your career progresses, you will have various resumes, background sheets, and so on. Keep copies of them in your book as well (even after you've replaced them with new ones). What about your networking and contact worksheets? They now have a place too.

We've discussed the importance of determining your markets and possible employers. This is where you can keep these lists as well. Then, when you find new possibilities, just jot them down in your book. With your personal career success book, everything will be at your fingertips.

If you are like most people, you may attend seminars or workshops and get handouts or take notes. You now know where to keep them so you can refer to them when needed. The same goes for conference and convention material. Keep it in your personal career success book.

You know how sometimes you just happen to see a company where you would love to work? You just know you would fit right in. Until you have a chance to brainstorm and get your foot in the door, jot down your ideas. You'll be able to come back to them later and perhaps find a way to bring that job to fruition.

You'll find that success is easier to come by if you're more organized and have everything you need in one place.

If you're asking yourself if there's a lot of work involved in obtaining the career you want, the answer is a definite yes.

"Can't I just leave everything to chance like most people and hope I get what I want?" you say.

You can, but if your ultimate goal is to succeed in some aspect of the health care industry, you need to do everything possible to give yourself the best opportunity for success.

4

GET READY, GET SET, GO: PREPARATION

Opportunity Is Knocking: Are You Ready?

Over the years, I've given a lot of seminars and workshops on a variety of subjects related to some aspect of getting what you want. Sometimes it's getting the career of your dreams; sometimes it's obtaining success in some other facet of life.

At every one of these, I always ask the audience the same question: If opportunity knocks, are you ready to open the door and let it in?

"What do you mean?" someone always asks. "If opportunity knocks, I'll *get* prepared."

Unfortunately, that's not the way it always works. Sometimes you don't have a chance to prepare. Sometimes you need to be prepared at that very moment or you could lose out on an awesome opportunity. Let's look at a few scenarios.

First, imagine you are walking along the beach thinking about your career. "I wish I could work in health care administration," you say out loud, even though no one is there. "I wish I could find a really great job opening as the top administrator of a really large, prestigious hospital," you continue, planning how

success might come your way. As you're walking, the surf washes up and you see something shiny. You reach down to see what it is and pick up what appears to be a small brass lamp. All this time, you're still planning your career as you're walking. "I wish I had an interview with the human resources director of a prestigious hospital," you say as you absentmindedly rub the side of the lamp.

You see a puff of smoke and a genie appears. "Thank you for releasing me," he says. "In return for that, I will grant you your three wishes."

Before you have a chance to ask, "What wishes?" you find yourself in a beautiful office sitting in front of a desk where the HR director of one of the biggest hospitals in the country is interviewing you. Evidently, the genie had been listening to you talking to yourself and picked up on your three wishes.

Here's the opportunity you've been wishing for! You're sitting at the interview you wished for, being interviewed by the HR director at one of the most prestigious hospitals in the country. Are you ready? Or is this big break going to pass you by because you're not prepared? Not sure? Read on.

Imagine you're looking for a job as the sales director for a major pharmaceutical company. You are on your way to a weekend vacation in Las Vegas. You sit down in your seat on the plane and a man sits down next to you. You've seen him before but where? You search your mind, and it comes to you. He is the CEO of one of the biggest pharmaceutical companies in the world. You remember seeing a story about him with his photo in one of the trades just last week. Can you take advantage of the opportunity sitting right next to you, or would you let the opportunity pass you by because you were just prepared to go on vacation?

Let's look at another scenario. Imagine you have a fairy godmother who comes to you one day and says, "I can get you a one-on-one meeting with the admissions director of the medical school of your choice. The only catch is you have to be ready to walk in his office door in half an hour." Would you be ready? Would you miss your big break because you weren't prepared? If your answer is "Hmm, I might be ready...well, not really," then read on.

Here's the deal on opportunity: It may knock. As a matter of fact, it probably will knock, but if you don't open the door, opportunity won't stand there forever. If you don't

The Inside Scoop

For some reason we never understood, my grandmother always kept a suitcase packed. "Why?" we always asked her. "You can never tell when you'll have an opportunity to go someplace," she replied. "If you're ready, you can go. If you're not prepared, you might miss an opportunity."

Evidently she was right. Here's her story.

My grandfather was a physician. After he died, my grandmother worked at a number of different jobs, both to keep herself busy and to earn a living. At one point she worked as a sales associate in a women's clothing store in a well-known resort hotel. The hotel always had the top stars of the day in theater, music, film and television performing nightclub shows on holiday weekends. One weekend, Judy Garland was doing a show at the hotel. According to the story we were told as children, Judy Garland wanted a few things from the clothing store and called the store to see if someone could bring up a few pieces for her to choose from.

The store was busy and the manager assigned my grandmother the job. She quickly chose some items and brought them up to the star's room. Judy was pleased with my grandmother's choices and after talking to her for a short time was evidently impressed with her demeanor and attitude.

While signing for the purchases, she said to my grandmother, "I need a nanny for my children. I think you would be the right one for the job. I'm leaving tomorrow morning. If you're interested, I need to know now." Without missing a beat, my grandmother took the job and by the next afternoon was on the road with Judy Garland serving as nanny to her children.

While clearly she didn't give two weeks notice to her sales job, being in the right place at the right time certainly landed her an interesting job she seemed to love. I don't really remember how long she kept the position. What I do know, however, is that when an opportunity presented itself, my grandmother was ready. Had she not been ready or hesitated, someone else would have gotten the job.

The moral of the story is when opportunity knocks, you have to be ready to open the door.

answer the door, opportunity, even if it's *your* opportunity, will visit someone else's door.

While you might not believe in genies, fairy godmothers, or even the concept that you might just be in the right place at the right time, you should believe this: You will run into situations where you need to be ready "now" or miss your chance. When opportunity knocks, you need to be ready to open the door and let it in.

How can you do that? Make a commitment to get ready now. It's time to prepare. Ready, set, let's go!

Look Out for Opportunities

Being aware of available opportunities is essential to taking advantage of them. While it's always nice when unexpected opportunities present themselves, you sometimes have to go out looking for them as well.

How many times have you turned on the television or radio and learned about an opportunity you wished you had known about so *you* could have taken advantage of it? How many times have you opened the newspaper and read about an opportunity someone else experienced?

Would you rather open up the newspaper and read a feature story profiling a new physician who moved into town and is building a practice or be the physician being profiled? Would you rather see an advertisement congratulating the new graduating class of nurses or be one of the nurses graduating?

Would you rather meet the human resources director of a large pharmaceutical company who is visiting your campus or hear from your friend that she met him and got the job?

Whether your goal is a career in patient care; the business or administrative side of the industry; teaching; sales; research; communications; or any other area of the industry, you want to be the one taking advantage of every available opportunity.

Here's the deal: If you don't know about opportunities, you might miss them. It's important to take some time to look for opportunities that might be of value to you.

Where can you find opportunities? You can find them all over the place. Read through the papers, listen to the radio, look through the trade journals, and watch television. Check out newsletters, hospitals, health care facilities, trade associations, organizations, Web sites, and college campuses.

Even if you're not a student, schools, universities, and colleges often offer seminars or have programs that might be of interest and are open to the public for a small fee. Contact associations and ask about opportunities. Network, network, and network some more, continually looking for further opportunities.

What kind of opportunities do you have? What types of opportunities are facing you? Is a pharmaceutical company sending a representative to your campus? Is a physician giving a seminar on alternative medicine? Is your local hospital giving a seminar on careers in health care? Have you heard that the newspaper is looking for ideas for a new weekly column? Is a public relations company looking for interns?

Is there an upcoming fund-raiser at the local hospital? Is a local civic organization looking for a speaker? Are internship opportunities at the local hospital going to be announced soon? Will a trade association conference be hosting a career fair? Is an acclaimed physician speaking at a conference? Is the hospital offering infor-

Opportunities Worksheet

Hospital is offering informational seminar on careers in health care. Participants have the opportunity to meet with department heads as well as hear about various careers. June 14, 9:00 a.m. to 2:00 p.m. Call 339-3999 to reserve a space.

Conference of Health Care Administrators coming to town. September 23. See if I can find a way to attend. Maybe do a story for local newspaper.

Newspaper had article on internships at hospital. Call 339-2000 to get applications.

Chamber of Commerce is holding large networking event and recognizing the medical community on August 16. Make reservation.

Daily News looking for people to interview to talk about why they are interested in a career in health care.

mational workshops on various careers in the health care industry?

Is there an opening at the hospital where you're working, in the department you want to work? Did you hear a news story on the radio discussing a new health care facility? These are all potential opportunities. Be on the lookout for them. They can be your keys to success.

Keep track of the opportunities you find and hear about in a notebook. If you prefer, use the blank Opportunities Worksheet provided.

Assessment and Taking Inventory

Let's now make sure you're ready for every opportunity. One of the best ways to prepare for something is by first determining what you want and then seeing what you need to get it. This is the time to do a self-assessment.

What's that? Your self-assessment involves taking an inventory of what you have and what you have to offer and then seeing how you can relate it to what you want to do. Self-assessment involves thinking about you and your career goals.

Self-assessment helps you define your strengths and weaknesses. It helps you define your skills, interests, goals, and passions, giving you the ability to see them at a glance. Your self-assessment can help you develop and write your resume and make it easier to prepare for interviews.

Do you know what you want? Do you know what your strengths and weaknesses are? Can you identify the areas in which you are interested? Can you identify what's important to you in your career?

"But I already *know* what I want to do," you say. "This is a waste of my time."

Well, that's up to you, but answering these questions now can help your career dreams come to fruition quicker. It will help give you the edge others might not have.

Opportunities Worksheet

_____

_____

_____

_____

_____

_____

_____

_____

_____

_____

_____

_____

_____

_____

_____

_____

_____

_____

_____

Doing a self-assessment is a good idea no matter what area of the health care industry you are interested in pursuing. Before someone takes a chance on you, they are going to want to know about you. If you have this done, you'll be prepared.

Strengths and Weaknesses

We all have certain strengths and weaknesses. Strengths are things you do well. They are advantages that others may not have. You can exploit them to help your career. Weaknesses are things that you can improve. They are things you don't do as well as you could.

What are your strengths and weaknesses? Can you identify them? Why are these questions important? Once you know the answers, you know what you have to work on.

For example, if you're shy and you don't like speaking in front of groups of people, you might take some public speaking classes, or you might force yourself to network and go into situations that could help make you more comfortable around people. If you need better written

Tip from the Top

If there is something that you need to do or determine can help you in your career, do it now! Don't procrastinate. In other words, don't put off until tomorrow what could have been done today (or at least this week). If you need more education, certification, additional skills, or anything else, don't put it off until you "have time." Get it now! If you need to work on your resume or your portfolio, do it now and get it done. Procrastinating can seriously affect your career because it means you didn't get something done that needed to be accomplished. Just the sheer thought of *having* to get something done takes time and energy. Instead of thinking about it, do it!

communication skills, you might take a couple of writing classes to make you a better writer.

Are you a good salesperson who could be great? Think about taking some classes or workshops in selling. Do your computer skills need tweaking? Consider taking a quick class or workshop. Do you want to improve your writing skills? Take a class!

Do you need to learn how to organize your time better? Look for a time management seminar. Are you always stressed? Take a course in stress management. Do your negotiation skills need fine-tuning? You know what you need to do. Take a class.

Do your math skills need some help? A class or seminar on math or accounting might be what you need.

Take some time now to define your strengths and weaknesses. Then jot them down in a notebook or use the Strengths and Weaknesses Worksheet. Be honest and realistic. Here are a couple of sample worksheets to help you get started.

Tip from the Coach

If a human resource director, headhunter, interviewer, or college admissions officer asks what your weaknesses are, try to indicate a weakness that might also be a strength. For example, you might say something like, "I'm a perfectionist. I like things to be done right." You wouldn't want to give someone any information on any of your *real* weaknesses. Remember that as friendly as these people might seem during interviews, their job is screening out candidates. You don't want to give an interviewer or anyone else a reason not to hire you.

Strengths and Weaknesses Worksheet—Patient Care Career

My strengths:
I have a lot of energy.
I can get along with almost everyone.
I can follow instructions.
I'm a team player yet can work on my own.
I'm organized.
I am good at teaching others.
I have a good memory.
I have a good bedside manner.
I make people feel comfortable.

My weaknesses:
I'm shy.
I need better written communication skills.
I'm not good with numbers.
I don't test well.

What's important in my career?
I want to be a registered nurse and work in a hospital on the critical-care floor. I want to make a difference, and think I can in this field. I also eventually want to teach other nurses.

Strengths and Weaknesses Worksheet—Business/Administrative Career in Health Care

My strengths:
I am organized.
I get along with others.
I have great communications skills.
I'm a team player.
I have gone through internships in health care marketing.
I have a bachelor's degree with a double major in business and health care administration.

My weaknesses:
I'm a perfectionist.
I am an overachiever.
I have a difficult time being on time for things.
I don't know how to use PowerPoint or Excel.

What's important in my career?
I want to work in a large hospital as a marketing director. I want to develop innovative marketing campaigns designed to help make the facility I represent really stand out in the field. I also eventually want to go into health care administration as the executive director of a prestigious facility.

Strengths and Weaknesses Worksheet

My strengths:

_____

_____

_____

My weaknesses:

_____

_____

_____

What's important in my career?

_____

_____

_____

Tip from the Coach

A good way to deal with an interviewer asking you how you will deal with a specific weakness that *they* identify is by telling them that you are actively trying to make it a strength. For example, if one of your weaknesses is you don't like speaking in public, you might say you are working on turning that into a strength by taking a public speaking class. Telling an interviewer you are working on your shortcomings helps him or her form a much more positive picture of you.

Now that you know some of your strengths and weaknesses, it's time to focus on your personal inventory. Your combination of skills, talents, and personality traits helps determine your marketability.

What Are Your Skills?

Skills are acquired things that you have learned to do and can do well. They are part of your selling tools. Keep in mind that there are a variety of relevant skills. There are job-related skills that you use at your present job. Transferable skills are skills that you used on one job and that you can transfer to another. Life skills are skills you use in everyday living such as problem solving, time management, decision making, and interpersonal skills. Hobby or leisure skills are related to activities you do during your spare time for enjoyment. These might or might not be pertinent to your career. There are also technical skills connected to the use of machinery. Many of these types of skills overlap.

Most people don't realize just how many skills they have. They aren't aware of the specialized knowledge they possess. Are you one of them?

While it's sometimes difficult to put your skills down on paper, it's essential so you can see what they are and where you can use them in your career. Your skills, along with your talents and personality traits, make you unique. They can set you apart from others and help you land the career of your dreams.

Once you've given some thought to your skills, it's time to start putting them down on paper. You can either use the worksheet or a page in a notebook. Begin with the skills you know you have. What are you good at? What can you do? What have you done? Include everything you can think of from basic skills on up, and then think of the things people have told you you're good at.

Don't get caught up thinking that "everyone can do that" and so a particular skill of yours is not special. *All* your skills are special. Include them all in your list.

Tip from the Top

Accept the fact that at almost every interview you will go on, you will be asked about your strengths and weaknesses. Preparing a script ahead of time so you know what you are going to say gives you the edge.

Tip from the Coach

Don't limit the skills you list to just those that relate to the area of health care in which you're interested. Include all your skills. Even when a skill seems irrelevant, you can never tell when it might come in handy.

Review these skill examples to help get you started. Remember, this is just a beginning.

◎ computer proficiency
◎ public speaking
◎ time management
◎ analytical skills
◎ organizational skills
◎ writing skills
◎ listening skills
◎ verbal communications
◎ management
◎ selling
◎ problem solving
◎ language skills
◎ leadership
◎ math skills
◎ decision-making skills
◎ negotiating skills
◎ money management
◎ word processing skills
◎ computer repair
◎ teaching
◎ customer service
◎ cooking
◎ Web design
◎ singing
◎ songwriting
◎ acting
◎ playing an instrument
◎ interior decorating

Skills Worksheet

> ⭐ **Tip from the Top**
>
> Keep in mind that some skills also require *talent*. For example, writing is a skill. It can be learned. To be a great writer, however, you generally need talent. Cooking is a skill. To be a great chef, you need talent. Surgery is a skill. The best surgeons, however, are also talented.

Your Talents

You are born with your talents. They aren't acquired like skills, but they may be refined and improved. Many people are reluctant to admit what their talents are, but if you don't identify and use them, you'll be wasting them.

What are your talents? You probably already know what some of them are. What are you not only good at but better at than most other people? What can you do with ease? What has been your passion for as long as you can remember? These are your talents.

Are you a talented negotiator? Can you bring two sides to an agreement when no one else can? Are you a talented diagnostician? A prolific writer? A great fund-raiser? Can you tell stories and jokes in such a manner that those listening just can't stop themselves from laughing? Can you make people feel comfortable with a simple look?

Does your talent fall in science? How about math? What about art? Do you have an "eye" to be able to see just the right employee for a specific job? Can you look at someone and just *know* that, with a little training and work, they can be great?

Think about it for a bit and then jot your talents in your notebook or in the Talents Worksheet. Here are a couple of examples to get you started.

My Talents Worksheet

I have good interpersonal skills. I get along with most people.

People feel comfortable telling me things.

I am multilingual and can speak English, Spanish, and French.

People feel they can relate to me.

I am funny and can break the ice with a joke to make people feel comfortable.

I have the ability to make people around me feel good about themselves.

My Talents Worksheet

I am a talented writer.

I am very creative.

I have a great sense of humor. I can make almost everyone I'm around feel better by making them laugh.

I have the ability to inspire people.

I have the ability to motivate people.

I am a great public speaker.

I am very persuasive.

Talents Worksheet

_____

_____

_____

_____

_____

_____

Personality Traits Worksheet

Your Personality Traits

We all have different personality traits. The combination of these traits sets us apart from others. Certain personality traits can help you move ahead no matter what aspect of the health care industry you want to pursue. Let's look at some of them.

- ability to get along well with others
- adaptable
- ambitious
- analytical
- assertive
- charismatic
- clever
- compassionate
- competitive
- conscientious
- creative
- dependable
- efficient
- energetic
- enterprising
- enthusiastic
- flexible
- friendly
- hard worker
- helpful
- honest
- imaginative
- innovative
- inquisitive
- insightful
- observant
- optimistic
- outgoing
- passionate
- personable
- persuasive
- positive
- practical
- problem solver
- reliable
- resourceful
- self-confident
- self-starter
- sociable
- successful
- team player
- understanding

What are your special personality traits? What helps make you unique? Think about it, and then jot them down in your notebook or in the Personality Traits Worksheet.

Special Accomplishments

What special accomplishments have you achieved? Special accomplishments make you unique and often will give you an edge over others.

Have you won any awards? Were you awarded a scholarship? Were you asked to deliver a paper at a national conference? Have you won a writing competition? Did you do especially well in school?

Were you the president of your class? Were you the chairperson of a special event? Have you won a community service award? Were you nominated for an award even if you didn't win? Has an article about you appeared in a regional or national magazine or newspaper? Have you been a special guest on a radio or television show? Are you sought out as an expert on some subject in health care or in some other area? Were you named employee of the month? How about employee of the year?

All these things are examples of some of the special accomplishments you may have experienced. Think about it for a while, and you'll be able to come up with your own list. Once you

Special Accomplishments Worksheet

identify your accomplishments, jot them down in your notebook or on your Special Accomplishments Worksheet.

Education and Training

Education and training are important to the success of your career no matter what you want to do.

If your dream career in medicine is as a doctor, nurse, dentist, or researcher, a college education is mandatory. Certain careers also require postsecondary education and continuing education.

Some careers may or may not require college. A college background can't guarantee you a job, but it often helps prepare you for life in the workplace. Depending on your specific career goal, most employers will generally at least prefer that you have a college background even if it is not a requirement. A college education will also be valuable in helping you hone skills, learn about the business, and make important contacts.

Education and training may be formal or informal. It may encompass classes, courses, seminars, workshops, programs, on-the-job training, and learning from your peers. Every opportunity you have to learn anything can be a valuable resource in your career.

What type of education and training do you already possess? What type of education and training do you need to get to the career of your dreams? What type of education and training will help you get where you want to go?

Would some extra classes help you reach your career goal? Is there a special seminar that will help give you the edge? How about a course in public speaking? What about a class in time management? How about a stress management seminar? Would classes that get you certified in your field help move your career in a forward direction?

Is a college degree what you're missing to give you the edge over other applicants seeking jobs in the same area in which you're interested? How about some workshops or seminars? What about attending conferences? The options are yours.

Now is the time to determine what education or training you have and what you need so that you can go after it.

Fill in the Education and Training Worksheet with your information so you know what you need to further your career and meet your goals.

Education and Training Worksheet

What education and training do I have?

_____

_____

What education or training do I need to reach my goals?

_____

_____

What classes, seminars, and workshops have I taken which are useful to my career aspirations?

_____

_____

_____

_____

What classes, seminars, workshops, courses, and other steps can I take to help my career?

_____

_____

_____

_____

_____

Location, Location, Location: Where Do You Want to Be?

Location can be an important factor in your career. Where should you live if you want a career in the health care industry? Here's the good news! Careers in the health care industry are available throughout the country.

There are a ton of options. You might choose to work in a prestigious facility in a major metropolitan city or in a facility in the suburbs or a rural area. Sometimes you get to choose. Other times you have to go where the jobs are.

Will the biggest cities be the best? Not always. If you're just starting out, you might find it easier to locate opportunities in smaller areas. That way you can get some experience, make some contacts, and hone your skills.

One thing you might want to think about is that in deciding where you want to be headquartered, remember that it is sometimes helpful to be *where it's happening*. You have more opportunities to meet the people you need to meet to help you get to the top of your career quicker. You will also have more opportunities to make important contacts necessary to your career success.

There's also something to be said about being in the right place at the right time. What does that mean? Let's say you happen to hear about a job opening in a hospital in New York City.

Words from the Wise

Before you pack up and move to a large city without a job, be aware that living in these areas can be quite expensive. If you come from a smaller area, city living can also bring a radically different lifestyle. Try to find a place to live before you make a big move. If you don't have a nest egg, come up with a plan on how you're going to survive until you start earning money. That way you can concentrate on your career.

Location Worksheet

Type of area I reside in now:

_____

Location of job or career choice I want:

_____

Other possible locations:

_____

_____

The job hasn't be advertised yet, but someone in your network of contacts heard about it and thought you would be perfect. If you live locally, you can grab your resume, fill in an application, and maybe even snag the opportunity. If you live in New Hampshire, by the time you get to New York City, the opportunity might be gone.

As we'll discuss throughout this book, success comes from a number of things, including talent, luck, perseverance, and being in the right place at the right time.

Reviewing Your Past

Let's look at your past. What have you done that can help you succeed in your career in the health care industry?

Make a list of all the jobs you have had and the general functions you were responsible for when you held them. Don't forget to make a list of the volunteer activities in which you have participated.

Look at this information and see what functions or skills you can transfer to your career in the health care industry.

You might say, "None of my former jobs or volunteer activities have anything to do with the health care industry."

That's okay. Many skills are transferable.

"Give me examples," you say.

Have you held a job as a reporter for a local newspaper? That shows that you know how to develop and write an article or news story and can do it in a timely fashion. These skills can easily be transferred if you are interested in a career as a medical journalist or writer. They can also be transferred to skills needed to be a publicist or publications director at a hospital.

Have you worked as a bookkeeper? What about a job in the bookkeeping department of a hospital? What about working as a bookkeeper for a medical or dental group? With some education and certification, you might be able to fulfill your goals of working as a CPA in a hospital.

Have you worked in retail sales? Have you sold advertising for a newspaper? How about selling commercials for television or radio stations? Have you worked as a real estate salesperson? Do you love selling? You could use your sales skills in a career as a sales rep for a pharmaceutical company.

Did you work in a health food store, giving lectures on alternative health care methods? Did you help arrange a lecture series in a variety of subject areas for the store? You might be able to transfer these skills to a career in the wellness promotion area of a hospital.

Have you volunteered and helped a not-for-profit organization execute a special event? Have you worked at a local hospital or health care facility in any capacity? Have you interned at a health care facility? A pharmaceutical company? A social service agency?

Were you the fund-raising chairperson for a local not-for-profit organization? Did you bring in thousands of dollars for the organization when you ran the membership drive? You might use those talents in the fund-raising department of a hospital. You might also transfer your skills to a position doing the fund-raising for an association related to the health care industry.

Remember that the idea is to use your existing education, training, talents, skills, and accomplishments to get your foot in the door. Once in, you can find ways to move up the ladder so you can achieve the career of your dreams. When going over your list of past positions, include both part-time jobs you had as well as full-time ones. Look at the entire picture, including not only your jobs but your accomplishments, and see what they might tell about you.

"Like what?" you ask.

Did you graduate from high school in three years instead of four? That illustrates that you're driven and can accomplish your goals. Were you the chairperson for a not-for-profit charity event? That illustrates that you take initiative, work well with people, and delegate and organize well. Do you sing in your church choir? Have you volunteered to handle the choir's music? This shows you can sing and that you have the dedication to attend rehearsals. Handling the music illustrates your organizational skills.

Now that you have some ideas, think about what you've done and see how you can relate it to your dream career. Everything you have done in your life, including your past jobs, volunteer and civic activities, and other endeavors, can help create your future dream career in the health care industry.

Using Your Past to Create Your Future

When reviewing past jobs and volunteer activities, see how they can be used to help you get what you want in the health care industry. Answer the following questions:

◎ What parts of each job accomplishment or volunteer activity did you love?
◎ What parts made you happy?
◎ What parts gave you joy?
◎ What parts of your previous jobs excited you?
◎ What skills did you learn while on those jobs?
◎ What skills can be transferred to your career in the health care industry?

> ### ★ Tip from the Top
> If you're just out of school, your accomplishments will probably be more focused on what you did while in school. As you get more established in your career, your accomplishments will be more focused on what you've done *during* your career.

◎ What accomplishments can help your career in health care?

Jot down your answers in your notebook or use the Using Your Past to Create Your Future worksheet provided on the next page.

The more ways you can find to use past accomplishments and experience to move closer to success in your career in the health care industry, the better off you will be. Look outside the box to find ways to transfer your skills and use jobs and activities as stepping-stones to get where you're going.

Passions and Goals

Once you know what you have, it's easier to determine what you need to get what you want. You've made a lot of progress by working on your self-assessment, but you have a few more things to do. At this point, you need to focus on exactly what you want to do.

In what area of the health care industry do you want to be involved? What are you interested in? Do you want to be a doctor, nurse, nurse practitioner, dentist, optometrist, or chiropractor? Do you want a career working in health care for animals as a veterinarian? Do you want a career as a health care administrator, a marketing director, public relations director, publications director, or health care writer? Do you want to work as a

Using Your Past to Create Your Future

Past Job/ Volunteer Activity/ Accomplishment	Parts of job/ Volunteer Activity/ Accomplishment that I Enjoyed	Skills I Learned and Can Transfer to Career in the Health Care Industry

therapist, social worker, accountant, or attorney in the health care industry? It's all up to you.

You began working on this task earlier in the book. Continue to refine your list of things that you enjoy and want to do. Previously you defined your career goals. Now that you've assessed the situation, are they still the same?

What are your passions? You owe it to yourself to have a career that you love, that you're passionate about, and that you deserve. Take the time now to make sure that you get it by going after your passions.

5

JOB SEARCH STRATEGIES

Health care is one of the fastest-growing industries in the country and is expected to continue growing. If you've decided that your dream career will be in the health care industry, you're in luck. There are millions of jobs in the various segments of the industry as well as the peripherals. One of them can be yours.

We've covered some of the various opportunities in previous chapters. Some jobs are easier to obtain. Some may be more difficult. This section will cover some traditional and not-so-traditional job search strategies.

It's important to recognize that *getting* the job is just the beginning. What you want is a career.

Using a Job to Create a Career

Unfortunately, you can't just go to the store and *get* a great career. Generally, it's something you have to work at and create. How do you create your dream career? Developing the ultimate career takes a lot of things, including sweat, stamina, and creativity. It takes luck and being in the right place at the right time. It takes talent, education, and training. It takes perseverance and passion. And it takes faith in yourself that if you work hard for what you want and don't give up, you will get it.

You have to take each job you get along the way and make it *work* for you. Think of every job as a rung on the career ladder, every assignment within that job as a stepping-stone. Completing the puzzle takes lots of pieces and lots of work, but it will be worth it in the end.

Every job you get along the way helps to sharpen your skills and adds another line to your resume. Every situation is an opportunity to network, learn, and, most of all, get noticed.

If you know what your ultimate goal is, it is much easier to see how each job you do can get you a little closer. Every situation, no matter how small or insignificant you think it may be, gives you another experience, hones your skills, helps you gain confidence, and gives you the opportunity to be seen and discovered. Every job can lead you to the career you've been dreaming about.

One of the things you should know is that while most anyone can get a job, not everyone ends up with a career. As discussed in a previous section of the book, the difference between a job and a career is that a job is a means to an end. It's something you do to get things done and to earn a living. Your career, on the other hand, is a series of related jobs you build using your skills, talents, and passions. It's a progressive path of achievement.

When you were a child, perhaps your parents dangled the proverbial carrot on a stick in front of you, tempting you to eat your dinner so that you could have chocolate ice cream and cake for dessert. Whether dinner was food you liked, didn't particularly care for, or a combination, you probably ate it most of the time to get to what you wanted—dessert. In this case, your dessert will be ultimate success in your career in the health care industry.

Use every experience, every job, and every opportunity for the ultimate goal of filling your life with excitement and passion while getting paid. Will there be things you don't enjoy doing and jobs you wish you didn't have along the way? Perhaps, but there will also be things you love doing and jobs you look back on and remember with joy.

Your Career: Where Are You Now?

Where are you in your career now? Are you still in school? Are you just starting out? Are you in another field and want to move into a career in the health care industry? Do you know what you want to do with the rest of your life?

If you already know what you want to do, great! You're in good shape. You need only to prepare by getting the education, training, and experience, and you're ready to find the job or jobs that will lead you to your dream career.

Career Changing: Moving into the Health Care Industry

Are you currently working in another industry but really want to have a career in some segment of health care? If so, you're not alone. Many people have dreamed about a career in health care from the time they were very young and for a variety of reasons ended up in other industries. Is this you? If so, read on.

Perhaps at the time, you needed a job. Possibly it looked too difficult to obtain the career you wanted. Maybe you just didn't know how to go about it. Maybe you weren't ready. Maybe people around you told you that you were pipe dreaming. Maybe you were scared or maybe someone offered you a job in a different industry and you took it for security. There might be hundreds of reasons why you wanted a specific career in the health care industry, but you didn't pursue it at the time. More important, do you want to be there now?

"Well," you say, "I do, but . . ."

Before you go through your list of *buts,* ask yourself these questions: Do you want to give up your dream? Do you want to live your life saying, "I wish I had," but never really trying? Wouldn't you rather try to find a way to do what you want rather than never really being happy with what you're doing? Wouldn't it be great to look at others who are doing what they want and know that *you* are one of them? Here's the good news. You can! You just have to make the decision to do it!

How can you move into a career in health care from a different industry? How can you change your career path? Of course, it will depend on what part of the health care industry you aspire to work in, but it's not as hard as you think. What you need to do is take stock of what you have and what you don't have.

Do you want to work in one of the peripheral areas of the health care industry? Do you want to work in a hospital or health care facility but not necessarily in direct patient care?

One of the easiest ways to move into the business or administrative area of the health care industry is by transferring skills. That means going over your skills and finding ways you can use them in the career of your choice.

Do you have strong writing skills? Consider seeking out a position as a grant writer for a health care association. Think about a career in public relations or marketing. Consider a job as a publications director. Think about handling the publicity or public relations for a medical group, a private doctor, or a pharmaceutical company. What about a job as a medical reporter for a newspaper or periodical? How about a technical medical writer?

Are your skills in the number-crunching area? What about seeking a position in a hospital or other health care facility's accounting or bookkeeping department?

How about a job handling the finances for a medical association or hospital foundation? What about working with a CPA who handles physicians and other clients in the health care field?

Do you have office skills? Are you a good manager? Do you have good organizational skills? Consider a job as an administrative assistant in the administration office of a hospital, health care facility, a medical group, a doctor or dental group. One of the exciting things about these types of positions is that you get to learn the ropes and often have a great chance of

---

⭐ Tip from the Coach

Are you living someone else's dream? You can't change your past, but you can change your future. If your dream is to work in an aspect of the health care industry, go for it. Things might not change overnight, but the first step you take toward your new career will get you closer to your dream. Every day you put it off is one more day you're wasting doing something you don't love. You deserve more. You deserve the best.

moving up the career ladder. What else? These positions generally offer good benefits that you might not always get in another industry.

Do you have information technology (IT) skills? Do you have other computer skills? Transfer them to the health care industry!

Are you a webmaster? Today, most hospitals, health care facilities, medical groups, doctors, dentists, pharmaceutical and medical equipment companies, and health-oriented companies, agencies, and businesses have a Web site even if they have no IT department.

Are your skills in marketing? Are you working in marketing in another industry? Consider a position in the marketing department of a hospital or other health care facility. What about a position in a pharmaceutical company? How about a job at a marketing firm that specializes in clients in the health care industry?

Are your skills in sales? Lucky you! The possibilities are endless. Every pharmaceutical company and medical equipment company needs talented salespeople. So do the advertising segments of health and medical-oriented Web sites and periodicals and other publications.

Are your skills in education? What about teaching health education in elementary or secondary school? What about becoming a nursing instructor? How about teaching new doctors or chiropractors or dentists the skills they need to excel? What about teaching specialized techniques? Depending on your skills, experience, and education, the options are endless.

"Wait a minute," you say. "What if I don't want to work in the area where my skills are? What if I want to do something totally different? What then?"

Here's the deal. If you can, try to use your skills and your talents to get your foot in the

---

⭐ **Words from the Wise**

If you are working at another job until you get the one you want, it's not a good idea to keep harping on the fact that you're only there until you get your big break or the job of your dreams. If your supervisor thinks you are planning on leaving, not only will you probably not get the choice assignments, but coworkers who are stuck in the job you are using as a stepping-stone often feel jealous.

---

door. Once in, you have a better opportunity to move into the area you want.

"What if I want to work in medicine or patient care? Don't I need to do more than just transfer skills?" you ask.

Yes, you do. You can still transfer any applicable skills, but if your dream is to work in medicine or patient care and you are either just starting out your career or want to move into one of those areas, you probably are going to have to get some additional education or training before going on your job search.

Can you do it? Yes! Thousands of people become doctors, nurses, therapists, technicians, technologists, dentists, chiropractors, optometrists, and more. You can do it too!

Should you quit your present job to go after your dream? And if so, when should you do it? Good questions. Generally, you are much more employable if you are employed. You don't have that desperate "I need a job" look. You don't have the worries about financially supporting yourself and your family if you have one. You don't have to take the wrong job because you've been out of work so long that *anything* looks good.

It's best to work on starting your dream career while you have a job to support yourself.

Ideally, you'll be able to leave one job directly for another much more to your liking.

Of course, in some situations, you might want to (or need to) devote most of your time to your career. For example, if you are going to medical school, it might be difficult to go to school and hold down a full-time job. Some people do it, but it can be difficult. Only you can make the decision on how to go about starting your career. Take some time to decide what is best for you.

You must focus on exactly what you want to do, set your goals, prepare your action plan, and start taking action now. You're going to have to begin moving toward your goals every day—a job in itself but one that can lead to the career of your dreams.

The question many ask is, "When do I quit the job that I have to go after the job that I want?" No one can answer this for you, but try to be realistic. You don't want to be in the position where you *can't* do what you want because you don't have any funds. Do you have a nest

egg put away? To have the best shot at what you want to do, you need to be as financially stable as possible.

We've already discussed that you are usually more marketable if you are currently employed. This doesn't mean you shouldn't work toward your goals. Continue searching out ways to get where you're going.

"Working takes all my energy," you say. "I don't have time to do everything. If I'm working, I just don't have enough time to put into creating my dream career."

You're going to have to make time. It's amazing how you can expand your time when you need to. Remember your action plan? It's imperative that you carve time out of your day to perform some of your actions.

If you think you don't have the time, look at your day a little closer. What can you eliminate doing? Will getting up a half an hour early give you more time to work on your career? How about cutting out an hour of TV during the day or staying off the computer for an hour? Even if you can only afford to take time in 15-minute increments, you usually can find an hour to put into your career.

Moving from One Segment of the Health Care Industry to Another

Are you working in one segment of the health care industry and want to work in another? Are you an LPN who wants to become an RN? Are you working in research and want to become a medical doctor? Are you a social worker who wants a career in hospital administration? Are you a physician who wants to become an administrator? Are you a dietician who wants to become a nurse?

What do you do? Check out the requirements. Look into what education you need to reach your goals. Find a mentor. Ask questions. Find what you need to do to get the career of your dreams and then do it!

What should you *not* do? To begin with, don't give up before you get started. Don't get so caught up in how difficult something will be that you don't look for a way to do it. Most of all, don't discount your dreams.

If you are an LPN and want to become an RN, for example, look into what classes you need. Is there a nursing program in the hospital at which you work that can help you advance your career from that of an LPN to an RN?

Does the nursing program at your local college offer an RN program? What do you need to do? In most cases, you can probably take the education you need to become an RN while still working at your job as an LPN.

Let's say you are a social worker who wants to go into hospital administration. What do you do? You know you already have a degree in social work. What classes have you taken that are applicable to the degree you might need for a career as a hospital administrator? What other types of classes do you need to take? What kind of program can help you move into the job of your dreams? If you research what you need to do and take it step by step, you will be on your way to getting the job of your dreams.

Finding the Job You Want

Perseverance is essential to your success no matter what you want to do, what area of the industry you want to enter, and what career level you want to achieve. It doesn't matter whether you want to work in medicine or patient care. It doesn't matter if you want to work in the business or administration segment of health care. It doesn't matter if you want to work in research or sales. It doesn't matter what portion of the industry in which you want to work.

Do you want to know why most people don't find their perfect job? They give up looking *before* they find it.

Difficult as it might be to realize at this point, remember that your job—your great career—is out there waiting for you. You just have to locate it. How do you find that elusive position you want? You look for it!

For the most part, jobs are located in two areas: the open job market and the hidden job market. What's the difference? The open job market is composed of jobs that are advertised and announced to the public. The hidden job market is composed of jobs that are not advertised or announced to the public.

Where can you find the largest number of jobs? Are they in the hidden job market or the open job market? A lot depends exactly on what you want to do in the industry, but you should be aware that a great many jobs just aren't advertised. Why?

There are a few reasons. Some employers don't want to put an ad in the classified section of the newspaper because there could be hundreds of responses, if not more.

"But isn't that what employers want?" you ask. "Someone to *fill* their job openings?"

Of course they want their job openings filled, but they don't want to have to go through hundreds of resumes and cover letters to get to that point. It is much easier to try to find qualified applicants in other ways, and that is where the hidden job market comes in.

This doesn't mean, however, that you shouldn't look into the open market. The smart thing to do to boost your job hunt is utilize every avenue to find your job. With that being said, let's discuss the open job market a bit, and then we'll go on to talk about the hidden job market in more detail.

The Open Job Market

When you think of looking for a job, where do you start? If you're like most people, you head straight for the classifieds. Although, as we just noted, this strategy may not always be the best bet, it's at least worth checking out. Let's go over some ways to increase your chances of success in locating job openings this way.

The Sunday newspapers usually have the largest collection of help-wanted ads. Start by focusing on those. You can never tell when a company will advertise job openings, though, so you might also want to browse through the classified section on a daily basis, if possible.

Will you find a job advertised in your local hometown newspaper? That depends on what type of job you're seeking and where you live.

If you live in a small town and you're looking for a position with a major teaching hospital, probably not. If you're looking for a position in a smaller or regional facility, your chances are better.

What do you do if you don't live in the area you want to look for a job? How can you get the newspapers?

There are a number of solutions. Larger bookstores and libraries often carry Sunday newspapers from many metropolitan cities in the country. If you're interested in getting newspapers from specific areas, you can also usually order short-term subscriptions. One of the easiest ways to view the classified sections of newspapers from around the country is by going online to the newspapers' Web sites. The home page will direct you to the classified or employment section. Start your search from there.

What do you look for once you get the papers? That depends on the specific job you're after, but generally look for keywords. If you want a job as a physical therapist, for example, you would look for keywords such as *physical therapist* or *therapist*. If you are looking for a job as a marketing director of a hospital, you might look for keywords such as *marketing director, health care, health care marketing, hospital marketing,* or *marketing*. If you are looking for a job as a physician, you might look for keywords such as *physician, medical doctor, oncologist, medical group physician, locum tenens,* or *emergency room*

⭐ **The Inside Scoop**

Locum tenens are physicians who substitute on a temporary basis for other physicians. They are often used in hospital emergency rooms as well as in other departments.

physician. Don't forget to look for specific company names as well.

In some cases, all the jobs in health care are in a specific section of the classifieds. In others, jobs are scattered throughout the classified section. Keep in mind that in many situations, large facilities or companies also use boxed or display classified ads. These are large ads that may advertise more than one job and usually have a company name and/or logo. There may also be employment agencies specializing in jobs in a specific area of the health care industry that may advertise openings in the employment agency area of the classifieds.

Trade Journals, Industry Publications, Newsletters, and Web Resources

Where else are jobs advertised? Trade journals are often a good source. Trades are periodicals geared toward a specific industry. Every industry has trade magazines and newspapers, and the health care industry is no exception.

Where do you find them? Contact the trade association geared toward the specific area of the industry in which you are interested. (Trade associations are listed in Appendix I at the back of this book.)

How can you use the trades to your advantage? Read them faithfully. If you don't want to invest in a subscription, go to your local or college library to see if they subscribe. You might also check with your local hospital, health care facility, or medical office. If all else fails, find someone who subscribes in your area and ask if it would be possible for you to look at their copy of the periodical. Many of the trades also have online versions of their publication. Browse through the help-wanted ads in the classified section each issue to see if your dream job is there.

Newsletters related to the various areas of the health care industry might offer other possibilities for job openings. What about Web sites such as Monster.com, Hotjobs.com, and other employment sites? Don't forget company Web sites. Hospitals, health care facilities, medical groups, physical therapists, dentists, physicians, nutritionists, pharmaceutical companies, and medical equipment companies generally host Web sites. Many of these sites have specific sections listing career opportunities at their company. It's worth checking out.

Are you already working in the industry and seeking to move up the career ladder? Do you have a job in a hospital in the fund-raising department and want to move up a rung on the career ladder? Many companies post their employment listings in the human resources department or in employee newsletters. What if you don't have a job there already and are interested in finding out about internal postings? This is where networking comes into play. A contact at the company can keep you informed.

If you're still in college or you graduated from a school that had programs in the area in which you are interested, check with the college placement office. In some cases, companies searching to fill specific positions may go to colleges and universities where they know there are specific programs.

★ Words from the Wise

If you are going to use an employment agency to help you find a job, remember to check *before* you sign any contracts to see who pays the fee—you or the company. There is nothing wrong with paying a fee. You simply want to be aware ahead of time as to what the fee will be.

Employment Agencies, Recruiters, Headhunters, and Executive Search Firms

Let's take a few minutes to discuss employment agencies, recruiters, and headhunters. What are they? What's the difference? Should you use them?

Employment agencies may fall into a number of different categories. They may be temp agencies, personnel agencies, or a combination of the two. Temp agencies work with companies to provide employees for short-term or fill-in work. These agencies generally specialize in a number of career areas. For example, an employment agency may specialize in providing clerical workers, food service workers, or nurses, among others. Some agencies even provide workers for longer-term projects.

How do they work? A company tells an agency what types of positions they are looking to fill, and the temp agency recruits workers who they feel are qualified for those positions. The business then pays the agency, and the agency pays the employee.

When you work in this capacity, you are not working for the company or hospital, for instance. You are an employee of the temp agency. Generally, in this type of situation, you do not pay a fee to be placed.

Personnel agencies, on the other hand, work in a different manner. These agencies try to match people looking for a job with companies that have openings. When you go to a personnel agency, they will interview you and talk about your qualifications. If the interviewer feels you are suitable, he or she will send you to speak to companies who have openings for which you are qualified. You may then meet with an HR director or someone else in the human resources department of the company with the opening.

Words from the Wise

Employment agencies in most states are required to be registered with the department of labor and licensed. Check out employment agencies before you get involved with them.

You may or may not get the job. There are no guarantees using a personnel agency.

If you do get the job, you will generally have to pay a portion of your first year's salary to the personnel company that helped you get the job. In some cases, the employer will split the fee with you. Check ahead of time so you will have no surprises.

You should not be required to pay anything up front. You may be asked to sign a contract. Before you sign anything, read it thoroughly and understand everything. If you don't understand what something means, ask.

Recruiters, headhunters, and executive search firms are all similar. These firms generally have contracts with employers who are looking for employees with specific skills, talents, and experience. Their job is to find people to fill those positions.

The difference between recruiters, headhunters, and executive search firms and the employment or personnel agencies we discussed previously is that you (as the job seeker) are not responsible for paying a fee. The employer will instead pay the fee.

How do these companies find you? There are a number of ways. Sometimes they read a story in the paper about you or see a press release about an award you received. Sometimes someone they know recommends you.

In some cases, they just cold-call people who have jobs like the ones they are trying to fill and ask if they know anyone who might be looking for a similar job whom you might recommend. You might recommend someone, or you might even say you are interested yourself.

What if no one calls you? Are you out of luck? Not at all. It's perfectly acceptable to call recruiters and headhunters yourself.

What you need to do is find firms that specialize in the industry you are looking for. For example, if you are a hospital administrator looking for a job in that field, you would look for executive recruiters who specialize in the administrative area of the health care industry.

How do you find them? There are over 5,000 executive recruiting agencies in the United States. You can search out firms on the Internet or look in the Yellow Pages of phone books from large, metropolitan areas.

You might also check out trade magazines and periodicals. Many have advertisements for recruiters in their specific career area.

Why do companies look to recruiters to find their employers? Generally, it's easier. They have someone screening potential employees, looking for just the right one. As recruiters don't generally get paid unless they find the right employee, they have the perfect incentive.

Should you get involved with a recruiter? As recruiters bring job possibilities to you, there really isn't a downside. As a matter of fact, even if you have a job that you love, it's a good idea to keep relationships with headhunters and recruiters. You can never tell when your next great job is around the corner.

Here are a few things that can help when you are working with a recruiter.

◎ Tailor your resume or curriculum vitae (CV) to the specific sector of the industry in which the recruiter works. You want your qualifications to jump off the page.

◎ Make sure you tell your recruiter about any companies to which you do not want your resume sent. For example, you don't want your resume sent to your current employer. You might not want your resume sent to a company where you just interviewed and so on.

◎ Call the recruiter on a regular basis.

The Hidden Job Market

Let's talk a bit about the hidden job market. Many people think that their job search begins and ends with the classified ads. If they get the Sunday paper and their dream job isn't there, they give up and wait until the next Sunday. I am betting that once you have made the decision to have a career in the health care industry, you're not going to let something small like not finding a job opening in the classifieds stop you. So what are you going to do?

While there may be job openings in which you are interested, advertised in the classifieds, it's essential to realize that many jobs are not advertised at all. Why? In addition to not wanting to be bombarded and inundated by tons of resumes and phone calls, some employers may not want someone in another company to know that they are looking for a new marketing director or a new director of publicity until they hire one. As a matter of fact, they may not want the person who currently holds the job to know that he or she is about to be let go. Whatever the reason, once you're aware that all jobs aren't advertised, you can go about finding them in a different manner.

Why do you want to find jobs in the hidden job market? The main reason is because you will have a better shot at getting the job. Why? To begin with, there is a lot less competition.

Because positions aren't being actively advertised, there aren't hundreds of people sending in their resumes. Not everyone knows how to find the hidden job market, nor do they want to take the extra time to find it, so you also have an edge over other job applicants. Many applicants in the hidden job market come recommended by someone who knew about the opening. This means that you are starting off with one foot in the door.

While there are entry-level jobs to be found in the hidden job market, there are also a good number of high-level jobs. This can be valuable when you're trying to move up the career ladder.

How does the hidden job market work? When a company needs to fill a position, instead of placing an ad, they quietly look for the perfect candidate. How do they find candidates without advertising? Let's look at some ways this is accomplished and how you can take advantage of each situation.

◎ Employees may be promoted from within the company.
  ▫ That is why it is so important once you get your foot in the door and get a job to keep yourself visible in a positive manner. You want supervisors to think about you when an opening occurs. For example, if you're working in the publicity department and your goal is a career in marketing, drop subtle hints during conversations with both supervisors of your department and the marketing department. You might say something like, "I love working in publicity. Learning how to publicize facilities, events, physicians, and programs was one of my goals when I decided to

work in this industry. I've also always wanted to learn about marketing." You're not saying you don't like your job. You're not saying you want to leave your job. You're planting a seed. If you have been doing an amazing job in your current position and anything opens up in marketing, you just might be suggested.

◎ An employee working in the company may recommend a candidate for the position.
  ▫ This is another time when networking helps. Don't keep your dreams to yourself. Tell others what type of job you're looking for and what your qualifications are. You can never tell when a position might become available. Employers often ask their staff if they know anyone who would be good for this job. If you shared your qualifications and dreams, someone just might recommend you.

◎ Someone who knows about an opening may tell their friends, relatives, or coworkers, who then apply for the job.
  ▫ In some cases, it's not another employee who knows about an opening, but it might be someone who has contact with the company. For example, the director of nursing at a hospital might hear that the facility is looking for a director of marketing and an administrative assistant. He or she might tell his or her daughter to call up and apply for one of the jobs. He or she might also mention it to a colleague, who might mention it to someone else.

- Sometimes it may be someone outside the company who hears about the job. The UPS delivery person may be delivering packages to a dentist's office and overhear a conversation about the dentist needing a dental hygienist. If you had networked with the UPS delivery person and mentioned you were looking for a job at a dentist's office, he or she might stop by and tell you about the opportunity. Then, all you would have to do is contact the dentist.

◎ People may have filled in applications or sent resumes and cover letters to the company asking that they be kept on file. When an opening exists, the human resources department might review the resumes and call one of the applicants.

- Even if no jobs are advertised, it is often worth your while to send a letter and your resume to the human resources department asking about openings. Be sure to ask that your resume be kept on file.

◎ Suitable candidates may place cold calls at just the right time.

- Difficult as it can be to place cold calls, it might pay off. Consider committing yourself to make a few cold calls every day. Do some research. Then, depending on the area of the health care industry in which you are interested in working, choose companies and call the director of human resources in an attempt to set up an interview. Who can you call? Depending on what type of job you are looking for, you might call hospitals, nursing

> ### ★ The Inside Scoop
> When making a cold call, try to get the name of the person you're trying to reach ahead of time so you can ask for someone by name. How? Just call up and ask the receptionist.

homes, health care facilities, clinics, medical offices, dental offices, or physical therapy groups. You might call health or medical-oriented trade associations. How about pharmaceutical companies or medical equipment manufacturers? What about marketing or publicity firms that specialize in the health care market? What about medical-oriented Web sites? The beauty of a cold call is that it can be made to anyone.

◎ People may have networked and caught the eye of those who need to fill jobs.

- Finding positions in the hidden job market is a skill in itself. One of the best ways to do this is by networking. Through networking you can make contacts, and your contacts are the people who will know about the jobs in the hidden market.

Networking in the Health Care Industry

Often, it's not just what you know but who you know. Contacts are key in every industry, and the health care industry is no exception. Networking is therefore going to be an important part of succeeding. It is so important that in some situations it can often make you or break you.

How so, you ask? If you don't have a chance to showcase your skills and your talents to the right people, it's difficult to get the jobs you want, the promotions you want, and the career of your dreams.

Networking is important in every area of the health care industry, no matter what segment you aspire to work in. Without the power of networking, it is often difficult to get your foot in the door. That doesn't mean you *can't* get your foot in the door; doing so is just harder.

Earlier chapters have touched on networking, and because of its importance to your career success, we will continue discussing it throughout the book. Networking isn't just something you do at the beginning of your career. It's something you're going to have to continue doing for as long as you work.

How do you network? You put yourself in situations where you can meet people and introduce yourself. Chapter 7 discusses more about networking basics and offers some networking exercises that you'll find useful. But what you should be doing at this point is learning to get comfortable walking up to people, extending your hand, and introducing yourself.

"Hi, I'm Dan James. Isn't this an interesting event? What a great opportunity this was to learn more about marketing," you might say at a seminar.

The person you meet will then tell you his or her name and perhaps something about him or herself. You can then keep talking or say, "It was nice meeting you. Do you have a card?"

Make sure you have your business cards handy, and when you are given a card, offer yours as well.

Every situation can ultimately be an opportunity to network, but some are more effective than others. Look for seminars, workshops,

> ### ★ Voice of Experience
>
> You never want to be in a position where someone remembers that you would be perfect for a job yet has no idea how to get hold of you. Don't be stingy with your business cards. Give them out freely.

and classes that professionals in the area of the health care industry in which you are interested might attend.

Why would an industry professional be at a workshop or seminar? There are many reasons. They might want to network just like you do, they might want to learn something new, or they might be teaching or facilitating the workshop.

Where else can you meet and network with professionals in the health care industry? What about at their place of work? Hospitals; doctor's offices; medical group offices; pharmaceutical companies; medical equipment companies; dental offices; urgi-centers; surgi-centers; health or medical-oriented trade associations; physical therapy offices; clinics; and the list goes on.

"But I can't just walk in someone's office I don't know and introduce myself," you say.

You're right. That probably won't work. You probably wouldn't walk unannounced into the office of a hospital administrator or marketing director and just say, "Hi." You probably wouldn't walk into the office of the executive director of a health care trade association or the CEO of a pharmaceutical company. So what can you do?

If you don't know someone in the type of company for which you want to work, you're going to have to get creative in your networking. How can you network with employees of those companies? Here's a strategy you might want to try.

> ### ⭐ Tip from the Top
>
> When networking at an event, don't just zero in on the people you think are the "important" industry insiders and ignore the rest. Try to meet as many people as you can. Always be pleasant and polite to everyone. You never can tell who knows whom and who might be a great contact later.

Find one or two of the organizations, companies, or facilities in which you might be interested in working and locate the physical address. It might be a hospital or other health care facility. It might be a laboratory or a medical group or one or more doctor's offices. Perhaps it's a pharmaceutical company, a medical supply company, or a firm that handles marketing for clients in the health care industry.

Choose a day when you have some time to spare. Generally, it needs to be on a weekday because those are the days most business takes place. Get dressed in appropriate clothing, and go to the location of the company or facility you've chosen. Now stand outside the building and look around. Are there restaurants, coffee shops, diners, or bars nearby? There probably are. If it's a hospital or other health care facility, is there a cafeteria or lunchroom? Is it open to the public?

Why does all this matter? Because people working in these offices have to eat lunch somewhere and get their coffee somewhere. After work on Friday, they might want to stop into the bar on the corner for happy hour.

What does that mean to you? If you can determine where the company employees hang out, you can put yourself in situations in which to network with them.

Can you find out which restaurants, diners, and coffee shops the employees frequent? You often can, if you stand outside around lunchtime and watch to see who goes where.

Some office buildings have thousands of employees in different businesses. How do you know which are the employees from the company you have targeted? You might have to eavesdrop a little and listen for clues in things people say as they walk out the door. You might stop in the building and ask someone. Get on the elevator for the floor on which the company is located and ask the elevator operator. Ask the security guard standing in the lobby. You might even stop into a couple of the coffee shops, diners, or restaurants and ask the host or hostess.

"Hi, I was supposed to have a lunch meeting with someone from DRG Pharmaceuticals, the company next door, and I'm embarrassed to say, I'm not sure which coffee shop the meeting was set for," you might say. "Do a lot of employees from the company come in here?"

At this point, the hostess will either give you a blank look that means you probably are in the wrong place (or she really doesn't know) or tell you that you are indeed in the right location. She might even say, "Yes, we just did a take out order for them a few minutes ago," or something to that effect.

Once you've found the correct location, wait until it's nice and busy and there is a slight line. People will usually talk to other people even if they don't know them when they are standing in lines. Start up conversations and hope that you're standing near the people from the company you're looking for. What about sitting at the counter? It you get lucky, you might end up sitting next to someone from the company.

This whole process is often a lot easier if you are trying to network with people who work at a hospital or other facility and there is a cafeteria or lunchroom, because the odds are you will be running into people who work in the facility.

The tricky part in this entire procedure is being able to network in this type of situation. Some people are really good at it and some people find it very difficult. What you're dealing with when doing this is first finding the correct people and then starting a conversation that may let you turn the person into a networking contact. If you do it right, it can pay off big time. You might meet someone, for example, who works in the hospital pharmacy and strike up a conversation.

You never can tell what happens from there. You might mention you were thinking about filling in an application because you were looking for a job in the marketing department. Your new contact might say, "I don't think there are any positions in that department, but the assistant director of volunteers just put in her letter of resignation." You might get a referral, set up an interview, or even end up with a job.

Does this technique always work? Sometimes it does and sometimes it doesn't. The important thing to know is that it might help you get your foot in the door where you otherwise might not have.

If you find networking in this manner difficult, it might be easier for you to do at a bar during happy hour because people tend to talk more in these situations. Remember, though, that while it's okay to drink socially, your main goal is to network and make contacts. You won't do yourself any favors becoming intoxicated and then acting outrageously or saying something inappropriate.

Where else might people who work in the health care industry congregate? What about joining the auxiliary at a hospital and volunteer-

The Inside Scoop

It's great to network with those at the top, but a good and often more practical strategy is to try networking with their assistants and support team. The people at the top might not always remember you; those a step or two down the line usually will. Additionally, a recommendation from these people about you to their boss can do wonders for your career.

ing to work on some events? What about volunteering to help with one of their fund-raisers? Even if the hospital staff doesn't get involved in the actual planning or execution of events, they generally attend them.

It is more effective to your career to meet the executive director of a hospital or the HR director when you're being introduced as a volunteer who helped pull an event together than knocking on his or her door and saying, "Hi, do you have a minute?"

How else can you get to the right people? Sometimes all it takes is making a phone call. Consider calling a pharmaceutical company, for example, asking to speak to the public relations director and telling him or her about your career aspirations. Ask if he or she would be willing to give you the names of a few industry people that you might call. Contact a nursing home and ask whom you might talk to if you were interested in a career as an activities director. Contact a trade association, ask to speak to the communications director, and ask about career opportunities in the industry. You just might be surprised.

"Why would anyone want to help me?" you ask.

Most people like to help others. It makes them feel good. Don't expect everyone to be courteous or to go out of their way for you, but if you find one or two helpful people, you may wind up with some useful contacts.

To get you started thinking, here's a sample script of how such a conversation might go.

Health Care Trade Association Executive Director: Hello, Mark Jones.

You: Hi, this is Samantha Thompson. I'm not sure if you're the right person to speak to about this, but would it be okay if I tell you what I'm looking for and you can point me in the right direction?

Health Care Trade Association Executive Director: Sure, go ahead.

You: Thanks. First of all, I'm not selling anything. I'm getting my bachelors degree in May with a major in marketing and administration. My goal is to get a job in some aspect of the health care industry, but I don't really know any of the right people. I was wondering if you might have some ideas about who I could talk to or how I can meet some people in the industry. I'm really interested in working at a hospital, but I know there are probably other opportunities. I'm not sure who to talk to, but I thought because most of the hospitals in the state belong to your association, you might be able to give me some suggestions.

Health Care Trade Association Executive Director: I wish I could help, but I'm not sure who I could suggest. Sorry.

You: Well, at this point, I'm just trying to get my foot in the door. Do you have any suggestions of people who might be able to give me a couple of names?

Health Care Trade Association Executive Director: You probably could contact any of the facilities in our member-

ship. I'm not sure who specifically could help you, though.

You: I would appreciate any help. Would it be a big imposition for me to come in one day when you're not too busy to just meet with you for a couple of minutes, just to get a couple of ideas? I would appreciate any help. I promise I won't take a lot of your time.

Health Care Trade Association Executive Director: I'm pretty busy for the next few weeks. We have our annual conference at the end of the month. I'm sorry. I'm really swamped. My assistant is on maternity leave and our conference coordinator was just in an accident, so things are really piling up.

You: Well, thanks for your time. Can I leave my number?

Health Care Trade Association Executive Director: Not a problem. Did you say you were getting your degree in marketing?

You: Yes, marketing and administration. I just finished up a really interesting seminar on marketing health care events.

Health Care Trade Association Executive Director: I don't know if you would be interested, but I could get you a pass to our conference. In addition to the seminars, we have a number of networking sessions. All our member hospitals and facilities send representatives. Are you interested?

You: Thanks. That would be great.

Health Care Trade Association Executive Director: Why don't you fax your information over and I'll make sure you get a conference pack. The number is 111-222-3333. Be sure to stop by at the conference and introduce yourself.

You: Thank you. That's great. I look forward to meeting you.

See how easy it is? You just have to ask.

"But what if someone says no?" you ask. "What if they won't help?"

That might happen. The conversation may not go in the direction you want it to. Some people will say no. So what? If you don't ask, you'll never know.

"But what do I say if someone says no?"

Simply thank them nicely for their time and hang up. Don't belabor the point. Just say, "Thanks anyway. I appreciate your time."

It will be difficult the first few times you make a call like that, but as you begin to reach out to others, it will get easier. Pretty soon, you won't even think about it.

Where else can you network? A lot of that depends on what segment of the health care industry you are trying to target. Look for opportunities.

"But how do I get through to the industry professionals?" you ask.

You're going to have to be creative. For example, let's say you read a press release in the paper about an upcoming event to benefit a hospital, health care facility, or health care organization. What do you do? First of all, make sure you go.

"I can't afford to go to a big fund-raiser," you say.

Get creative. Volunteer to be a host or hostess. Offer to help serve. See if you can cover the event for the newspaper. Think outside of the box.

Events don't always have to be oriented just to the health care industry to be good networking opportunities. For example, you might want to join Kiwanis or Rotary and go to their meetings. You might want to join the chamber of commerce and go to their events. Why? Industry professionals attend these events. It's a good place to meet people on a more even playing field.

Remember that these are business functions. Behave professionally and make sure to watch for any opportunities to network—the main reason that you're there. Here are some tips on what to do and what not to do:

◎ Do not bring anyone with you. Go alone. It will give you more opportunities to meet people.
◎ Do not smoke even if other people are. You can never tell what makes someone remember you. You don't want it to be that you smell of tobacco.
◎ Don't wear strong perfume, cologne, or aftershave. Aside from the possibility of some people being allergic to it, you don't want this to be the reason people remember you.
◎ Do not use drugs, even if other people are.

Here are some things you *should do.*

◎ Do bring business cards to give out to everyone.
◎ Do bring a pen and small pad to take down names and phone numbers of people who don't have cards.
◎ Do meet as many people as possible. If given the opportunity, briefly tell them what your goal is and ask if they have any suggestions about who you can contact.

Follow up on the contacts and information you gather at these meetings. Don't neglect this step, or you will have wasted the opportunity. Call, write, or e-mail contacts you have made in a timely fashion. You want them to remember meeting you.

Tip from the Coach

Remember that networking is a two-way street. If you want people to help you, it's important to reciprocate. When you see something you can do for someone else's career, don't wait for them to ask for help. Step in and do it graciously.

The Right Place at the Right Time

Have you ever looked down while you were walking and seen some money sitting on the ground? It could have been there for a while, but no one else happened to look down at that time. You just happened to be in the right place at the right time.

It can happen anytime. Sometimes you hear about an interesting job opening from an unlikely source. You might be standing in a long line at the bakery. The woman in back of you asks if you would mind very much if she went ahead of you because she is rushing out of town to visit her son. It seems she needs to pick up the bakery's famous cheesecake because the cheesecake is her son's favorite and he misses it since moving away to take a job as the administrator of a large hospital.

You of course agree to let her get ahead of you. While standing in line chatting, you mention that you also work in health care in the local hospital as a health promotion coordinator. The woman then tells you she came to a seminar you put together at the hospital on women's health.

A few moments later, the woman gets her cheesecake, thanks you for letting her get ahead of you, and tells you how much she enjoyed chatting. A couple months later, you get a call from the woman's son, who tells you he is looking for someone to put together a wellness department at his hospital and his mother had told him all about you. With a little bit of investigative work, he found you and you had the possibility of a new job.

Think it can't happen? It can and it does. It's just a matter of being in the right place at the right time.

There is no question that being in the right place at the right time can help. The question is, however, what is the right place and the right time and how do you recognize it?

It's almost impossible to know what the right place and right time is. You can, however, stack the deck in your favor. How? While you never know what the right place or the right time to be someplace is, you can put yourself in situations where you can network. Networking with people outside of the industry can be just as effective and just as important as networking with industry professionals.

The larger your network, the more opportunities you will have to find the job you want. The more people who know what you have to offer and what you want to do, the better. Who do you deal with every day? Who do these people know and deal with? Any of these people in your network and your extended network may know about your dream career in the health care industry.

If you aren't employed and don't have to worry about a current boss or supervisor hearing about your aspirations, spread the news about your job search. Don't keep it a secret. The more people who know what you're looking for in a career, the more people who potentially can let you know when and where there is a job possibility.

If I haven't stressed it enough, if at all possible do not keep your career aspirations to yourself. Share them with the world.

Cold Calls

What exactly is a cold call? In relation to your career, a cold call is an unsolicited contact in person, by phone, letter, or e-mail with someone you don't know in hopes of obtaining some information, an interview, or a job. It is a proactive strategy.

Let's focus on the cold calls you make by phone. They are much like the call we just discussed with the health care trade association executive director.

Many find this form of contact too intimidating to try. Why? Because not only are you calling and trying to sell yourself to someone who may be busy and doesn't want to be bothered, but you are also afraid of rejection. None of us like rejection. We fear that we will get on the phone and try to talk to someone, and they will not take our call, will hang up on us, or will say no to our requests.

The majority of telemarketing calls made to homes every day are cold calls. In those cases, the people on the other end of the phone aren't trying to get a job or an interview. Instead, they are attempting to sell a product or service. When you get those calls, the first thing on your mind is usually how to get off the phone. The last thing you want to do is buy anything from someone on the other end. But the fact of the matter is that people do buy things from telemarketers if they want what they're selling.

With that in mind, your job in making cold calls is to make your call compelling enough that the person on the other end responds positively. Why would you even bother making a cold call to someone? It's simply another job search strat-

Cold Call Tracking Worksheet					
Company	**Phone Number**	**Name of Contact**	**Date Called**	**Follow-up Activities**	**Results**
Health Care Execs Recruitment	111-111-1111	Audrey James	5/6	Send resume.	Asked for resume, will get back to me after reviewing my qualifications.
Rindolow Medical Group	222-222-3333	Sheila Bower	5/9	Send resume.	Will keep resume on file, not hiring now. Call back in a few months.
Middletown Urgi-Center	222-222-4444	Simon Jackson	5/9	E-mailed resume.	Will review resume and get back to me.
Community Regional Hospital	888-999-0000	Ms. Joanne Johnson HR director	5/11		Said to come in and fill in application.

egy, and it's one that not everyone attempts, which gives you an edge over others.

How do you make a cold call? It's really quite simple. If you want to make a cold call to a potential employer, you just identify who you want to call, put together a script to make it easier for you, and then make your call. Keep track of the calls you make. You may think you'll remember who said what and whom you didn't reach, but after a couple of calls, it gets confusing. Check out the Cold Call Tracking Worksheet sample below for the type of information you should record. Then use the Cold Call Tracking Worksheet provided.

Voice of Experience

You will find it easier to make cold calls if you not only create a script but practice it as well. To be successful in cold calling, you need to sound professional, friendly, and confident.

Who do you call? That depends on who you're trying to reach. If, for example, you are pursuing a career as a pharmacist, you might call pharmacies, hospitals, health care facilities, surgi-centers, or urgi-centers. If you are seeking

Cold Call Tracking Worksheet

Company	Phone Number	Name of Contact	Date Called	Follow-up Activities	Results

a position in health care marketing, you might call hospitals, health care facilities, trade associations, pharmaceutical companies, physicians, dental groups, or medical groups.

If you are a homeopathic physician trying to build a practice, you might call a health spa or a hospital with a complimentary medicine department. If you are a nutritionist, you might want to call spas, gyms, hospitals, or camps. You might even want to call some sports teams or athletes. Every call you make is a potential opportunity that can pan out for you.

Here's an example.

You: Hi, Ms. Mason. This is Steve Jackson. I'm not sure you're the right person to speak to, but I was hoping I could tell you what I was looking for and perhaps you could point me in the right direction. Are you in the middle of something now or would it be better if I called back later?

Ms. Mason: What can I do for you?

You: I just got my bachelor's degree in physical therapy and I'm working on getting my master's. I was wondering if you knew of any opportunities in facilities like yours. I don't have a lot of actual work experience, but I had a 4.0 grade point average in school and some great references from my professors. I know I could probably get a job at one of the hospitals, but I really am interested in working with children with special needs.

Ms. Mason: Have you worked around children with special needs before?

You: I grew up with a close cousin with special needs. I saw what her physi-

cal therapist did for her. That's what prompted me to go into the field. I checked out your Web site and didn't see and positions open, but I just thought I would give it a try.

Ms. Mason: We don't have any positions open at the moment, but we did just get a grant to hire an additional physical therapist. The position won't be available for a couple of months. You said you were getting your master's?

You: Yes. I'm starting in September, but I think I can handle the course load and a full-time job.

Ms. Mason: Why don't you come in and fill out an application and then we could talk for a bit. I'm going to put you on with Marie, my secretary, and she'll set up an appointment.

You: Thanks for your time. I look forward to meeting with you.

Ms. Mason: See you then. Hold for Marie please.

It's not that difficult once you get someone on the phone.

"But what if they say no?" you ask.

So they say no. Don't take it personally. Just go on to your next call and use your previous call as practice.

Where do you find people to call? Browse company Web sites for names. Read trade journals. Read the newspaper. Look for magazine articles and feature stories. Watch television and listen to the radio. Go through the yellow pages. You can get names from almost anyplace. Call up. Take a chance. It may pay off.

Depending on where you're calling and the size of the company, in many cases when

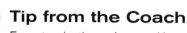

Tip from the Coach

Expect rejection when making cold calls. Some people may not want to talk to you. Rejection is a lot easier to deal with when you decide ahead of time it isn't personally directed toward you.

you start your conversation during a cold call, the person you're speaking to will direct you to the human resources (HR) department. If this is the case, ask whom you should speak to in HR. Try to get a name. Then thank the person who gave you the information and call the HR department, asking for the name of the person you were given. Being referred by someone else in the company will often get you through. Try something like this:

You: Good afternoon. Would Sara Johnston be in please?

Secretary: Who's calling?

You: This is Connie Owens. Mr. Adams suggested I call her.

Believe it or not, the more calls you make, the more you will increase your chances of success in getting potential interviews.

If you're really uncomfortable making the calls or you can't get through to the people you're trying to reach by phone, consider writing letters. It takes more time than a phone call, but it is another proactive method for you to get through to someone.

Creating Your Own Career

Do you want one more really good reason to find the hidden job market? If you're creative and savvy enough, you might be able to *create* a

position for yourself even if you are only on the first or second rung of the career ladder. What does that mean? Here's an example.

Let's say you're working as an administrative assistant in a medical group. In the course of your job, you get an idea: Wouldn't it be great to have a newsletter with health tips and health news that goes out once a month to patients? It could be sent out both via mail and e-mail. The e-mail version could provide links to interesting medical and health news. You do a prototype, develop the idea, and bring it to your supervisor. You explain that it would not only help keep patients in the loop; it would help market the medical group. It could also be sent out to potential patients. As it would be informational, the local newspaper might even print it as a public service. Your supervisor speaks to the physicians in the office, and they think it's a great idea. While there was no position planned, they see value in your idea and ask you if you would be interested in taking over this project. Voila! You've created your own position and you've moved up the ladder.

"What if I don't yet have a job? Is it still possible to create a position?"

If you are creative, have some initiative, and are assertive enough to push your idea, you can. What you have to do is come up with something that you could do for the company you want to work for that isn't being done now or that you could do better. Do you have any ideas? What about suggesting becoming a concierge for employees in the hospital? What about suggesting the possibility of you becoming a nutritionist or personal trainer for employees in a corporation? How about seeing if a popular spa might be interested in using your services as a physician to give lectures on alternative health, stress management, or a healthy lifestyle? What about suggesting that a recording group use your services as a nurse while the group is on tour?

Put fear aside and think outside the box. Get creative. Come up with an idea, develop it fully, put it on paper so you can see any problems, and fine-tune the idea. Then call up the company that you want to work with, lay out the idea, and sell them on it. You've just created your own job!

6

TOOLS FOR SUCCESS

Every trade has its own set of tools that help the tradesman (or woman) achieve success. Whatever area of the health care industry you are pursuing, certain tools can help you achieve success faster. These may include things such as your resume, CV, business and networking cards, brochures, career portfolio, and professional reference sheets.

This chapter will help get you started putting together these tools. Some of these tools will be helpful to those on the business and administrative end of the industry. Others are geared toward those pursuing a career in medicine or the allied health areas. Some can be useful to everyone.

Your Resume as a Selling Tool

There is virtually no successful company that does not market their products or services in some manner. Some may utilize ads in newspapers or magazines or television or radio commercials. Others may use billboards, banners, the Web, or a variety of additional marketing vehicles. Still others use publicity, promotion, or some other form of marketing.

Why do they do this? The main reason is to make sure others are aware of their product or service so they can then find ways to entice

potential customers to buy or use that product or service.

What does this have to do with you and your career? When trying to succeed, no matter what area of the health care industry you are pursuing, it is a good idea to look at yourself as a *product*.

In a broad sense, that means you will be marketing yourself so people know you exist; so they begin to differentiate you from others; so they see you in a better light. How can you entice potential employers to hire you?

The answer is simple: Start by making your resume a selling tool! Make it your own personal marketing piece. Everyone sends out resumes. The trick is making yours so powerful that it will grab the attention of potential employers.

Resumes are important no matter what area of the health care industry you are pursuing. Does your resume do a great job of selling your credentials? Does it showcase your skills, personality traits, and special talents? Is your resume the one that is going to impress the employers or human resources directors who can call you in for that all important interview and ultimately land you the job you're after? Is it going to land you the job you've been dreaming about?

If an employer doesn't know you, their first impression of you might very well be your resume. This makes your resume a crucial part of getting an interview that might ultimately lead to your dream job.

A strong resume illustrates that you have the experience and qualifications to fill a potential employer's needs. How can you do this? To begin with, learn to tailor your resume to the job you're pursuing. One of the biggest mistakes people make in job hunting is creating just one resume and using it every single time they apply for a position, no matter what the job.

If this is what you've been doing, it's time to break the habit. Begin by crafting your main resume. Then edit it to fit the needs of each job opening or opportunity you are applying for.

"But," you say, "I want to work in health care administration. Can't I use the same resumes for jobs in the same area?"

Here's the answer in a nutshell. You can use the same resume only if you are going for the exact same type of job. For example, let's say you apply for a position as an administrative assistant in one hospital. You then apply for a similar position as an administrative assistant in a different hospital. In this instance, you can probably use the same resume.

On the other hand, let's say you're pursuing a job in the public relations department of a hospital. Another opening in which you're interested is in the public relations department of a pharmaceutical company. In a case like this, while your resume might generally be the same, you should change it slightly by highlighting your skills and experiences most relevant to each position.

Before computers became commonplace, preparing a different resume for every job was far more difficult. In many cases, people would prepare one resume and have it professionally printed by a resume service or printer. That was it. If you wanted to change your resume, you had to go back to the printer and have it done again, incurring a major expense.

Today, however, most of us have access to computers, making it far easier to change resumes at will. Do you want to change your career objective? What about the order of components on your resume? Do you want to add something? You can create the perfect resume every time with the click of a mouse.

Always keep copies of your resume on your computer and make sure you note the date each was done and its main focus. For example, you might save your resumes as "marketing resume;" "PR resume;" "communications director resume;" "resume for jobs in hospitals and health care facilities;" "resume for jobs in pharmaceutical companies;" and so on. If you don't have

---

Words from the Wise

If you're using different resumes, make sure you know which one you send to which company. Keep a copy of the resume you use for a specific job with a copy of the cover letter you send. Do this *every* time. Otherwise, when sending out numerous resumes and letters, it's very easy to get confused.

Tip from the Top

When replying to a job advertisement, use words from the advertisement in both your resume and your cover letter. It makes you look like more of a fit with the company's expectations.

> ### ⭐ Tip from the Top
>
> Keep updated copies of your resume on a CD, DVD, or flash drive as well as your computer. You can never tell when your computer hard drive will die just when someone tells you about a great opportunity or you see an advertisement for the perfect job. If your resume is on a CD or other media, you simply need to put it in another computer, tailor it for that particular job, and send it off. You can also toss a CD or a USB flash drive in your briefcase or bag to keep with you if you are away from home and find that you need to add something to your resume quickly. Adding a handwritten line when you change your phone number or address or even whiting out the wrong information just is not acceptable.

your own computer, keep your resume on a CD, DVD, or flash drive so you always have access to it without having to type it all over again.

How can you make your resume a better marketing tool? Present it in a clear, concise manner, highlighting your best assets. Organize it in an order that makes it easy for someone just glancing at your resume to see the points that sell you best.

The decision about the sequence of items in your resume should be based on what is most impressive in relation to the position you are pursuing. Do you have a lot of experience? Put that information first. Are your accomplishments extraordinary? If so, highlight those first. Do you have little experience but just graduated cum laude? Then perhaps your education should be where your resume should start.

Sometimes it helps when creating your own resume to imagine that you just received it in the mail. What would make you glance at it and say, "Wow," and keep on reading? Or would

you glance at it and hope that there is a more interesting one coming in?

One of the most important things to remember is that no matter what anyone tells you, there really is no *right* or *wrong* type of resume. The right one for *you* will end up being the one that ultimately gets you the position you want.

There are so many ways to prepare your resume that it is often difficult to choose one. My advice is to craft a couple different ones, put them away overnight, and then look at them the next day. Which one looks better to you? That probably will be the style you want to use.

Here are some tips that might help:

◎ Tailor every resume for every position.
◎ Make sure you check for incorrect word usage. No matter what position you're pursuing, most employers prefer to have someone who has a command of the English language. Check to make sure you haven't inadvertently used the word "their" for "there," "to" for "too" or "two," "effect" for "affect," "you're" for "your," "it's" for "its," and so on.
   ▫ Don't rely solely on your computer's spell and grammar checker. Carefully go over your work yourself as well.
◎ Every time you edit your resume or make a change, check carefully for errors.
   ▫ It is very easy to miss a double word, a misspelled word, or a wrong tense. Have a friend or family member look over your resume. It is often difficult to see mistakes in your own work.
◎ Tempting as it is to use colored inks when preparing your resume, don't. Use only black ink.
◎ Use a high-quality paper at least 40 pound weight for printing your resumes. Paper with texture often *feels* different, so

it stands out. While you can use white, beige, or cream papers, soft, light colors such as light blue, salmon pink, gray, or light green will help your resume stand out from the hundreds of white and beige ones.

◎ Make sure your resume layout looks attractive. You can have the greatest content in the world, but if your resume just doesn't look right, people may not actually read it.

  ▫ You know the saying, "You can't judge a book by its cover?" Well, you really can't, but if you don't know anything about the book or its contents, you just might not pick it up *unless* the cover looks interesting.

◎ When sending your resume and cover letter, instead of using a standard number 10 business envelope and folding your resume, use a large manila envelope. That way you won't have to fold your resume and your information gets there looking clean, crisp, and flat.

◎ Don't use odd fonts or typefaces. Why? In many large companies, resumes are scanned by machine. Certain fonts don't scan well. What should you use? Helvetica, Times, Arial, and Courier work well.

◎ Similarly, many fonts don't translate well when e-mailing. What looks great on the resume on your computer screen may end up looking like gibberish at the recipients end, and you probably will never know. Once again, use Helvetica, Times, Arial, or Courier. You might want to e-mail a copy of your resume to a friend's computer to check to see what it looks like.

◎ When preparing your resume, make your name larger and bolder than the rest of your resume. For example, if your resume is done in 12-point type, use 14-, 16- or even 18-point type for your name. Your name will stand out from those on other resumes.

◎ Remember to utilize white space. Margins should be at least one inch on each side as well as on the top and bottom of each page. White space also helps draw the reader's attention to information.

Redefining Your Resume

You probably already have a resume in some form. How has it been working for you? Is it getting you the interviews you want? If it is, great! If not, you might want to consider redefining it.

You want your resume to stand out. You want it to illustrate that you are successful in your accomplishments. You want potential employers to look at your resume and say to themselves, "That's who I want working here!"

How do you do that? Make your resume compelling. Showcase your accomplishments. Demonstrate through your resume that you believe in yourself, because if *you* don't believe in *you*, no one else will. Show that you have the ability to solve problems and bring fresh ideas to the table.

★ Words from the Wise

Whatever color paper you use for your resume and cover letters, make sure they photocopy well. Some colored papers photocopy dark or look messy.

First decide how you want to present yourself. What type of resume is best for you? There are a couple of basic types of resumes. The chronological resume lists your jobs and accomplishments beginning with the most current and going backwards. Functional resumes, which may also be referred to as skills-based resumes, emphasize your accomplishments and abilities. One of the good things about this type of resume is that it allows you to lay it out in a manner that spotlights your key areas, whether they be your qualifications, skills, or employment history.

What's the best type of resume for you? That depends on a number of factors, including where you are in your career. If you are just entering the job market and you haven't held down a lot of jobs but you have relevant experience through internships and/or volunteer activities, you might use the functional type. If, on the other hand, you have held a number of jobs in the field and climbed the ladder each time you moved, you might want to use the chronological variety. You can also combine elements from both types. This is called a combination resume. As I noted earlier, there is no one right way. You have to look at the whole picture and make a decision.

Use common sense. Make sure your best assets are prominent on your resume. Do you have a lot of experience? Are your accomplishments above the bar? Did you graduate cum laude? Do you have a master's degree? Do you have a doc-torate? Determine what would grab your eye and find a way to focus first on that.

What Should Your Resume Contain?

What should you have in your resume? Some components are required and some are optional. Let's look at some of them.

What do you definitely need? You definitely need your name, address, phone number, and e-mail address, if you have one. You also should have your education and any training as well as your professional or work experience.

You want to include your work accomplishments and responsibilities so potential employers know what you have done and what you can bring to the table. What else? Certifications, licenses, professional affiliations and memberships, honors, awards, and professional accomplishments.

What else might you want to put in your resume? What about your career objective, a summary of skills, and a career summary?

What should you not put in your resume? Your age, marital status, religion, any health problems, current or past salaries, and whether or not you have children. What else should you not put down? Any weakness you have or think you have.

⭐ Tip from the Coach

I often facilitate seminars or workshops for job hunters. During the resume section of the workshop, there are always a lot of questions everyone has on what *not* to include on your resume.

"Shouldn't I tell potential employers about my weaknesses?" a woman at one of the seminars asked. "You know, the things I'm not good at? Don't you think they should know, for example, that I really can't stand being around blood?"

"Are you pursuing a job where you're going to have to see a lot of blood?" I asked. "Are you going to be working in medicine or patient care in some manner?"

"No," she said. "I'm hoping to get a job in health care administration. But it's still in a hospital. Don't you think I should tell them ahead of time?"

"No, it definitely isn't something I would mention," I told her. "Chances are you won't run into blood on a daily basis. There really is no sense in giving someone a reason *not* to hire you."

"What about that I'm not good with numbers?" someone else asked.

Are you going to be dealing with numbers as part of your job," I asked. "Are you going to be an accountant or expected to do budgets?"

"No, not really," the man replied. "I'm hoping to find a job in health care promotion or wellness promotion."

"Are you bad at math or you do you just not like dealing with numbers?" I asked.

"I just don't feel comfortable dealing with numbers. I'm not even really bad at math; I just don't like it."

"Then why do want to give someone a reason *not* to hire you?" I asked. One of the problems with putting something in writing is that you sometimes can't explain what you mean. It can be limiting to your career. You don't have the option of saying, "I really am capable of handling projects involving math, but I just don't really like having to deal with it." When you put something in writing, it almost sets it in stone. It also might hurt your chances of advancement down the line.

Career Summary

Let's discuss your career summary. While a career summary isn't a required component of your resume, it often is helpful when an employer gets huge numbers of resumes and gives each a short glance. A career summary is a short professional biography no longer than 12 sentences that tells your professional story. You can do it in a number of ways. Here's an example:

> Bachelor's degree with a major in marketing and coursework toward my MBA. Seminars and workshops in grant writing, fund-raising, and marketing. Proven ability to plan, direct, and implement fund-raising programs in health care facilities. Fully knowledgeable in all aspects of fund-raising, development, marketing public relations, publicity, advertising, and marketing of health care facilities. Have brought in over 10 million dollars to facilities through a combination of grants and fund-raising programs as well as successfully cultivating both corporate and private donors. Fluent in English, French, Spanish, and German. Energetic, passionate, and articulate team player with a good sense of humor and the goal of making a success out of every opportunity.

A potential employer looking at this might think, "This Rick King might not have his masters yet, but he does have a proven track record. He appears to understand all aspects of fund-raising and development. The ability to speak more than one language is always a plus. Why don't I give him a chance to tell me more? I think I want to bring him in for an interview."

"What if I'm just out of college and have no experience?" you ask. "What would my career summary look like?"

In situations like this, you have to look toward experience and jobs you held prior to graduating. How about this?

Recent graduate of State University with a major in health services administration and a minor in communications with a GPA of 4.0. Intern in rotating departments at large metropolitan hospital. Proven ability to handle various tasks quickly, effectively, and efficiently. Ability to bring a project to fruition on time. Member of college student government and campus activities board. Member of local hospital auxiliary, co-chairing two fund-raisers and handling publicity for various events.

If you prefer, you can use a bulleted list to do your career summary.

- Recent graduate of State University with a major in health services administration and a minor in communications. GPA of 4.0.
- Intern at City Hospital (rotating in various departments).
- Member of college campus activities board, assisting in the booking of speakers and seminars.
- Member of local hospital auxiliary.
- Co-chair of two hospital auxiliary fund-raisers.

Career Objective

Do you need a career objective in your resume? It isn't always necessary, but in certain cases it

helps. If you are just starting out in your career, having a career objective or a specific goal illustrates that you have some direction. It shows that you know where you want to go in your career.

When replying to a job opening, make sure your career objective on your resume is as close to the job you are applying for as possible. For example, if you are applying for a job as a publications assistant at a hospital, you might make your career objective "To work in the marketing or communications department of a health care facility in a position where I can fully utilize my creativity and writing skills."

If, on the other hand, you are sending your resume to a company "cold" (not sending it for a specific job opening), don't limit yourself unnecessarily by stating a specific career objective. If you use a career objective in this type of situation, make sure it is general.

Sometimes you might want to send copies of your resume with a cover letter to companies you want to work for who aren't actively looking to fill a job. Your hope is to garner an interview. If your resume indicates, for example, that your sole goal is to work in a hospital's publications department, depending on who opens it first, you might be overlooked for a position in the marketing or public relations department. Your career goal in this situation instead might be "To work in the marketing, public relations, development, or other department of a major health care facility where my writing, marketing, and public relations skills can be utilized." Remember, what you want is the person reviewing your resume to think of all the possible places you might fit in the organization.

Education and Training

Where should you put education on your resume? That depends. If you recently have graduated from college and especially if you have a degree in something related to the area of the health care industry you are pursuing, put it toward the top. If you graduated a number of years ago, put your education toward the end of your resume.

Should you specify the year you graduated? Recent graduates might want to. Other than that, just indicate the college or university you graduated from, your degree, and major.

"What if I went to college but didn't graduate? What should I put on my resume?" you might ask.

If you went to college but didn't graduate, simply note that you attended or are taking coursework toward a degree. Will anyone question you on it? That's hard to say. Someone might. If questioned, simply say something like, "I attended college and then unfortunately found it necessary to go to work full time. I plan on getting my degree as soon as possible. I only have nine credits left to go, so it will be an easy goal to complete."

In addition to your college education, you should also include courses, seminars, and workshops geared toward licensing and credentialing you have completed. Don't forget to include any relevant noncredit courses, seminars, and workshops you have attended. While you probably wouldn't want to add classes like flower arranging (unless this had to do with your job in someway), you might include educational courses that are not industry oriented but might help you in your career, such as public speaking, writing, grant writing, communications, or team work.

Licensing and Credentialing

Potential employers want to know if you hold the necessary licenses and credentials for your job area, so you are going to want to list any special licensing or credentials you have related to the health care industry. If you hold state licenses, it's a good idea to indicate the specific states in which you are licensed.

Professional and Work Experience/ Employment History

Potential employers always want to know your work history. List your work experience in this section of your resume. What jobs have you had? Where did you work? What did you do? What were your responsibilities? What did you accomplish?

How far back do you go? That once again depends where you are in your career. You don't want to go back to your job as a babysitter when you were 15, but you need to show your work history.

In addition to your full-time jobs in or out of the health care industry, include any part-time work that relates to the area of the industry you are pursuing or illustrates transferable job skills, accomplishments, or achievements.

Remember when listing your employment history to start at the point where you are currently in your career and then go backwards.

Skills and Personality Traits

There's an old advertising adage that says, "Don't sell the steak, sell the sizzle." When selling yourself through your resume, do the same. You don't want only to state your skills and personality traits—you want to make them sizzle! Do this by using descriptive language and key phrases.

Need some help? Here are a few words and phrases to get you started.

◎ creative
◎ dedicated
◎ hard working
◎ highly motivated

◎ energetic
◎ self-starter
◎ fully knowledgeable
◎ strong work ethic
◎ team player
◎ problem solver
◎ compassionate
◎ empathetic
◎ patient
◎ resourceful
◎ positive
◎ positive attitude
◎ effective in streamlining productivity
◎ team spirited
◎ highly professional
◎ successful leader
◎ articulate

Accomplishments and Achievements

What have you accomplished in your career in or out of the health care industry? Were you named employee of the year? How about employee of the month? Have you increased sales? Have you increased attendance? Have you coordinated a program for women's health?

Have you put together the speakers for a health fair? Were you the driving force for bringing 200 uninsured, low-income people to a hearing clinic? Are you a nurse recognized for your compassion when dealing with children? Do you write a weekly column on staying healthy? Have you won an industry award? Done the publicity for a fund-raiser? Written a large innovative grant? Your achievements inform potential employers not only about what you have done but also about what you might do for them.

Sit down and think about it for a while. What are you most proud of in your career? What have you done that has made a difference or had a positive impact on the facility or company for which you worked? If you are new to

> **Tip from the Top**
>
> One of the mistakes that many people make when preparing their resume is that they keep adding accomplishments without deleting any of the earlier or less important ones. While it's very tempting to do this, it's not always the best idea.

the workforce, what did you do in school? What about in a volunteer capacity?

Just as you made your skills and personality traits sizzle with words, you want to do the same thing with your accomplishments and achievements. Put yourself in the position of a human resources director for a moment. You get two resumes. Under the accomplishments section, one says, "Helped execute hospital health fair." The other says, "Planned, coordinated, and successfully executed five health fairs annually from inception through fruition, resulting in 300 new patients." Which resume would catch your eye?

You can help your accomplishments and achievements "sizzle" by adding action verbs to your accomplishments. Use words like achieved, administered, applied, accomplished, assisted, strengthened, and others.

Honors and Awards

When drafting your resume, include any honors you have received, whether they have anything to do with the health care industry or not. These honors help set you apart from other candidates. They show that you are a hard worker and good at what you do.

Was one of your articles accepted by a medical journal? Did one of your newspaper stories win a journalism award? Were you named secretary of your chapter of the nurses association?

Were you named president of the PTA? Elected to your local library board of directors? The recipient of a community service award?

Each of these honors helps make you more special.

Community Service and Volunteer Activities

If you perform community service or volunteer activities on a regular basis, include it on your resume. Community service and volunteer activities you perform illustrate to potential employers that you "do a little extra." Additionally, you can never predict when the person reviewing your resume might be a member of the organization with which you volunteer. An unexpected connection like that can help you stand out. Additionally, many hospitals and other health care facilities are not-for-profits. Illustrating that you are involved in the not-for-profit world may be a plus to potential employers.

Hobbies and Interests

What are your hobbies and interests? Do you raise bulldogs? Do you go to concerts? Do you go to plays? Do you collect cookbooks? Do you collect NASCAR memorabilia? Are you a hiker? Do you volunteer with a literacy program? Are you a CASA volunteer? While many career counselors feel that hobbies or personal interests have no place on a professional resume, I disagree.

Here's a secret. You can never tell what will cause the person or persons reviewing the resumes to make a connection. Perhaps he or she has the same hobby as you. Perhaps he or she is a volunteer with a literacy program in which you participate. Anything that causes you to stand out in a positive manner or that causes a connection with your potential interviewer will help your resume garner attention, helping you land an interview.

One situation where you may not want to add unrelated hobbies or interests is when you are sending your resume to a recruiter. The job of a recruiter is to find the *perfect* candidate for an employer. He or she will generally not know the personal hobbies or interests of the person doing the hiring, so adding your information probably won't be of any value.

References

The goal for your resume is to have it help you *obtain* an interview. If you list your references on your resume, be aware that someone may check them to help them decide if they should interview you. You don't really want people giving their opinions about you *until* you have the chance to sell yourself. With this in mind, it usually isn't a good idea to list your references on your resume.

If you are uncomfortable with this, include a line on your resume stating that "References are available upon request."

Your Resume Writing Style

How important is writing style in your resume? Very important. Aside from conveying your message, your writing style helps to illustrate that you have good written communication skills.

"But I'm not going for a business or administrative job," you say. "I'm pursuing a career in a lab."

It doesn't matter what type of career you are pursuing. Good written communication skills will always be helpful in your career.

When preparing your resume, write clearly and concisely, and do not use the pronoun "I" to describe your accomplishments. Instead of writing "I have experience in critical care. I have experience in the patient transport area.

> ### ★ Tip from the Coach
>
> Don't stress yourself out if you can't get your resume on one or two pages. While most career specialists insist a resume should only be one or two pages at most, I strongly disagree. You don't want to overwhelm a potential employer with a ten-page *book,* but if your resume needs to be three or four pages to get your pertinent information in, that's okay. Keep in mind, though, that lengthy resumes or CVs (curriculum vitae) like these are generally used by high-level professionals who have many years' experience and work history to fill the additional pages.
>
> If your resume is longer than normal, you should use a brief career summary at the beginning so a hiring manager can quickly see what your major accomplishments are. If they then want to take their time to look through the rest of the resume, your information will be there.

I have strong problem solving skills. I have supervisory experience," try this: "Six years of experience in critical care; three years of experience in patient transport; two years of supervisory experience; strong problem-solving skills."

Instead of "I developed key PR campaigns for health care facilities. I got the hospital over 1,000 appearances and mentions in major media," try "Developed key PR campaigns for health care facility, resulting in over 350 feature stories, positive mentions, and press release placements in a three-month period." Note the inclusion of a time period. It's good to be specific about your achievements.

Creating Industry-Specific Resumes

How can you create resumes specific to the area of the health care industry you are pursuing? Once you've created your basic resume, tailor each resume for the specific position or area you are pursuing, and find ways to relate your existing skills to that resume.

The placement of each of the components of your resume will also help you better tailor your resume to specific jobs.

Use all your experiences, talents, and skills to obtain the career you want. Learn how to transfer skills and experience. Remember that if you can sell one product or service, with a little training, you can usually sell another. If you can publicize one product or service, you can publicize another. If you are an office manager in one industry, you can become an office manager in another.

One thing you should *never* do is lie on your resume. Don't lie about your education. Don't lie about experience. Don't lie about places you've worked. Don't lie about who you know or people with whom you have worked. If you haven't picked up on it yet, *do not lie*. Once someone knows you have lied, that is what they will remember about you, and they may pass on that information to others.

"Oh, no one is going to find out," you might say.

Don't bet on it. Someone might find out by chance, deduce the truth based on knowledge within the industry, or hear the facts from a coworker or industry colleague. Someone just by chance may be surfing the net and see your name. When the truth comes out, it can end up blowing up in your face.

"By that time, I'll be doing such a good job, no one will fire me," you say.

The Inside Scoop

I recently heard a story of a woman who had worked in the administrative area of a health care facility for over 20 years. She had great work reviews and consistently received promotions throughout her career. She was well respected and liked by her colleagues and supervisors. One day, she was called into the human resources office and fired. Why? It seems that 20 years ago when she had applied for the job, the woman had indicated she had a bachelor's degree. In reality, she was two credits away from her degree and never graduated. Evidently, someone did some research on her background for a press release announcing an upcoming promotion and found out she had lied on her application, resulting in her termination.

The moral of the story is don't lie on your resume. No matter what you think the chances are that your lie will not be found out, it might be, and it is not worth the chance.

Tip from the Top

If you are pursuing a career in the clinical area, when preparing your resume, be sure to add any administrative or managerial skills you have in addition to your clinical skills. In the same vein, if you are pursuing a career in the administrative or management area of the health care field, be sure to include any clinical skills you have as well as your administrative and management skills.

That's the best-case scenario and there's a chance that could happen, but think about this. Once someone lies to you, do you ever trust him or her again? Probably not, and no one will trust you or anything you say. That will hurt your chances of climbing the career ladder. The worst-case scenario is that you will be fired, left without references, lose some of your contacts, and make it much more difficult to find your next job.

If you don't have the experience you wish you had, try to impress the hiring manager or recruiter with other parts of your resume and your cover letter. If you have the experience and you are trying to advance your career, this is the time to redefine your resume. Add action verbs. Add your accomplishments. Make your new resume shine. Create a marketing piece that will make someone say, "We need to interview this person. Look at everything he's done."

When creating your resume for a career in the health care industry, you want it to reflect your knowledge of the industry and its challenges. Be sure your resume shows evidence of skills, experience, productivity, and your personal commitment to quality in health care.

Your CV—Curriculum Vitae

What exactly is a CV? CV is short for *curriculum vitae*. What's the difference between a CV and a resume? That depends on who you ask. Some people use the words interchangeably. Some say a resume is a one- or two-page summary of your employment history, experience, and education, and a CV is a more comprehensive synopsis of your qualifications, education, and experience. So what's the answer?

Generally, it's somewhere in between. Your resume is a summary of your employment history and education that highlights your skills, talents, and education. Your CV would be a longer, detailed synopsis of these things, plus teaching and research experience you might have, articles or papers you have published, research projects you have done, presentations you have made, and so on. The CV gives you the opportunity to list every paper, project, and presentation.

How do you know which type of document to use? Generally, it depends on the type of job for which you are applying. Usually, you would use a CV instead of a resume if you were applying for a job in research, education, or certain parts of medicine (for example, if you were applying for a teaching position at a medical school or a job in research at a hospital or pharmaceutical company).

Words from the Wise

As people often use the words *CV* and *resume* interchangeably, don't assume that just because someone asks you for your CV they actually want that particular document. They might really want your resume.

What About References?

References are another of your selling tools. Basically, references are the individuals who will vouch for your skills, ethics, and work history when a potential employer calls. A good reference can set you apart from the crowd and give you the edge over other applicants. A bad one can seriously hinder your career goals.

It's always a good idea to bring the names, addresses, and phone numbers of the people you are using for references with you when you apply for a job or when you are going on an interview. If you're asked to list them on an employment application, you'll be prepared.

Who should you use for references? To begin with, you're going to need professional references. These are people you've worked with or know you on a professional level. They might be current or former supervisors or bosses, the director of a not-for-profit organization you've volunteered with, internship program coordinators, a former professor, and so on.

Do your references need to be part of the health care industry? If you have references in the industry, it can't hurt. In the industry or not, however, what you are looking for are people who you can count on to help sell you to potential employers.

Always ask people if they are willing to be a reference before you use them. Only use people you are absolutely positive will say good things about you. Additionally, try to find people who are articulate and professional.

Who would be a bad reference? A boss who fired you, a supervisor you didn't get along with, or anyone you had any kind of problem with whatsoever. Do not use these people for references even if they tell you that they'll give you a good one. They might keep their word, but they might not, and you won't know until it's too late.

You might be asked to list references on an employment application, but it's a good idea to prepare a printed sheet of your professional references that you can leave with the interviewer as well. This sheet will contain your list of three to five references, including their names, positions, and contact information. As with your resume, make sure it is printed on a good quality paper.

Here's an example to get you started.

Professional References for Kay Mandel

Mr. Gerry Brown
CEO
Sunset General Hospital
222 Sunset Road
Anytown, NY 11111
(222) 333-3333
browng@sunsetgeneral.org

Ms. Christine Woodruff
Lab Manager
Green Tree Urgi-Center
303 4th Avenue
Anytown, NY 11111
(111) 333-2222
cwoodruff@greentree.com

Mr. Vince Marino
Lab Manager
Sunset General Hospital
222 Sunset Road
Anytown, NY 11111
(222) 333-3333
marinov@sunsetgeneral.org

The Inside Scoop

If you give your references an idea of what type of job you're pursuing, what skills are important in that position, or even what you want them to say, you stand a better chance of them leading the conversation in the direction you want it to go.

Personal References

In addition to professional references, you might be asked to provide personal references. These may be friends, family members, or others with whom who you don't have a professional relationship. You probably won't need to print out a reference sheet for your personal references, but make sure you have all their contact information in case you need it quickly.

As with professional references, make sure the people you are using know you are listing them as references. Give them a call when you're going on an interview to let them know someone might be contacting them and ask them to let you know if they get a call.

Letters of Recommendation

As you go through your career, it's a good idea to get letters of recommendation from people who have been impressed with your work. Along with references, these help give potential employers a better sense of your worth. How do you get a letter of recommendation? It's simple. You usually just have to ask. For example, let's say you are close to completing an internship.

Say to your supervisor, "I've enjoyed my time here. Would it be possible to get a letter of recommendation from you for my files?"

Most people will be glad to provide a letter. In some cases, people might even ask you to write it yourself for them to sign. Don't forego these opportunities even if you feel embarrassed about blowing your own horn.

The easiest way to do it is by trying to imagine you aren't writing about yourself. In that way, you can be honest and write a great letter. Give it to the person and say, "Here's the letter we discussed. Let me know if you want anything changed or you aren't comfortable with any piece of it." Nine times out of 10, the person will sign the letter as is without making changes.

Whom should you ask for letters of recommendation? You might ask professors with whom you have developed a good relationship, internship coordinators, supervisors, former and current employers, executive directors of not-for-profit, civic, or charity organizations you have volunteered with, and so on.

Letters of recommendation can become another powerful marketing tool in your quest to career success. Make sure you copy each letter you get on good quality white paper. Once that's done, you can make them part of your career portfolio, send them with your resume when applying for a position, or bring them with you to interviews.

Creating Captivating Cover Letters

Unless instructed otherwise by a potential employer or in an advertisement, always send your resume with a cover letter. Why? Mainly be-

---

★ Words from the Wise

Don't wait until the last minute to ask people to write letters of recommendation. Give them enough time so they will not be under pressure and be able to write the best letter possible for you.

---

cause if your resume grabs the eye of someone in the position to interview you, he or she often looks at the cover letter to evaluate your written communication skills as well as to get a sense of your personal side. If your letter is a good one, it might just get you the phone call you've been waiting for. On the other hand, a poorly written letter might just keep you from getting that call.

What can make your letter stand out? Try to make sure your letter is directed to the name of the person to whom you are sending it instead of "Hiring Manager," "To Whom It May Concern," or "Sir or Madam."

"But, what if the name of the person isn't in the ad?" you say. "How do I know what it is?"

You might not always be able to get the correct name, but at least do some research. You might, for example, call the company and ask the name of the person to which responses are directed.

If you are sending your resume to a company cold, it's even more important to send it to a specific person. It gives you a better shot at someone not only reviewing it but taking action on it.

It's okay to call the company and say to the receptionist or secretary, "Hi, I was wondering if you could give me some information? I'm trying to send my resume to someone at your company and I'm not sure who to send it to. Could you please give me the name of the human resources director?" (or whoever you are trying to target).

★ The Inside Scoop

Letters of recommendation may be used for other purposes than obtaining a job. You may also need them when applying for scholarships, fellowships, graduate school, med school, and so on.

In hospitals or other health care facilities, this is not usually a problem. In some other companies, however, receptionists may not be open with the information. If he or she won't give it to you for some reason, say thank you and hang up.

How do you get around this? Wait until lunch time or around 5:15 p.m. when the person you spoke to might be at lunch or done with work, call back, and say something to the effect of, "Hi, I was wondering if you could please give me the spelling of the name of your director of sales?" (Or the HR director or whoever you are trying to find.)

If the person on the other end of the phone line asks you to be more specific about the name, simply say, "Let's see, I think it was Brownson or something like that. It sounded like Brown something."

Don't worry about sounding stupid on the phone. The person at the other end doesn't know you. This system usually works. Believe it or not, most companies have someone working there whose name sounds like Brown or Smith.

The person on the phone may say to you, "No, we don't have a Brownson. What department are you looking for?" When you say sales, he or she will probably say, "Oh, that's not Brownson, it's John Campbell. Is that who you're looking for?"

Then all you have to say is, "You know what, you're right, sorry, I was looking at the wrong notes. So that's C-A-M-P-B-E-L-L?"

Voila. You have the name. Is it a lot of effort? Well, it's a little effort, but if it gets you the name of someone you need and ultimately helps get you an interview, isn't it worth it?

By the way, this technique not only works for getting names you need but other information as well. You might have to be persistent and it might take you a few tries, but it generally always gets you the information you need.

You sometimes can get names from the Internet. Perhaps the company Web site lists the names of their key people. Key names for large companies may also often be located on Hoovers.com, an online database of information about businesses. Do what you can to get the names you need. It can make a big difference when you direct your letters to someone specific within the company.

Those who are in the position to hire you, no matter which segment of the health care industry you are pursuing, receive a large number of resumes, letters, and phone calls. What can help your letters stand out? Make them grab the attention of the reader. How? Make sure your cover letters are creative.

Take some time and think about it. What would make *you* keep reading? While there will be situations where you might be better off sending the traditional "In response to your ad letter," what about trying out a couple of other ideas?

Take a look at the first sample cover letter. Would this letter grab your attention? Would it make you keep reading? Chances are it would. After grabbing the reader's attention, it quickly offers some of the applicant's skills, talents, and achievements. Would you bring in Mike Richards for an interview? I think most employers would.

MIKE RICHARDS
211 Avenue J
Different Town, NY 22222
666-777-7777
mrichards@moreinernet.com

Ms. Paula Carlson
Human Resources Manager
Crescent Regional Medical Center
P.O. Box 332
Crescent City, NY 11111

Dear Ms. Carlson:
    CONGRATULATIONS!

I'm pleased to inform you that you have just received the resume that can end your search for the Crescent Regional Medical Center's new marketing director. In order to claim your "prize," please review my resume and call as soon as possible to arrange an interview. I can guarantee you'll be pleased you did!

As the assistant marketing director for a 275-bed community hospital, I helped coordinate the marketing activities of the facility for a year before being promoted to the position of full-fledged marketing director. During my two-year tenure in this position I developed and implemented a number of creative, innovative programs to help bring new patients to the facility. These programs additionally helped promote community awareness and support of the CRMC Foundation. Bottom-line revenue has increased dramatically and donations have jumped 200 percent this year.

In this position I have also worked with large corporate businesses developing partnership and sponsorship opportunities, saving monies for the facility while generating large amounts of media attention for both entities.

While I love what I do now, my dream and passion has been a career in marketing at a health care facility in the area where I grew up and my family still resides.

I welcome the challenge and opportunity to work with the Crescent Regional Medical Center and believe my experience, skills, talents and passion would be an asset to your organization.

I look forward to hearing from you.

Sincerely yours,
Mike Richards

Now check out some other creative cover letters.

SEAN ROPER
609 East 41st Avenue
Different Town, NY 33333
999-999-9999
seanroper@moreinternet.com

Mr. Jack Ritter
Human Resources Director
State Street Family Health Clinic
411 State Street
Anytown, NY 11111

Dear Mr. Ritter:
IS YOUR CLINIC IN NEED OF FUNDS?
Thousands of dollars can be yours with just one call…to me!!!

I was excited to learn about your opening for a Director of Fund-Raising and Development for the State Street Family Health Clinic. How lucky for me that just as I moved back into the area, the perfect job became available.

I have recently graduated from Lerner University with a major in health services administration and a minor in communications. Before you pass by my resume for lack of experience, I urge you to read on. I'm sure you will agree that what I lack in professional experience in fund-raising, I more than make up for in my volunteer activities.

While still in college, I volunteered to work on the fund-raising committee for the local hospital auxiliary. I began by assisting in the coordination of a number of fund-raising events. I soon was helping develop and implement fund-raising events and activities helping to raise over $300,000. After researching and writing a number of grants, I was also able to secure two grants totaling close to $100,000 to be used for volunteer training.

I know your clinic, like other not-for-profit organizations depends on grants, donations, sponsorships, and bequests for a large part of your funding. While, of course, I can't guarantee the exact amount I can help you raise, I can promise you that I will work tirelessly using every avenue possible to secure funds.

I strongly believe in the mission of the State Street Family Health Clinic and believe that it is essential that everyone has the right to have good quality medical care regardless of their ability to pay.

I'm an enthusiastic, creative, motivated team player who can also work effectively on my own. I am focused and goal oriented. If you give me the chance, I'll be your clinic's number one cheerleader. I believe with my passion for the mission and proven ability to secure funds, I have the skills and talents to be an asset to the State Street Family Health Clinic.

I have enclosed my resume, copies of news stories on grants and fund-raising programs I was involved with as well as a brief outline of a number of ideas I developed for fund-raising and development for the Southern Tier Community Hospital.

I would very much appreciate the opportunity to meet with you to discuss this exciting opportunity.

Thanks for your consideration. I look forward to hearing from you.

Sincerely yours,
Sean Roper

Does your cover letter always have to be creative? It doesn't have to, but it should at least always grab the attention of the reader. It should create a strong impact and make the reader want to further review your resume.

To do this, you might want to do some research on the potential employer. Surf the net a bit and you might find, for example, that the hospital to which you are applying for a job

The Inside Scoop

When I was first entering the workforce, I replied to an advertisement, sending my resume and a cover letter. The contact name was "Marsha Wilson." About a week after I sent my letter out, I received a phone call from a secretary who referred to the job and asked me to hold for what sounded like *Marshall Wilson.* I panicked. I had sent my letter to Ms. Marsha Wilson.

"How stupid could I have been?" I asked myself. I quickly came up with a plan.

"Hello, Shelly," the person on the other end of the phone said in a deep voice.

"Hi, Mr. Wilson," I said. "How are you?"

"It's Ms. Wilson," she said shortly. "I have a deep voice, but I am a woman."

The phone interview went downhill from there.

Had I simply asked the secretary, "Did you say Marsha or Marshall?" I would not have been in that predicament. From that point on, if I have a question, I try to *ask or find out* ahead of time. Before you put yourself in a situation like this, learn from my mistake and don't assume.

Words from the Wise

Never guess at someone's gender when writing a letter. If you don't know if someone is a Ms. or a Mr. (and you can't find out by calling before you send your letter), and you know their name, just use their full name. For example, if you don't know if Tony Lyon is a male or a female, just write *Dear Tony Lyon.* If you don't know the person's name at all, use the salutation *Dear Sir or Madam.*

recently was accredited or has one of the largest pediatric units in the country or was named one of the best health care facilities to work for. What do you do with this information?

Craft part of your letter around it. For example, you might write, "I was excited to learn that your facility has a large and progressive oncology unit utilizing some new complimentary care therapies. I have just completed a seminar dealing with a number of complimentary therapies in cancer care and found them extremely effective in the treatment of patients both physically and emotionally."

Here are a few more sample letters.

Pauline Samuels
32 Garden Street
Some Town, NY 11111
555-555-5555

Ms. Leah Robbins-Hiring Manager
See Bright Ophthalmologic Associates
PO Box 9002
Some Town, NY 11111

Dear Ms. Robbins:

Almost no one wants to be sitting in an ophthalmologist's office getting their eye pressure taken, their eyes tested, or having any other test or procedure done. They simply aren't the activities of choice. And while I might not be able to change that, I can promise you that given the chance, I will make sure the patients I deal with in your office always have a caring smile, lots of kind words, and a positive experience.

I will be one of your office's most cheerful ophthalmologic technicians, helping break any tensions that might arise during the day with humor and a laugh.

I'm an enthusiastic, energetic, and personable individual with a knack for making people smile. I knew the first day I started the training to become an ophthalmologic technician that I had a passion for work in this field. Now, with three years of experience, I am sure I made the right career choice!

While I was sad to have to leave my previous position in Chicago when my husband was transferred back to New York, I am thrilled to be back "home." I was even more excited when I saw this opening, because I had been a patient of your ophthalmologic group when I was 10 years old. During my initial visit, the ophthalmologic technician was so caring and made me feel so comfortable that I decided on the spot that was what I wanted to do "when I grew up."

I'm a quick and efficient learner and adapt well to new situations, and I'm sure that I will be an asset to your office. I have enclosed my resume and letters of reference from my former employer for your review. I would very much ap-preciate the opportunity to meet with you for an interview so I can learn more about the job.

Thanks for your consideration. If I don't hear from you within a couple of weeks, I'll give you a call.

I look forward to hearing from you.

Sincerely yours,
Pauline Samuels

Here's a sample of a letter similar to one many people send with their resumes. If you were a human resources manager, which letter would catch your eye?

DON PHILLIPS
919 Main Street
Some City, NY 11111
333-333-3111
donphillips@bestinternet.com

Mr. Harrison Hannity
Human Resources Director
LaSalle Hospital
Some Town, CA 22222

Dear Mr. Hannity:

I would like to apply for the physical therapist position you advertised in the October 29 issue of the *Times*. I am enclosing my resume for your consideration.

I look forward to hearing from you.

Sincerely yours,
Don Phillips

More Selling Tools—Business and Networking Cards

The best way to succeed at any project is to do everything possible to stack the deck in your favor. Most people use a resume to sell themselves. As we just discussed, done right, your resume can be a great selling tool. It can get you in the door for an interview. However, putting all your eggs in one basket is never a good idea. What else can you do to help sell yourself? What other tools can you use?

Business cards are small but powerful tools that can positively enhance your career if used correctly. We've discussed the importance of business cards throughout the book. Let's look at them more closely.

Whatever level you're at in your career, whatever area of the industry you're interested in pursuing, business cards can help you get further. If you don't have a job yet, business cards are essential. At this point, they may also be known as networking cards because that is what they are going to help you do.

If you already have a job, business cards can help you climb the ladder to success. Get your business cards made up, and get them made up now!

Why are cards so important? For a lot of reasons but mainly because they help people not only remember you but find you. Networking is essential to your success. Once you go through all the effort of doing it, if someone doesn't remember who you are or how they can contact you, it's almost useless.

How many times have you met someone during the day or at a party and then gone your separate ways. A couple days later, something will come up where you wish you could remem-

ber the person's name or you do remember their name but have no idea how to get a hold of them. How bad would you feel if you found out that you met someone, told him or her that you were looking for a job, they ran into someone else who was looking for someone with your skills and talents, and they didn't know how to get a hold of you? Business cards could have solved that problem.

When was the last time you ran into someone successful who didn't have business cards? They boost your prestige and make you feel more successful. If you feel more successful, you'll be more successful.

What is your next step? Start by determining what you want your business cards to look like. There are a variety of styles to choose from. You might want to go to a print shop or an office supply store such as Staples or Office Max to look at samples or you can create your own style.

Order at least 1,000 cards. What are you going to do with 1,000 cards? You're going to give them to everyone. While everyone might not keep your resume, most people in all aspects of business keep cards.

Samples of Business and Networking Cards

Ernest Davis

Executive Management Position in Health Care Organization
BA Health Services Administration
MBA Health Services Administration
Creative thinker, problem solver, commitment to quality
Ability to assess needs and develop effective solutions

P.O. Box 320   Phone: 444-444-9999
Anytown, NY 11111   Cell: 888-999-1111
E-mail: edavis@moreinternet.com

---

912 Spring Street
Anytown, NY 11111

Tamara Rosen

Excellent verbal and written communication skills
Accomplished publicist and marketing professional

Phone: 111-111-1111
Cell: 888-999-0000
E-mail: trosen@moreinternet

---

450 South Main Street   Phone: 222-111-1111
Anytown, NY 11111   Cell: 111-999-0000
E-mail: bettysavoy@moreinternet.com

Betty Savoy–Registered Nurse
BSN
Licensed in NY, NJ, CT, and PA

Reliable, compassionate, ethical health care provider
Available for private nursing assignments

Gayle James

Medical Office Manager
Organized, experienced problem solver

P.O. Box 140.   Phone: 444-444-4444
Anytown, NY 11111   Cell: 999-999-9999
E-mail: gaylejames@bestnet.com

Stanley Johnson

Seeking challenging position as a
Physical Therapist

Graduating with MPT, December 2007

P.O. Box 1240   Phone: 111-444-5555
Anytown, NY 11111   Cell: 111-888-9999
E-mail: stanleyjohnson@bestnet.com

Dr. James Michaels

Chiropractor

Good Adjustments Chiropractic Center

1200 Broadway   Phone: 222-333-4444
Anytown, NY 11111

http://www.goodadjustments.com

Simple cards are the least expensive. They probably will cost approximately $20 to $40 to print an order of 1,000. The more features you add, the more the cost goes up.

What should your cards say? At minimum, include your name, address, and phone number (both home and cell, if you have one). It's a good idea to add your job or your career goal or objective. You might even briefly describe your talents, skills, or traits. Your business card is your selling piece, so think about what you want to sell. Check out some of the samples to get ideas.

At every career-oriented seminar I give, when we get to the section on business cards, someone always raises a hand and says something to the effect of "I don't have a job yet. What kind of cards do I make up? What would they say—*unemployed?*"

So before you think it or say it, the answer is no. You definitely don't put the word *unemployed* anywhere on your card. You will put your name, contact information, and career goals on your business card and then use them to become employed in your career of choice.

Remember that cards are small, which limits the number of words that can fit so the card looks attractive and can be read easily. If you want more room, you might use a double-sided card (front and back) or a double-sized card folded over, giving you four times as much space. I've seen both used successfully. The double-sized card can be very effective for a mini-resume.

You have a lot of decisions on how you want your business cards to look. What kind of card stock do you want? Do you want your card smooth or textured? Flat or shiny? What about color? Do you want white, beige, or a colored card? Do you want flat print or raised print?

> ### Tip from the Coach
> Look at other people's business cards to try to find a style you like. Then fit your information into that style.

What fonts or typefaces do you want to use? Do you want graphics? How do you want the information laid out? Do you want it straight or on an angle? The decisions are yours. It just depends what you like and what you think will sell you the best.

Brochures Can Tell Your Story

While you're always going to need a resume or a CV, consider developing your own brochure, too. A brochure can tell your story and help you sell yourself. Sometimes, something out of the ordinary can also help grab the attention of someone important in your career.

What's a brochure? It is a selling piece that gives information about a product, place, event, or person, among other things. In this situation, the brochure is going to be about you. While your resume tells your full story, your brochure is going to illustrate your key points.

Why do you need one? A brochure can help you stand out from other job seekers.

What should a brochure contain? While it depends to a great extent on what segment of the industry you're pursuing, there are some basic things you should include.

Definitely include your name and contact information. Then add your selling points. Maybe those are your skills. Perhaps they are your accomplishments or talents. What about something unique or special that you do or have done?

You want to try to illustrate what *you* can do for an employer and what benefits they will obtain by hiring you. You want them to see what you can bring to the table. A brief bio is often helpful to illustrate your credentials and credibility. What about three or four quotes from some of your letters of recommendation? For example:

◎ "One of the best interns we ever had participate in our internship program." Jack Anderson, Internship Coordinator, City Hospital

◎ "A real team player who motivates the team." Patti Riley, CEO, Morgantown UrgiCenter.

You might want to use a number of quotes from letters from your patients, customers, or supervisors. Always get permission first. Keep your wording simple. Make it clear, concise, and interesting.

What should your brochure look like? The possibilities are endless. Brochures can be simple or elaborate. Your brochure can be designed in different sizes, papers, folds, inks, and colors. You can use photographs, drawings, illustrations, or other graphics.

If you have graphic-design ability and talent, lay out your brochure yourself. If you don't, ask a friend or family member who is talented in that area. There are also software programs that help you design brochures. With these programs you simply type your information and print it out.

If you want to design your brochure but want it printed professionally, consider bringing

---

The Inside Scoop

You don't need 1,000 brochures. Start off with 100 or so and see how they work for you. If you're not seeing results, you may need to rework it. Remember that for brochures to be effective, you have to send them out, so be sure you start working on a list of companies or people you want to target.

---

your camera-ready brochure to a professional print shop. Camera-ready means your document is ready to be printed, and any consumer print shop should be able to help guide you through the steps needed to prepare your work for them. In addition to print shops, you might also consider office supply stores such as Staples and Office Max that do printing.

If you don't feel comfortable designing your own brochure, you can ask a printer in your area if there is an artist on staff. Professional design and printing of a brochure can get expensive. Is it worth it? Only you can decide, but if it helps get your career started or makes the one you have more successful, the answer is likely yes.

Can brochures be effective? I certainly think so. Not only do I know a great number of people who have used them successfully in every industry; I personally used one when I was breaking into the music business and have continued using them ever since. Here's my story.

At the time, I was sending out a lot of resumes and making a lot of calls in an attempt to obtain interviews. I had learned a lot about marketing and noticed that many companies used brochures. My father, who was a marketing professional, suggested that a brochure might just be what I needed. By that time, I had realized that if I wanted to *sell* myself, I might need to

---

Tip from the Coach

You are going to use your brochure in addition to your resume, not in place of it.

market myself a little more assertively than I was doing, so I decided to try a brochure idea.

We designed a brochure printed on an 11-by-17-inch paper folded in half, giving me four pages to tell my story. We mounted a head shot on the front page and had it printed it in hot pink ink. The inside was crafted with carefully selected words indicating my accomplishments, skills, talents, and areas in which I could help a company who hired me.

The brochures were professionally printed. I researched companies I might want to work with and sent the brochures to various record labels, music instrument manufacturers, music publishers, music industry publicity companies, artist managers, and so on.

I started getting calls from some of the people who received the brochure, obtained a number of interviews, and even landed a couple of job offers. None of them, however, was the job of my dreams.

Five years after I sent out my first brochure, I received a call from a major record company who told me that at the time they first received it they didn't need anyone with my skills or talents, but they thought the brochure was so unique that they kept it on file. Voila. Five years passed, they needed an individual with my skills, someone remembered my brochure, pulled it out, and called me. By that time I was already on the road with another group and couldn't take the job, but it was nice to be called.

⭐ Words from the Wise

It is very easy to miss errors. Before you have your brochure printed, proofread it and proofread it again. Then ask a friend or family member to proofread it as well.

⭐ Words from a Pro

If you want to try out the brochure concept on an inexpensive basis, lay out your brochure on your computer. You can do it on your own if you are computer savvy or use a brochure software program. Then print it out using good quality paper. You can even try glossy photo paper to make your brochures slick. You can leave your paper flat, fold it in half crosswise, or even make a tri-fold and design your brochure accordingly. Remember, you don't need a lot of words for your brochure to be effective; you just need the words you use to be effective.

Why am I sharing this story with you? To show you the power of what brochures can do for your career. What is really interesting is that companies and people I originally sent that first brochure to years ago still remember it. They can describe it to a tee and many of them still have it in their files. My brochure ended up becoming a networking tool.

When creating your brochure make, sure it represents the image you want to portray. Try to make it as unique and eye-catching as possible. You can never tell how long someone is going to keep it.

Your Career Portfolio: Have Experience Will Travel

People in creative careers have always used portfolios to illustrate what they have done and can accomplish. You can do the same.

What is a career portfolio? It's a portfolio or book that contains your career information and illustrates your best work. Your portfolio is a visual representation of your potential. Why do you need one? Because your career portfolio can help you get the positions you want, and that is what this is all about.

Consider this question. What would you believe more? Something someone told you or something you saw with your own eyes? If you're like most people, you would believe something you saw. And that's what a good career portfolio can do for you. It can provide actual illustrations of what you've done and what you can do.

For example, you might tell a potential employer that you can write press releases. Can you really? If you have samples in your portfolio, you can pull out a couple and show your work.

You might tell potential employers you can manage their medical office, but if you have letters from former employers that are full of praise, it's generally means more.

What would be more impressive to you? Reading over someone's resume and reading that they won the salesperson of the month award or actually seeing a copy of the award certificate? Reading in someone's resume that they wrote successful grants or seeing the articles in the newspaper discussing the big grant that they got?

Have you written press releases about your accomplishments that led to articles in the paper? Have others done articles or feature stories about you that appeared in the media?

Copies of all these documents can be part of your career portfolio. Often, if you have buzz around you, potential employers feel you will be a commodity to their company.

Don't think that your portfolio is only going to be useful when you're first obtaining a job. If you continue adding your accomplishments, new skills, and samples of projects you've worked on, your portfolio will be especially useful in advancement throughout your career. Of course, as time goes on, omit some of your earlier documents and replace them with

> **Tip from the Top**
> When compiling your portfolio, be careful not to use any confidential work or documents from a company, even if you were the one who wrote the report or the letter. You also need to make sure you don't use anything that might infringe on the privacy of any patients. Potential employers might be concerned about how you will deal with their confidential issues if you aren't keeping other confidences.

more current ones. Having an organized system to present your achievements and successes is also helpful when going through employment reviews or asking for a promotion or a raise. It also is very effective in illustrating what you've done if you're trying to move up the ladder at a different company.

I consistently get calls from people who have been to our seminars or called for advice who continue to use their career portfolios successfully in their careers. Work on developing your career portfolio, and this simple tool can help you achieve success as well.

Your portfolio is portable. You can bring it with you when you go on interviews so you can show it to potential employers. You can make copies of things in your portfolio to give to potential employers or have everything at hand when you want to answer an ad or send out cold letters.

How do you build a detailed portfolio illustrating your skills, talents, and accomplishments? What goes into it? You want your portfolio to document your work-related talents and accomplishments. These are the assets that you will be *selling* to your potential employers. Let's look at some of the things you might want to include.

- your profile
- resume
- bio
- reference sheets
- skill and abilities
- degrees, licenses, and certifications
- experience sheet
- summary of accomplishments
- professional associations
- professional development activities (conferences, seminars, and workshops attended as well as any other professional development activities)
- professional presentations you have given
- papers or articles you have written and have been published.
- awards and honors
- volunteer activities and community service
- supporting documents
- samples of work
- newspaper, magazine, and other articles and/or feature stories about you
- reports you've done
- letters or notes people have written to tell you what a good job you've done
- photos of you accepting an award or at an event you worked on
- photos of events you were involved in (a health fair, women's wellness day, community hearing clinics, and so on)
- news stories or feature articles generated by your execution of a project (for example, if you did the publicity for a golf tournament to benefit a hospital and the paper did a feature story on the event)

Remember that this list is just to get you started. You can use anything in your portfolio that will help illustrate your skills, talents, and accomplishments.

Here are some sample portfolio documents:

Sample of Profile for Portfolio

PROFILE: Andrew Dyano

Education:
- State University—Master's degree in gerontology
- State University—Bachelor of Science degree
  - Major: Social work with emphasis in gerontology

Additional Training:
- Seminar: Geriatric Training for Emergencies
- Seminar: Assessment Techniques for geriatric assessment coordinators
- Conference: Geriatric Assessment
- Conference: American Geriatrics Society
- Grant writing

Goals:
- To work in a major health care facility as a geriatric assessment coordinator.

Qualifications:
- Hard working, focused, motivated, energetic
- Creative thinker
- Proven ability to develop plan of care
- Compassionate
- Detail oriented
- Ability to work equally well with the elderly and their families
- Computer skills: Microsoft Office and various other programs
- Verbal and written communication skills

Sample of Professional Development Sheet

Certificates of Professional Development

ANDREW DYANO

COMMUNICATIONS
◎ Certificate of Completion: Writing Assessment Reports
◎ Toastmasters Certification

GRANT WRITING
◎ Certificate of Completion: Grant Writing

GERONTOLOGY
◎ Certificate of Completion: Aging and the Family
◎ Certificate of Completion: Geriatric Assessment Methods

Make sure your information is well organized so you can locate what you need quickly. Many find using dividers or tabs helpful. You can compile your portfolio in a variety of booklets, binders, and so on. Whatever format you choose should be clean, neat, and professional.

⭐ Tip from the Top

Make good quality copies of key items in your portfolio to leave with interviewers or potential employers, agents, etc. Visit an office supply store to find some professional looking presentation folders to hold all the support documents you bring to an interview.

Press Kits Tell the Story

"Press kits—aren't those the things entertainers use?" you ask. "You know, famous people."

Entertainers do utilize press kits. So do famous people. But they aren't the only ones. Press kits might be of assistance to those in a variety of other career areas.

"Like who?" you ask?

Physicians, chiropractors, and dentists for starters. Physical therapists, veterinarians, psychologists, psychiatrists, personal trainers, nutritionists—and the list goes on.

Why? There are a number of reasons. You might be trying to build a practice, become recognized in your field, or want to become the professional that the media calls when they need an expert. Some might just hope it happens. If you want to be pro-active in your career, however, you're going to have to *help* it happen.

To make these things happen, you sometimes have to help them along. You might have to become your own publicist. If you have already achieved a level of success, you might have a publicist or public relations counselor handling your publicity and press relations. You might be working at a medical group or health care facility that does this for you. If you are not in this position yet, or even if you are and you want to stay on top of your own publicity, read on.

Press kits might be called media kits, promo kits, or press packs. A well-designed press kit can be an effective marketing and selling tool. It can be yet another key element in your success.

What's a press kit? Your press kit is a sales pitch. Done right, it's a chance to shine, to set yourself apart, and to get noticed.

Press kits are handy to give to those who might need professional information about you. This includes:

⭐ The Inside Scoop

Many physicians, dentists, chiropractors, therapists, nutritionists, and trainers use press kits very effectively for expanding their business. One physician I know who specializes in alternative health sent his press kit to health spas all over the country and was invited to speak on the subject. In the process, he also obtained a number of new clients in his home area.

- the media
- health care, medical, and general editors and reporters—local, regional, and national media
- TV and radio producers
- civic groups

How do you put together a press kit? Depending on where you are in your career and your financial resources, you can retain a publicist or publicity firm to handle the task, or you might want to try your hand at putting together a press kit yourself.

If you are interested in learning more about putting together a press kit, check out the section on press kits in Chapter 11: Succeeding in Your Career as a Physician.

Quote Sheets

If you are lucky enough to have professionals from the health care industry make positive comments about you either verbally or in writing, you can use these by adding quote sheets to your press kits. Remember to get permission from that person.

Put the quotes on a sheet under a heading like "Here's What They're Saying About (your name)." Don't overwhelm people. Just choose a few selected quotes with the person's name and title.

It's www—Your Personal Web Address

If you're a physician, dentist, chiropractor, psychologist, veterinarian, or any other medical professional building a practice, you're probably going to need a Web site. Why? Because the Internet is where it's at today. Your competition probably has a Web site, which means that you need one too! It's yet another of the key elements for your success and a marketing tool you really can't do without.

What can a Web site do for you? When people are searching for health-oriented information today, the Internet is often the first place they look. If you have a Web site, they might find you too.

Whether you're trying to build a practice, communicate with current or potential patients, inform people about medical or health care news, or let people know what you're doing, a Web site can help.

If you're interested in knowing more about developing a Web site, be sure to check out the information in Chapter 11: Succeeding in Your Career as a Physician.

Your Web site can be simple or elaborate, as long as it showcases you in a professional manner and accurately portrays your image. Once you have your site up and running, use your Web address on everything. Emblazon it on your business cards, in your advertisements, on your stationary, and so on.

Get the edge over others by using every tool you can, not only to get the career of your dreams but to succeed as well.

7

GETTING YOUR FOOT IN THE DOOR

Whether giving seminars or just speaking to people looking for career advice and hoping to get that perfect job, people tell me, without fail, that if they only could get their foot in the door, they would be on their way. In a way they're right.

One of the keys to a great career is getting your foot in the proverbial door. If you can just get that door open—even if it's just a crack—you can slip your foot in, and then you're on the road to success. Why? Because once you get your foot in, you have a chance to sell yourself, sell your talent, and sell your products and services.

It may seem easy, but sometimes the hardest part is getting your foot in the door. Whether you simply walk in off the street to see someone or call to make an appointment, you often are faced with the same situation. You need to get past the receptionist, the secretary, or whoever the "gatekeeper" happens to be between you and the person with whom you want to speak.

Here's what you need to know. Whenever there is a job opening, someone will get the job and unfortunately someone won't. Rejection is often part of the process in getting a job. However, feeling rejected when you haven't even had the chance to be rejected because you can't get through to someone is quite another thing.

It's not personal, but the secretary, receptionist, assistant, and even the person you're trying to reach often think of you and most other unsolicited callers as unwanted intruders who waste their time. It doesn't really matter whether you're trying to sell something or get a job, unless they can see what you can do for them, it's going to be hard to get through.

In reality *you* are trying to sell something. You're trying to sell *you, your skills,* and *your talents.* You're trying to get a job. What you need to do, however, is try not to let these gatekeepers know exactly what you want.

I am in no way telling you to lie or even stretch the truth. I'm telling you to find a way to change their perception of you. Get creative.

Some areas of the health care industry are easier to enter than others. Some segments of the industry are more competitive. And while there generally always is a gatekeeper, sometimes it's easier to get past him or her.

You might not think you have to worry about getting past a gatekeeper if you are pursuing a career in one of the segments of the industry such as nursing, which is in great demand, but you can never tell. You might, for example, want to interview in a hospital where it may be more difficult to get jobs. You might want to go after a nursing supervisor position. You might want to work as a nurse at a large corporation or go after a position as a nurse on the road with a recording group or a prizefighter. There are so many possibilities where there *could* be a gatekeeper in your way that it is always good to be prepared.

In many situations, you might be answering an advertisement or visiting the human resources office of a health care facility to fill out an application. If, for example, you are applying for an advertised job as a phlebotomist in a health care facility, you might not have to *worry* about getting past the gatekeeper, but that doesn't mean he or she isn't there.

No matter which segment of the industry you are pursuing, there will be times when you need to get past a gatekeeper so you can get your foot in the door. Before you rush in and find the door locked, let's look at some possible keys to help you get in.

Will you need every key? Probably not, but once you learn what some of the keys are, you'll have them if you need them.

Getting Through to People on the Phone

Let's start with the phone. If your goal is to talk to a specific person or make an appointment, it's important to know that many high-level business people don't answer their own phone. Instead, they rely on secretaries, receptionists, or assistants to handle this task. And that's not even counting the dreaded *voicemail.*

You can always try the straightforward approach. Just call and ask to speak to the person you are looking for. If that works, you have your foot in the door. If not, it's time to get creative.

Let's look at a few scenarios and how they might play out.

Scenario 1

Receptionist: Good afternoon, Center City Medical Group.

You: Hello, this is Joan Walsh. Can I please speak to Dr. Bishop?

Receptionist: Does he know what this is in reference to?

You: No, I'm looking for a job and would like to see if I could set up an interview.

Receptionist: I'm sorry; Dr. Bishop isn't looking to fill any positions at this time. Thank you for calling.

You: Thanks. Good-bye.

With that said, you're done. Is there something you could have said differently that might have led to a better ending? Let's look at another scenario.

Scenario 2

Secretary: Good afternoon, Center City Medical Group.

You: Is Dr. Bishop in?

Secretary: Who's calling?

You: Joan Walsh.

Secretary: May I ask what this is in reference to?

You: Yes, I was trying to set up an informational interview. Would Dr. Bishop be the person who handles this or would it be someone else?

[Asking the question in this manner means that you stand a chance at the gatekeeper giving you a specific name that you can call if Dr. Bishop is the wrong person.]

Secretary: Informational interview for what purpose?

You: I was interested in some information on a career at your medical group. Would Dr. Bishop be the right person to speak to about that?

[Make sure you are pleasant. This helps the person answering the phone want to help you.]

Secretary: No, he doesn't handle that. You need to speak to Meredith Jones. Would you like me to switch you?

[What you are really doing is helping her get you off the phone even if it means she is dumping you on someone else.]

You: "Yes, that would be great. What was your name?

[Try to make sure you get the name. In this manner, when you get transferred, the person answering at the other end will be more apt to help you.]

Secretary: Janice Little.

You: Thanks for your help. I really appreciate it.

Secretary: I'll switch you now.

Meredith Jones: Meredith Jones, may I help you?

You: Hi, Ms. Jones, Janice Little suggested you might be the right person for me to speak to. I'm interested in setting up an informational interview regarding the possibility of working with you at Center City Medical Group?

At this point, she probably will either say sorry we have no openings, ask you some additional questions, or set up a time. If she says, sorry we have no openings at this time, say something like: "I understand. Would it be possible for me to send my resume for you to review and keep on file?" If this is the case, make sure you ask to whose name your information should be directed as well as getting the exact addresses and her extension.

If she starts to question you about what type of job you are looking for, make sure you have an answer prepared. *Never* say: "Oh, I don't care; any job would be fine."

Instead, have a definitive answer. For example: "I'm interested in working in the pharmacy department. I was a pharmacy tech while in the service and I really enjoyed it. I've heard such good things about your center that I really would like to explore the options of working there."

Or, "I was interested in working in your communications or marketing department. When I was still in school I worked on my school paper and also interned in the public relations department of the local hospital for a semester and then volunteered to work on the publicity committee of their auxiliary. I just graduated with a BA in communications and moved back to the area."

Have your calendar in front of you so that if she wants to set up an interview, you can make every effort to go with the time and date she suggests.

⭐ Tip from the Top

Remember that skills are transferable. If you've done publicity for a radio station, a school system, a bank, a college, a not-for-profit, or any other type of business, you can usually do publicity for a hospital or health care facility. If you have handled marketing for a corporation, you can do marketing for a hospital.

Scenario 3

Sometimes mentioning a job to the gatekeeper is not a good idea. Let's say you are trying to create your own position or you are going after a position so coveted that those already working in the company may not be willing to help outsiders. What can you do?

Creativity is the name of the game. You might want to try this.

Receptionist: Good afternoon, Center City Medical Center.

You: I'm working on a project involving various upper-level careers in the health care industry, and, with your center's stellar reputation, you are one of the best ones to talk to. Do you know whom in your company I might speak to?

[Here is where it can get a little tricky. If you are very lucky, he or she will just put you through to someone in publicity, public relations, or human resources. If you're not so lucky, he or she will ask you questions.]

Receptionist: What type of project?

You need to be ready with a plausible answer. What you say will, of course, depend on your situation. If you are in college, you can always say you are working on a project for school. If not, you can say you are doing research on career opportunities. If you have writing skills, you might contact a local newspaper or magazine to see if they are interested in an article on careers in the health care industry (or whatever segment of the industry you are targeting). If you can't find someone to write for, you can always write a story on "spec." This means that if you write a story, you can send it in to an editor on speculation. They might take it, and they might not. Don't think about money at this point. Your goal here is to get the "right people" to speak to you and get an appointment.

This method of getting to know people is supposed to give you credibility. The idea will only be effective if you *really* are *planning* on writing an article or a story and carry through.

One of the interesting things about writing an article (whether on spec or on assignment) is that you can ask people questions and they will usually talk to you. They won't be looking at you as they would if you were looking for a job.

What you've done in these situations is changed their perception about why you're talking to them. One of the most important bonuses of interviewing people about a career in various industries is that you are making invaluable contacts. While it might be tempting, remember to use this opportunity to ask questions and network; do not try to sell yourself. After you write the article, you might call up one of the people you interviewed, perhaps the human resources director, and say something like, "You made a career in health care sound so interesting that I'd like to explore a career in the industry. Would it be possible to come in for an interview or to fill out an application?"

What can you do if none of these scenarios work? The receptionist may not be very eager to help. He or she may have instructions on "not letting anyone through." It may be his or her job

***

★ Voice of Experience

Make sure you get the correct spelling of the name of everyone who helps you. Send a short note, thanking them for their help immediately. This is not only good manners; it helps people remember who you are in a positive way.

to block unsolicited callers and visitors from the boss. What can you do?

Here are a few ideas that might help. See if you can come up with others.

◎ Try placing your call before regular business hours. Many executives and others you might want to talk to come in early before the secretary or receptionist is scheduled to work.

◎ Try placing your calls after traditional business hours when the secretary probably has left. The executives and others you want to reach generally don't push a time clock and often work late. More important, even if people utilize voicemail, they may pick up the phone themselves after hours in case their family is calling.

◎ Lunch hours are also a good time to attempt to get through to people. This is a little tricky. The executive may use voicemail during the lunch hour period, or he or she may go out to lunch. On the other hand, you might get lucky.

◎ Sometimes others in the office fill in for a receptionist or secretary and aren't sure what the procedure is or who everyone is. While you might not get through on the first shot, you might use this type of opportunity to get information. For example, you might ask for the person you want to speak to, and when the substitute tells you he or she isn't in and asks if you want to leave a message, say something like, "I'm moving around a lot today. I'll try to call later. Is Mr. Brown ever in the office after 6:00 p.m.?" If the answer is yes, ask if you can have his direct extension in case the switchboard is closed.

> ### ★ Words from the Wise
> Friday afternoon is the worst time to call someone when you want something. The second worst time is early Monday morning.

Remember the three "Ps" to help you get through. You want to be:

◎ Pleasant
◎ Persistent
◎ Positive

Always be pleasant. Aside from it being general good manners to be nice to others, being pleasant to gatekeepers is essential. Gatekeepers talk to their bosses and can let them know if you were annoying or obnoxious. When someone tells you their boss "never takes unsolicited calls or accepts unsolicited resumes," tell them you understand. Then ask what they suggest. Acknowledge objections, but try to come up with a solution.

Be persistent. Just because you don't get through on the first try doesn't mean you shouldn't try again. Don't be annoying, and don't be pushy, but don't give up. People like to help positive people. Don't moan and groan about how difficult your life is to the secretary. He or she will only want to get you off the phone.

Persistence and the Guilt Factor

Don't forget the guilt factor. If you consistently place calls to "Mr. Keane" and each time his secretary tells you he is busy, unavailable, or will call you back and he doesn't, what should you do? Should you give up? Well, that's up to you. Be aware that persistence often pays off. In many cases, after a number of calls, you and the secretary will have built up a "relationship" of

Voice of Experience

While persistence can work, don't be annoying. Calling more than once a day or, in most cases, even more than once a week (unless you are given specific instructions by the secretary, receptionist, or person's assistant to do so) will put you on the annoying list.

sorts. As long as you have been pleasant, he or she may feel "guilty" that you are such a nice person and his or her boss isn't calling you back. In these cases, the secretary may give you a tip on how to get through, tell you to send something in writing, or ask the boss to speak to you.

Voicemail is another obstacle you might have to deal with. This automated system is often more difficult to bypass than a human gatekeeper. Many people don't even bother answering their phone, instead letting their voicemail pick up the calls and then checking their messages when convenient.

Decide ahead of time what you're going to do if you get someone's voicemail. Try calling once to see what the person's message is. It might, for example, let you know that the person you're calling is out of town until Monday. What this will tell you is that if you are calling someone on a cold call, you should probably not call until Wednesday, because they probably will be busy when they get back in town.

If the message says something to the effect of "I'm out of town; if you need to speak to me today, please call my cell phone" and then provides a phone number, don't. You don't *need* to speak to him or her; you *want* to. There is a big difference between *need* and *want*. You are cold-calling a person who doesn't know you to ask for something. It is not generally a good idea to bother them outside the office.

If you call a few times and keep getting the voicemail, you're going to have to make your move. Leave a message something like this.

You: Hi, this is Samantha Harris. My phone number is (111) 222-3333. I'd appreciate if you could give me a call at your convenience. I'll look forward to hearing from you. Have a great day.

If you don't hear back within a few days, try again.

You: Hi, Mr. Redner. This is Samantha Harris. (111) 222-3333. I called a few days ago. I know you're busy and was just trying you again. I look forward to hearing from you. Thanks. Have a great day.

You might not hear from Mr. Redner himself, but one of her assistants might call you. What do you do if you don't get a call back? Call again. How many times should you call? That's hard to say. Persistence may pay off. Remember that the person on the other end may start feeling guilty that he or she is not calling you back and place that call.

Be prepared. When you get a call back, have your ducks in a row and be ready to sell yourself. Practice ahead of time if need be and leave notes near your phone.

I suggest when making any of these calls that you block your phone number so that no one knows who is calling. To permanently block your phone number from showing on the receiver's caller ID, call your local phone company. Most don't charge for this service. You can also block your phone number on a temporary basis by dialing *67 before making your call. Remember that as soon as you hang up, this service will be disabled, so you will need to do this for each call.

Getting Them to Call You

While persistence and patience in calling and trying to get past the receptionist is usually necessary, you may need something else, too. You want something to set you apart, so the busy executives not only want to see you but remember you. You want them to give you a chance to sell yourself.

What can you do? Creativity to the rescue! The amount of creativity will depend to a great extent on the specific company or organization to which you are trying to get through.

Your goal is to get the attention of the important person who can give you a chance to sell yourself. Once you have his or her attention, it's up to you to convince them that they should work with you.

Let's look at some ideas that I have either personally used or others have told me worked in their quest to get an individual's attention so they could get a foot in the door. Use these ideas as a beginning, but then try to develop more of your own. You are limited only by your own creativity and ability to think outside the box.

My Personal Number-One Technique for Getting Someone to Call You

I am going to share my number one technique for getting someone to call you. I have used this technique successfully over the years to get people to call me in an array of situations and in a variety of industries at various levels in my career. I first came up with it after I graduated from college when I was entering the workforce and wanted to get a job in the music industry.

At the time, there was no book to give me ideas. There was no career coach. There was no one who really wanted to help, and I desperately needed help to get a job.

I had tried all the traditional methods. I tried calling people, but most of the time I couldn't get past the gatekeeper. When I did, no one called me back. I had tried sending out resumes. As I had just graduated college, I had no "real" experience. I didn't know anyone and didn't even know anyone who knew anyone. I needed a break. Here's what I did.

When I was younger, my parents used to take raw eggs, blow out the contents, and then decorate the shells. Every one always commented on how nice they were and how different they were. One day, for some reason, the eggs popped into my mind, and I came up with my method to get people to call me back. Here's how it works.

Get a box of eggs. Extra-large or jumbo work well. While either white or brown eggs can be used, because of the coloration differences in brown eggs, start with white ones. Wash the raw eggs carefully with warm water. Then dry the shells well.

Hold one egg in your hand and using a large needle or pin, punch a small hole in the top of the egg. The top is the narrower end. Then carefully punch a slightly larger hole in the other end of the egg. You might need to take the needle or pin and move it around in the hole to make it larger. Keep any pieces of shell that break off.

Next, take a straw and place it on the top hole of the egg. Holding the egg over a bowl, blow into the straw, blowing the contents of the egg out. This may take a couple of tries. Because of concerns with salmonella, do not put your mouth directly on the egg.

Keep in mind that the bigger you have made the hole, the easier it will be to blow the contents out of the egg. However, you want the egg to look as "whole" as possible when you're done. The bigger the hole, the harder this is to accomplish.

After blowing the contents out of the egg, carefully rinse out the shell, letting warm water run through it. Get the egg as clean as possible. Shake the excess water out of the egg and leave it to dry thoroughly. Depending on the temperature and humidity when you are preparing the eggs, it might take a couple of days.

Do at least three eggs at one time in case one breaks or cracks at the next step. You might want to do more. After you get the hang of this, you're going to want to keep a few extra prepared eggs around for when you want to get someone's attention fast and don't have time to prepare new ones.

Next, go to your computer and type the words, "Getting the attention of a busy person is not easy. Now that I have yours, could you please take a moment to review my resume?" You can customize the message to suit your purposes by including the name of the recipient if you have it or specifying your background sheet, CV, or whatever you want the recipient to look at and consider. Then type your name and phone number.

Use a small font to keep the message to a line or two. Neatly cut out the strip of paper with your message. Roll the strip around a toothpick. Carefully insert the toothpick with the strip of paper into the larger of the holes in the egg. Wiggle the toothpick around and slowly take

the toothpick out of the egg. The strip of paper should now be in the shell.

Visit your local craft store and pick up a package of those small moveable eyes, miniature plastic or felt-shaped feet, and white glue or a glue gun. Glue the miniature feet to the bottom of the egg, covering the hole. Make sure you use the glue sparingly so none goes on your message. Now, glue on two of the moving eyes, making the egg look like a face.

Go back to your computer and type the following words: "CRACK OPEN THIS EGG FOR AN IMPORTMANT MESSAGE." Print out the line and cut it into a strip. You might want to use bright-colored paper. Glue the strip to the bottom of the feet of the egg.

Now you're ready. Take the egg and place it in a small box that you have padded with cotton, bubble wrap, or foam. These eggs are very fragile, and you don't want the egg to break in transit!

Wrap the egg-filled box in attractive wrapping paper and then bubble wrap to assure it won't move around. Put your resume (or CV, background sheet, and so on) and a short cover letter into an envelope. Put it on the bottom of a sturdy mailing box. Place the egg box over it.

Make sure you use clean boxes and pack the egg as carefully as possible. Address the box. Make sure you include your name and return address. Then mail, UPS, FedEx, Airborne, or hand deliver it to the office of the person you are trying to reach. Even if that person has a secretary opening his or her mail, the chances are good that the "gift" will be opened personally. In the event that a secretary opens the package, he or she will probably bring the egg to the boss to crack.

So now the recipient has the egg. He or she will probably break it open, see the message, and glance at your resume. Here's the good news. By the time the person breaks open the egg, he or she won't even notice the hole on the bottom and usually has no idea how you got the message in there. Generally, people who have seen this think it is so neat that they want to know how you did it, so they call you to ask. (Believe it or not, everyone has someone they wish they could get to call them back.)

Once you have them on the phone, your job is to get an interview. You want to get into their office and meet with them. When you get that call, tell the recipient you would be glad to show him or her how you did it, but it's kind of complicated telling them on the phone. Offer to show them how it is done and ask when they would like you to come in.

Voila, you have an appointment. Now all you have to do is sell yourself.

Is your resume sitting in a pile of countless others? Do you want your resume to stick out amongst the hundreds that come in? Do you want an interview but can't get one? Are you having difficulties getting people to call you back?

While I love the egg idea and have used it to obtain appointments and call backs and to get noticed throughout my career, there are other ideas that work too. You might want to try a few of these.

Have you ever considered using these simple items to help you succeed? If you haven't, perhaps now is the time.

◎ fortune cookies
◎ chocolate chip cookies
◎ candy bars
◎ mugs
◎ pizzas
◎ roses

Fortune Cookies

Almost no one can resist cracking open a fortune cookie to see what the "message" says. This can be good news for your career.

Some fortune cookie companies make cookies similar to the ones you get in Chinese restaurants but with personalized messages inside. What could you say? That depends on what you are looking for. How about something like, "Human Resources Director who interviews Robert Jarvis will have good luck for the rest of the day. Robert's lucky number: 111-222-3333."

Whatever message you choose, remember that you generally need to make all the messages the same or it gets very expensive to have the cookies made. You also need to print cards on your computer or have cards printed professionally that read something to the effect of "Getting the attention of a busy person is not easy. Now that I have yours, could you please take a moment to review my resume?" Or "Getting the attention of a busy person is not easy. Now that I have yours, I was hoping you could take a few moments to give me a call." (Or set up an appointment or anything else you want.) Make sure your name and phone number are on the card.

Put a few cookies with the card and your resume or other material in a clean, attractive mailing box and address it neatly. Make sure you address the box to someone specific. For example, don't address it to CEO, PRG Pharmaceuticals. Instead, address it to Ms. Leslie Targeti, CEO, PRG Pharmaceuticals.

"I've heard of sending fortune cookies," you say. "What else can I do?"

Here's a twist. Send the same package of cookies, the card, and whatever else you sent (your resume, CV or background sheet, and so on) every day for two weeks. Every day, after the

Words from the Wise

Make sure cookies are individually wrapped and factory sealed. Otherwise, some people may just toss them.

first day, also include a note that says, "Cookies For [Name of person] For Day 2," "Cookies For [Name of Person] For Day 3," and so on. At the end of the two-week period, stop. By now your recipient will probably have called you. If not, he or she will at least be expecting the cookies. So, if you don't hear from your recipient, feel free to call the office, identify yourself as the fortune cookie king or queen, and ask for an appointment.

This idea can be expensive, but if it gets you in the door and you can sell yourself or your idea, it will more than pay for itself.

Another great idea that can really grab the attention of a busy executive, or anybody else, for that matter, is finding a company that makes gigantic fortune cookies with personalized messages. These cookies are often covered in chocolate, sprinkles, and all kinds of goodies and almost command people to see who sent them. Send these cookies with the same types of messages and supporting material as the others. The only difference is that if you choose to send the gigantic cookies, you probably only need to send one. If you don't get a call within the first week, feel free to call the recipient yourself.

Chocolate Chip Cookies

Chocolate chip cookies are a favorite of most people. Why not use that to your advantage? Go to the cookie kiosk at your local mall and order a gigantic pizza-sized cookie personalized

with a few words asking for what you would like done. For example:

◎ "Please Review My Resume . . . Kelly Jackson"
◎ "Please Call Me For An Interview . . . Pat Hendricks"

Keep your message short. You want the recipient to read it, not get overwhelmed. Generally, the cookies come boxed. Tape a copy of your resume or whatever you are sending to the inside of the box.

Write a short cover letter to your recipient stating that you hope he or she enjoys the cookie while reviewing your resume, giving you a call, and so on. Put this in an envelope with another copy of your resume, your demo, or other material. On the outside of the box, neatly tape a card with the message we discussed previously stating *"Getting the attention of a busy person is not easy. Now that I have yours, would you please take a moment to review my resume."* Or ask them to give you a call or whatever you are hoping they will do. Make sure your name and phone number are on the card.

If the cookie company has a mail or delivery service, use it even if it is more expensive than mailing it yourself. It will be more effective. If there is no mail or delivery service, mail or deliver the cookie yourself. You should get a call from the recipient within a few days.

The Inside Scoop

To avoid potential problems with people who have allergies, do not send any food with nuts as an ingredient. Nothing can ruin your chances of getting a job better than causing an allergic reaction in the person you're trying to impress.

Voice of Experience

Do not try to save money by making the cookies yourself. In today's world, many people won't eat food if they don't know where it came from or if it was not prepared by a commercial eatery.

Candy Bars

A number of studies tout chocolate as a food that makes people happy or at least puts them in a good mood. Keeping this in mind, you might want to use chocolate to grab someone's attention and move them to call you. Most people love chocolate and are happy to see it magically appear in their office. There are a number of different ways you can use chocolate to help your career.

◎ Buy a large, high-quality chocolate bar. Carefully fold your resume or a letter stating what you would like accomplished and slip it into the wrapping of the chocolate bar.

◎ Buy a large, high-quality chocolate bar. Wrap the chocolate bar with your resume or the letter stating what you would like accomplished.

◎ There are companies that create personalized wrappings for chocolate bars. Use one to deliver your message.

◎ Create a wrapping on your computer, but if you do this, make sure you leave the original wrapping intact and cover it.

Whatever method you choose, put the candy bar in an attractive box, and attach the card with the message, "Getting the attention of a busy person is never easy. Now that I have yours, could you please take a moment to review my resume?" (Or whatever action you are asking your recipient to take.) Add a cover letter and send it off.

Mugs

When was the last time you threw out a mug? Probably not for a while. How about using this idea to catch the attention of a potential employer? Depending on your career aspiration, have mugs printed with replicas of your business or networking card, key points of your resume, CV, or background sheet, along with your name and phone number.

Add a small packet of gourmet or flavored coffee or hot chocolate and perhaps an individually wrapped biscotti or cookie and, of course, the card with the message stating, "Getting the attention of a busy person is never easy. Now that I have yours, could you please take a moment to check out my resume?" (Or whatever else you are requesting.) Put the mug, a short cover letter, and your resume, background sheet, or other material in a box and mail or deliver it to your recipient. Remember to put your return address on the box.

Pizza

Want to make sure your resume or background sheet gets attention? Have it delivered to your recipient with a fresh, hot pizza. This technique can be tricky but effective. It does have some challenges, however.

To guarantee the pizza gets there with your information, you really need to be in the same geographic location as the company or organization you're trying to reach. You will need to personally make sure that your information is placed in a zip-lock bag or, better yet, laminated and then taped to the inside cover of the pizza box. You not only have to know the name of the person for this to be delivered to but that he or she will be there the day you send it and doesn't have a lunch date. It's difficult to call an office where no one knows you and ask what time the recipient goes to lunch. So you are taking the risk that you will be sending a pizza to someone who isn't there. One way to get around this is by sending it in the late afternoon instead. That way your recipient can have a mid-afternoon pizza break.

If you do this, make sure that you have the pizzeria delivering the pizza tape the card with the message about getting a busy person's attention on the front of the box, so even if the receptionist gets the pizza, he or she will know who it came from.

If you don't get a thank-you call that day, call the recipient the next morning. You probably will speak to the secretary or receptionist first. Just tell whomever you speak to that you were the one who sent the pizza the day before in hopes of getting the attention of the recipient so you might set up a job interview.

Roses

A very effective but pricey way to get your recipient's attention is to have a dozen roses delivered to his or her office. No matter how many things you have tried with no response, there are very few people who will not place a thank-you call when they receive a dozen roses.

Talk to the florist ahead of time to make sure that the roses you will be sending are fragrant. Send the roses to your recipient with a card that simply says something to the effect of "While you're enjoying the roses, please take a moment to review my resume, sent under separate cover." Sign it "Sincerely hoping for an interview," and include your name and phone number.

It is imperative to send your information so it arrives on the same day or, at the latest, the next day so the roses you sent are still fresh in the recipient's mind.

It's Who You Know

While, of course, there are some areas of the health care industry that are easier to get into,

there generally still is always some amount of competition to get most jobs. There are also talented and skilled individuals who never get past the front door. Knowing someone who can get you in the door most certainly will help.

Before you say, "Me? I don't know anyone," stop and think. Are you sure? Don't you know someone, anyone, even on a peripheral basis, who might be able to give you a recommendation, make a call, or be willing lend his or her name?

What about your mother's aunt's husband's friend's neighbor's boss? Sure, it might be a stretch. But think hard. Who can you think of who might know someone who might be able to help? This is not the time to be shy.

Call your aunt. Explain what you're trying to do with your career. Then ask if she would be willing to talk to her husband's friend about talking to their neighbor about using their name to make an appointment with the neighbor's boss.

"But I don't need any help," you say. "I can do it on my own."

You might be able to and you might not, but why wouldn't you give yourself every edge possible? You're going to have to prove yourself once you get in the door. No one can do that for you.

What if you don't have a relative who has a contact down the line? What about your physician? Does he or she know someone at the hospital where you want to apply? What about a friend who already works in the hospital? How about someone on the hospital board of directors? What about someone on the hospital foundation or auxiliary? What about the pharmacist at the drug store you use? What about the medical group office manager?

What about your hair stylist? Your UPS delivery person? Your mailman? Your clergyman or woman? The possibilities are endless if you just look.

The trick here is to think outside the box. If you can find someone who knows someone willing to help you to get your foot in the door, all you have to do is sell yourself. If someone does agree to lend their name, make a call, or help you in any manner, it's important to write thank-you notes immediately. These notes should be written whether or not you actually get an interview or set up a meeting.

If you do go on an interview, it's also a good idea to either call or write another note, letting your contact know what happened.

Meeting the Right People

You think and think and you can't come up with anyone you know with a connection to anyone at all in the area of the health care industry in which you are trying to succeed. What can you do? Sometimes you have to find your own contacts. You need to meet the right people. But how can you do this? The best way to meet the right people in the health care industry is to be around people in the health care industry. There are several possible ways you might do this.

To begin with, consider joining industry organizations and associations. Many of these organizations offer career guidance and support. They also may offer seminars, workshops, and other types of educational symposiums. Best of all, many have periodic meetings and annual conventions and conferences. All of these are treasure troves of possibilities to meet people in the industry. Some of them may be industry experts or insiders. Others may be just like you: people trying to get in and succeed. The important thing to remember is to take advantage of every opportunity.

> ### ★ Tip from the Top
> At industry events, it is important to have a positive attitude and to avoid any negative conversation with anyone about anything at the seminar or in the industry. You can never tell who is related to whom or what idea someone originated. Be remembered for being bright and positive.

Workshops and seminars are great because not only can you make important contacts, but you can learn something valuable about the industry. Most of these events have question and answer periods built into the program. Take advantage of these. Stand up and ask a good question. Make yourself visible. Some seminars and workshops have break-out sessions to encourage people to get to know one another. Use these to your advantage as well. Walk around and talk to people. Don't be afraid to walk up to someone you don't know and start talking. Remember to bring your business or networking cards and network, network, network!

After the session has ended, walk up, shake the moderator's hand, and tell him or her how much you enjoyed the session, how much you learned, and how useful it will be in your career. This gives you the opportunity to ask for a business card so that you have the correct spelling of the person's name, their address, and their phone number. This is very valuable information. When you get home, send a short note stating that you were at the session they moderated, spoke to them afterward, and just wanted to tell them again how much you enjoyed it.

You might also ask, depending on their position, if it would be possible to set up an informational interview with them at their convenience or if they could suggest who you might call to set up an appointment. If you don't hear back within a week, feel free to call up, identify yourself, and ask again.

Another good way to meet people in the industry is to attend industry or organization annual conventions. These events offer many opportunities you might not normally have to network and meet industry insiders.

There is usually a charge to attend these conventions. Fee structures may vary. Sometimes there is one price for general admission to all events and entry to the trade-show floor. Other times, there may be one price for entry just to the trade-show floor and another price if you also want to take part in seminars and other events.

The cost of attending these conventions may be expensive. In addition to the fee to get in, if you don't live near the convention location, you might have to pay for airfare or other transportation as well as accommodations, meals, and incidentals. Is it worth it? If you can afford it, absolutely! If you want to meet people in the industry, these gatherings are the place to do it.

How do you find these events? Look in the appendix of this book for industry associations in your area of interest. Find the phone number and call up and ask when and where the annual convention will be held. Better yet, go to the organization's Web site. Most groups put information about their conventions online.

If you are making the investment to go to a convention or a conference, take full advantage of every opportunity. As we've discussed throughout this book, network, network, and network some more! Some events to attend at conventions and conferences might include

- opening events
- keynote presentations
- educational seminars and workshops
- certification programs
- break sessions
- breakfast lunch and/or dinner events
- cocktail parties
- trade show exhibit areas
- career fairs

There is an art to attending conventions and using the experience to your best benefit. Remember that the people you meet are potential employers and new business contacts.

This is your chance to make a good first impression. Dress appropriately and neatly.

It's important to remember not to get inebriated at these events. If you want to have a drink or a glass of wine, that's probably okay, but don't over-drink. You want potential employers or people you want to do business with to know you're a good risk, not someone who drinks at every opportunity.

It is essential to bring business cards with you and give them out to everyone you can. You can never tell when someone hears about a position, remembers meeting you and getting a card, and will give you a call.

Collect business cards as well. When you arrive home from the convention or trade show, you will have contact names to call or write regarding business or job possibilities.

Walk the trade-show floor. Stop and talk to people at booths. They are usually more than willing to talk. This is a time to network and try to make contacts. Ask questions and listen to what people are saying.

If you have good writing skills, a good way of meeting people in the industry is to write articles, do reviews, or interview people for local, regional, or national periodicals or newspapers. We discussed the idea earlier when talking about using your writing skills to help you obtain interviews. It can be just as effective in this situation.

How does this work? A great deal of it depends on your situation, where you live, and the area of the industry you are targeting.

You have to develop an angle or hook for a story on the segment of the health care industry in which you are interested in meeting people.

For example, is one of the doctors in the area also a musician who plays in a band? Does one of the phlebotomists who works at the hospital lab also volunteer in the children's wing performing as a clown? Does one of the local dentists not only collect art but write about it in a major art magazine? These are angles or hooks you might use to entice a local or regional periodical to let you do an article.

Your next step is to contact someone who might be interested in the story. If you're still in school, become involved with the school newspaper. If you're not, call up your local newspaper or a regional magazine and see if they might be interested in the article or feature story you want to write.

You probably will have to give them some samples of your writing and your background sheet or resume. You might also have to write on "spec" or speculation. This means that when you do the story, they may or may not use it. If they do, they will pay you. If not, they won't.

Your goal here (unless you want to be a health or medical writer or journalist) is not to make money (although that is nice.) Your goal is to be in situations where you have the opportunity to meet industry insiders. If you're successful, not only will you be meeting these people; you'll be meeting them on a different level than if you were looking for a job.

Networking Basics

It's not always what you know but who you know. With that in mind, I'm going to once again bring up the importance of networking. You can never tell who knows someone in some area of the industry, so it is essential to share your career dreams and aspirations with those around you. Someone you mention your goals to might just say, "My cousin is a personal trainer and nutritionist too." Or, "Really, I know someone who was looking for someone with skills like yours."

Think it can't happen? Think again. It's happened to me, it's happened to others, and it can happen to you!

I know a woman who was a certified personal trainer and nutritionist who lived in a big apartment building. She was in the elevator one day and just so happened to mention to another woman in the elevator that she was going to meet a client. They briefly chatted about what she did. A few weeks later, she ran into the same woman she had been chatting with about her work. It turned out the woman was the editor of a magazine who asked her if they could interview her regarding some aspect of fitness and nutrition on which they were doing a story. And it didn't stop there. After the article came out, the trainer was called by a prestigious spa to give a number of workshops. Soon after that, she was retained by the spa to work with their clients.

Want to hear another one?

A couple of years ago, a woman called asking my advice on how she could find a job as an activities director in a nursing home. She had a degree, she had worked as a recreational staff member in another industry, and she had volunteered in a nursing home, but she couldn't find a job doing what she wanted. At the time she called, she had been substituting in a local school.

"I want to work as an activities director in a nursing home so badly," she told me. "It's my passion. I saw what a difference the activities director made in my grandmother's life, and I want to do that for other people. I enjoy working with the elderly, and it's what I want to do.

"I've sent out resumes and made a couple calls, but there are a limited number of positions where I live, and they all are taken by people who have been in them forever. Maybe I should just give up."

"Are you telling people about what you want to do?" I asked.

"Just my family," she said. "I don't want anyone else to know that I can't get what I want. It's embarrassing. I almost feel like a failure. Everyone else seems so happy with their work."

"There's no reason to feel like a failure," I told her. "It takes a while for everyone to create their dream career. You'll get there too, if you don't give up. Why don't you try to network a bit more and tell everyone what you're looking for? Tell everyone about your dream."

"I'll try," she said. "But I think I'm going to have to relocate to find a job and right now that would be difficult."

"Keep mentioning your dreams," I told her. "The more people who know what you want to do, the better your chances are of finding a job."

A couple of months later, I received a call from the woman. "Guess what?" she asked me excitedly.

"Tell me what's happening," I replied.

It turned out that one day the woman was substituting in the high school and sitting in the teacher's lounge. Another teacher was talking about her mother, who was in a nursing home located within the local hospital.

"It's a very nice facility," she said. "They always keep her busy. They have a great activities director over there."

"It's been my dream to have a job like that," the woman said. "I just can't find an opening."

"When I was visiting my mother, I heard that the assisted living facility was looking for an activities director," the other teacher mentioned. "There's talk at the nursing home that the activities director is going to go over there. You might want to check it out too."

The woman didn't miss a beat and called the assisted living facility. But she didn't stop there. She also placed a call to the nursing home at the hospital, asking if she could send her resume to be kept on file.

It turned out that the activities director did take the job at the assisted living facility, and the woman's resume arrived at the human resources office just at the right time. After a number of interviews, she beat out the competition and got the job.

People always ask, "But do those things really happen?" The answer is an unequivocal *yes*. These are not isolated incidents. Things like this happen all the time. Networking and sharing your dreams can and does work for others and can work for you. But in order for it to happen, you have to be proactive.

Knowing how important networking can be to your career, let's talk about some networking basics.

The first thing you need to do is determine exactly who you know and who is part of your network. Then you need to get out and find more people to add to the list.

When working on your networking list, add the type of contact you consider each person. Primary contacts are people you know: your family members, teachers, friends, and neighbors. Secondary contacts are individuals referred to you by others: a friend of a friend, your aunt's neighbor, your attorney's sister, and so on.

You might also want to note whether you consider each person a close, medium, or distant relationship. Close, for example, would be family, friends, employers, and current teachers. Medium would be people you talk to and see frequently such as your dentist or attorney or your UPS, FedEx, or mail delivery person. Distant would include people you talk to and see infrequently or those you have just met or have met just once or twice.

Here's an example.

Networking Worksheet			
Name	Relationship/ Position	Type of Contact (Primary or Secondary)	Closeness of Contact (Close, Medium, or Distant)
James Davidson	Former Health Education Teacher	Primary	Medium
Lea Willis	Bank Teller	Primary	Distant
Bob	UPS Delivery Person	Primary	Medium
Mike Rowe	Newspaper Reporter	Secondary	Distant
Gina	Sister-in-law	Primary	Close
Dr. Rodgers	Dentist	Primary	Medium
Rob Secra	Attorney	Primary	Medium
Antonio Fast	Medical Reporter	Secondary	Distant
Dr. Cessario	Medical Doctor	Primary	Medium
Ann Marie	President of the Hospital Auxiliary	Secondary	Medium

Networking Worksheet

Name	Relationship/ Position	Type of Contact (Primary or Secondary)	Closeness of Contact (Close, Medium, or Distant)

It would be great to have a network full of people in the area of the health care industry where you hope to have your career. However, that may not be the case. That does not mean, though, that other people can't be helpful. Your network may include a variety of people from all walks of life. These may include:

◎ family members
◎ friends
◎ friends of friends
◎ coworkers and colleagues
◎ teachers or professors
◎ your doctor and dentist
◎ your pharmacist
◎ your mail carrier
◎ your hairstylist
◎ your personal trainer

◎ your priest, pastor, or rabbi
◎ members of your congregation
◎ UPS, FedEx, Airborne, or other delivery person
◎ your auto mechanic
◎ your attorney
◎ the server at the local diner or coffee shop
◎ bank tellers from your local bank
◎ your personal physician
◎ your neighbors
◎ friends of your relatives
◎ business associates of your relatives
◎ people you work with on volunteer not-for-profit boards and civic groups

Now look at your list. Do you see how large your network really is? Virtually everyone you come in contact with during the day can become part of your network. Just keep adding people to your list.

Expanding Your Network

How can you expand your network? There are a number of ways. Networking events are an excellent way to meet people. Industry networking events are, of course, the best, but don't count out nonindustry events. For example, your local chamber of commerce may have specific networking programs designed to help business people in the community meet and "network" with each other.

How do you know if the people at the event have any possibility of being related to the area of the health care industry in which you're interested? First, as we've discussed, you don't know who people know. People you meet may know others who *are* in the part of the industry you want to pursue. Second, no matter how small your area is, you never really know who is involved in what. For all you know, someone in your area may be:

◎ an investor in a medical group
◎ a lawyer who represents a doctor or the local hospital
◎ someone who is on the hospital board of directors
◎ a physician, chiropractor or other health care professional
◎ a member of the hospital auxiliary
◎ the public relations or advertising agency for a hospital

Civic and other not-for-profit groups also have a variety of events that are great for networking. Whether you go to a regular meeting or you attend a charity auction, cocktail party, or large gala to benefit a not-for-profit, you will generally find business people in the community you might not know. As a bonus, many larger not-for-profit events have media coverage meaning that you have the opportunity to add media people to your network.

Those who take advantage of every opportunity to meet new people will have the largest networks. The idea in building a network is to get out of your comfort zone. If you just stay with people you know and are comfortable with, you won't have the opportunity to get to know others. You want to continually meet new people; after all, you never know who knows whom.

Networking Savvy

You are now learning how to build your network. However, the largest network in the world will be useless unless you know how to take full advantage of it. So let's talk a little about how you're going to use the network you are building.

We've discussed the difference between skills and talents. Networking is a skill. You don't have to be born with it. You can acquire the skill to network, practice, and improve. What that means is that if you practice networking, you can get better at it, and it can pay off big in your career!

Get out. Go to new places. Meet new people. The trick here is when you're in a situation where there are new people, don't be afraid to walk up to them, shake their hand, and talk to them. People can't read your mind, so it's imperative to tell them about your career goals, dreams, and aspirations.

When you meet new people, listen to them. Focus on what they're saying. Ask questions. Be interested in what *they* are telling you. You can never tell when the next person you talk to is the one who will be able to help you open the door or vice versa.

If you're shy, even the thought of networking may be very difficult for you. However, it is essential to make yourself do it anyway. Successful networking can pay off big in your career! In some situations, it can mean the difference between getting a great job or not. Isn't it worth the effort?

Just meeting people isn't enough. When you meet someone you add to your network, the idea is to try to further develop the relationship. Just having a story to tell about who you know is not enough. Arrange a follow-up meeting, send a note or letter, or make a phone call. The more you take advantage of every opportunity, the closer you will be to getting what you want.

A good way to network is to volunteer. We've mentioned attending not-for-profit events and civic meetings to expand your network, but how about volunteering to work with a not-for-profit or civic group?

I can imagine you saying, "When? I'm so busy now; I don't have enough time to do anything."

Make time. It will be worth it. Why?

People will see you on a different level. They won't see you as someone looking for a job or trying to succeed at some level. Generally, people talk about their volunteer work to friends, family, business associates, and other colleagues. This means that when someone is speaking to someone else, they might mention in passing that one of the people they are working with on

---

The Inside Scoop

Volunteer to do projects that no one else wants to do, and you will immediately become more visible.

---

their event or project is trying to get a job in the hospital, trying to succeed as a medical reporter, or working as an intern with the marketing department of a pharmaceutical company.

Anyone these people mention you or your situation to is a potential secondary networking contact. Those people, in turn, may mention it to someone else. Eventually, someone involved in the area of the industry you are pursuing might hear about you.

Another reason to volunteer is so people will see that you have a good work ethic. Treat volunteer projects as you would work projects. Do what you say you are going to do, and do it in a timely manner. Do your best. Showcase your skills and your talents, and do everything you do with a positive attitude and a smile.

This also gives you the opportunity to demonstrate skills and talents people might not otherwise know you have. Can you do publicity? Can your write? How about organizing things? Do you get along well with others? What better way to illustrate your skills than utilizing them by putting together an event, publicizing it, or coordinating other volunteers?

Best of all, you can use these volunteer activities on your resume. While volunteer experiences don't take the place of work experience, they certainly can fill out a resume short of it.

Don't just go to meetings. Participate fully in the organization. That way, you'll not only be helping others; you will be adding to your network.

Tip from the Coach

While volunteering is good for networking, don't get involved with too many organizations. Depending on your schedule, one, two, or even three are probably fine. Anything more than that and you're on the road to burnout.

Where can you volunteer? Pretty much any not-for-profit or civic organization is a possibility. The one thing you should remember, however, is that you should only volunteer for organizations in whose causes you believe.

To make the most of every networking opportunity, it's essential for people to remember you. Keep a supply of your business cards with you all the time. Don't be stingy with them. Give them out freely to everyone. That way, your name and number will be close at hand if needed. Make sure you ask for cards in return. If people don't have them, be sure to ask for their contact information.

Try to keep in contact with people in your network on a regular basis. Of course, you can't call everyone every day, but try to set up a schedule of sorts to do some positive networking every day. For example, you might decide to call one person every day on your networking list. Depending on the situation, you can say you were calling to touch base, say hello, keep in contact, or see how they were doing. Ask how they have been or talk about something you might have in common or they might think is interesting. You might also decide that once a week you will try to call someone and set up a lunch or coffee date.

Be on the lookout for stories, articles, or other tidbits of information that might be of interest to people in your network. Clip them out and send them with a short note saying you saw the story and thought they might

---

Tip from the Coach

Have you ever received a birthday card from someone who wasn't a close friend or relative, someone who you just happened to mention to that your birthday was coming up in a few days? Remember how when you opened that card and read who it was from, it put a smile on your face? Remember thinking how nice the person who sent you the card was? Remember thinking about what you could do for them? You might not have known them well, but you probably won't forget them now. If you do the same type of thing for others, you will stand out as well.

---

be interested. If you hear of something they might be interested in, call them. The idea is to continue cultivating relationships by keeping in contact with people in your network and staying visible.

Keep track of the contacts in your network. You can use the sample sheet provided, a card file using index cards, or a database or contact software program on your computer. Include as much information as you have about each person. People like when you remember them and their interests. It makes you stand out.

Then use your networking contact list. For example, a few days before someone's birthday, send him or her a card. If you know that someone collects old guitars, for example, and you see an article on old guitars, clip it out and send it. Don't be a pest, but keep in contact. People in sales have been using this technique for years. It works for them, and it will help you in your career as well.

You might want to use some of the items here and then add information as it comes up. You don't have to ask people for all this information the first time you meet them. Just add it when you get it.

Words from a Pro

Keep a scrapbook of articles, photos, programs and other supporting material from volunteer events you have participated in. It will be useful when putting together your career portfolio.

Networking Contact Information Sheet

Name
_____

Business Address
_____

Business Phone
_____

Home Address
_____

Home Phone
_____

E-mail
_____

Web Address (URL)
_____

Birthday
_____

Anniversary
_____

Where and When Met
_____

Spouse or Significant Other's Name
_____

Children's Name(s)
_____

Dog Breed and Name
_____

Cat Breed and Name
_____

Hobbies
_____

Interests
_____

Things Collected
_____

Honors
_____

Awards
_____

Interesting Facts

Tip from the Top

After you have worked on a volunteer project, ask the director or board president if he or she would mind writing you a letter of recommendation for your file.

Networking And Nerve

Successful networking will give you credibility and a rapport with people in and out of the industry. But networking sometimes takes nerve, especially if you're not naturally outgoing. You have to push yourself to get out and meet people, talk to them, tell them what you are interested in doing, and then stay in contact. On occasion, you may have to ask people if they will help you, ask for recommendations, ask for references, and so on. Don't let the fear of doing what you need to do stop you from doing it. Just remember that the result of all this effort will be not only entry into a career you want but a shot at success.

Tip from the Coach

If someone asks you to be their mentor or asks for your help and you can, say yes. As a matter of fact, if you see someone you might be able to help, do just that. You might think that you don't even have your own career on track or you don't have time. You might be tempted to say no. Think again. You are expecting someone to help you. Do the same for someone else. There is no better feeling than helping someone else. And while you shouldn't help someone for the sole purpose of helping yourself, remember that you can often open doors for yourself while opening them for someone else.

Words from the Wise

It is not uncommon to run into someone who doesn't want to help you. This may be for any number of reasons, ranging from they really don't know how they can help, they don't have the time in their schedule, or they think that if they help you in your career, it puts their position at risk. If you do ask someone to be your mentor and he or she says no, just let it go. Look for someone else.

As long as you're pleasant, there is nothing wrong with asking for help. Just remember that while people can help you get your foot in the door, you are going to have to sell yourself once you open it.

Networking is a two way street. While it might be hard for you to imagine at this moment, someone might want you to help them in some segment of their career. Reciprocate and do so graciously. As a matter of fact, if you see or know someone you might be able to help even in a small way, don't wait for them to ask; offer your help.

Finding a Mentor or Advocate

Mentors and advocates can help guide and boost your career. A mentor or advocate in the health care industry also often provides you valuable contacts, which, as we now know, are essential to your success. The best mentors and advocates are supportive individuals who help move your career to the next level.

Can't figure out why anyone would help you? Many people like to help others. It makes them feel good and makes them feel important. How do you find a mentor? Look for someone who is successful and ask. Sounds simple? It is simple. The difficult part is finding just the right person or persons.

While someone in the area of the health care industry you are pursuing would be the ideal, don't let that exclude others outside of that area or even the entire industry.

Sometimes you don't even have to ask. In many cases, a person may see your potential and offer advice. They may not call it mentoring, but with any luck, that's what it turns into. Time is a valuable commodity, especially to busy people. Be gracious when someone helps you or even tries to help. Make sure you say thank you to everyone who shares his or her time, expertise, or advice. And don't forget to ask if there is any way you can return the favor.

8

THE INTERVIEW PROCESS

Getting the Interview

You can have the greatest credentials in the world, wonderful references, and a stellar resume, but if you don't know how to interview well, it's often difficult to land the job.

Whether your dream is to work in the area of medicine, allied health, business, administration, or anywhere in between, the first step is always getting the job.

One of the keys to getting most jobs is generally the interview. Landing a job in every segment of the health care industry is no different. Let's take some time to discuss how to get that all-important meeting.

The interview is your chance to shine. During an interview, you can show what can't be illustrated on paper. This is the time your personality, charisma, and talents can be showcased. This is where someone can see your demeanor, your energy level, and your attitude. Obtaining an interview and excelling in that very important meeting can help get you the job you want.

If you do it right, the interview can help make you irresistible. It is your chance to persuade the interviewer to hire you. It is your main shot at showing why *you* would be better than anyone else, why hiring *you* would benefit

the organization, and why *not* hiring *you* would be a major mistake.

There are many ways to land job interviews:

- responding to advertisements
- recommendations from friends, relatives, or colleagues
- making cold calls
- writing letters
- working with executive search firms, recruiters, or headhunters
- working with employment agencies
- attending job and career fairs
- finding the jobs that have not been advertised (the hidden job market)

Responding to an advertisement is probably the most common approach people take to obtaining a job interview. Where can you look for ads for jobs in the health care industry? Depending on the exact type of job you're looking for, here are some possibilities.

- newspapers
- trade magazines
- association Web sites
- company and organization Web sites
  - hospitals and other health care Web sites

- ▢ nursing homes
- ▢ medical groups
- ▢ dental groups
- ▢ pharmaceutical companies
- ▢ medical equipment companies
- ▢ marketing firms specializing in the health care industry
- ▢ publicity and public relations agencies specializing in the health care industry
- ▢ fund-raising firms specializing in the health care industry
- ▢ career-oriented Web sites
- ◎ health care or medical-oriented Web sites

Let's say you open up the paper or a trade magazine or even see an advertisement on the Web that looks like this.

Green Community General Hospital seeking to fill the following positions: Director of Marketing, Publicity Assistant, Administrative Assistant to PR director, Phlebotomist, Radiologist, Registered Nurses, Nursing Assistants. For consideration for these positions either fax resume to (111) 000-1111 or mail to P.O. Box 1111, Some Town, NY 11111.

Once you see the ad, you get excited. You have been looking for a job just like one of the positions in the advertisement. You can't wait to send your resume.

★ The Inside Scoop

No matter where you live, you can usually view the classified ads for most of the major newspapers throughout the country online. Go to the newspaper's main Web site and look for *classifieds*, *jobs*, or *employment*.

Want a reality check? There may be hundreds of other people who can't wait either. Here's the good news. With a little planning, you can increase your chances of getting an interview from the classified or display ad, and as we've just discussed, this is your key to the job.

Your resume and cover letter need to stand out. Your resume needs to generate an interview. Most important, in a broad sense, you want your resume to define you as the one *in* a million candidates an employer can't live without instead of one *of* the million others applying for a job.

In essence, it's essential that your resume and cover letter distinguish you from every other applicant going for the job. Why? Because if yours doesn't, someone else's will, and he or she will be the one who gets the job.

Let's look at the journey a resume might take after you send it out in response to a classified ad. Where does it go? Who reads it? That depends. In smaller companies or organizations, your resume and cover letter may go directly to the person who will be hiring you. It may also go to that person's receptionist, secretary, administrative assistant, or an office manager. This might be the case, for example, if you are replying to an ad for a job in a physician's office, dental office, or smaller medical group.

In larger organizations, your resume and cover letter may go to a hiring manager or human resources director. This would probably occur if you are answering an ad for a position at a hospital or other health care facility, large medical group, urgi-center or surgi-center, or a job with a large pharmaceutical company.

If you are replying to an advertisement placed by an employment agency, your response will generally go to the person at the employment agency responsible for that client and job.

Tip from the Top

Here is what you need to know. The requirements set forth in an advertisement are the ideal requirements that the company would like, not necessarily what they are going to end up with. Yes, it would be great if they could find a candidate with every requirement, but in reality, it doesn't always work like that. In many cases, while there may be a candidate who has all the qualifications, someone who is missing one or two stands out and ultimately is the one who lands the job.

In any of these cases, however, your resume may take other paths. Depending on the specific job and organization, your response may go through executive recruiters, screening services, clerks, secretaries, or even receptionists. Whoever the original screener of resumes turns out to be, he or she will have the initial job of reviewing the information to make sure that it fits the profile of what is needed. But that doesn't mean that if you don't have the exact requirements you should not reply to a job.

The trick is to tailor your resume as much as possible to the specific job and write a great cover letter. For example, let's say the job requirements for a job at a hospital or other health care facility in the marketing department might look something like this:

ASSISTANT DIRECTOR OF MARKETING: KING VALLEY HOSPITAL Creative, enthusiastic, team player with proven track record. Must have strong organizational skills and excellent verbal and writing skills. Minimum requirements include bachelor's degree and four years' experience in health-oriented marketing; media and community contacts helpful.

Now let's say that while you are creative and enthusiastic and have excellent verbal and writing skills, you don't have four years' experience working in health care marketing. Instead, you have two years of experience handling marketing for a sports team. Prior to your current job, you were a journalist for a local newspaper. You have media contacts, but they're not in the community in which you're applying for a job, nor are your community contacts. Should you not apply for the job? If you want it, I say go for it.

Here is what you need to know. When you are working on your resume and your cover letter in response to an ad, remember that skills are transferable. Skills for specific areas might need to be fine-tuned, but sales skills are sales skills, writing skills are writing skills, and publicity and public relations skills are publicity and public relations skills. Stress what you have done successfully, not what you haven't done. Use your cover letter to help showcase these accomplishments.

No matter who your resume and cover letter go to, your goal is to increase your chances of it ending up in the pile that ultimately gets called for an interview. Whoever the screener of the resumes is, he or she will probably pass over anything that doesn't look neat and well thought out or anything where there are obvious errors.

What can you do? First, go over your resume. Make sure it is perfect. Make sure it is perfectly tailored to the job you are going after. Make sure it is neat, clean, and not wrinkled, crumpled, or stained. If you are going to mail it, make sure it's printed on good quality paper.

Human resources departments often receive hundreds of responses to ads. While most people use white paper, consider using off-white or even a different color such as light blue or light mauve. You want your resume to look sophisticated and classy but still stand out. Of course, the color of the paper will not change what is in your resume, but it will at least help your resume get noticed in the first place.

If the advertisement directs you in a specific method of responding to the ad, use that method. For example, if the ad instructs applicants to fax their resumes, fax yours. If it says to e-mail your resume, use e-mail and pay attention to whether the ad specifies sending the file as an attachment or in the body of your e-mail. The company may have a procedure for screening job applicants.

If given the option of methods of responding, which should you use? Each method has its pros and cons.

- ◎ E-mail
  - ▫ On the pro side, e-mail is one of the quickest methods of responding to ads. Many companies utilize the e-mail method.
  - ▫ On the con side, you are really never assured someone gets what you sent, and even if they do, you're not sure that it won't be inadvertently deleted. Another concern is making sure that the resume you sent reaches the recipient in the form in which you sent it. If you are using a common word processing program and the same platform (Mac or PC) as the recipient, you probably won't have a problem. If you are using a Mac and the recipient is using a PC or you are using different word processing programs, you might.
- ◎ Fax
  - ▫ On the pro side, faxing can get your resume where it's going almost instantaneously.

  - ▫ On the con side, if the recipient is using an old-fashioned fax, the paper quality might not be great. The good news is that most companies now are using plain paper faxes.
- ◎ Mailing or Shipping (USPS, FedEx, Airborne, UPS, and so on)
  - ▫ On the pro side, you can send your resume on good quality paper so you know what it is going to look like when it arrives. You can also send any supporting materials that might help you get the coveted interview. You can send it with an option to have someone sign for it when it arrives so you definitely know when it arrives.
  - ▫ On the con side, it may take time to arrive by mail. One of the ways to get past this problem is to send it overnight or two-day express. It will cost more, but you will have control over when your package arrives.

Tip from the Coach

Don't be in such a rush to get your resume out that you make errors or don't produce a neat and tailored resume. If you're not ready, send your information out in a few days instead.

When is the best time to send your response to an ad in order to have the best chance at getting an interview? If you send your resume right away, it might arrive with a pile of hundreds of others, yet, if you wait too long, the company might have already found the right candidate and stopped seriously looking at new resumes.

Many people procrastinate, so if you can send in your response immediately, such as the day the ad is published or the very next morning, it will probably be one of the first ones in. At that time, the screener will be reading through just a few responses. If yours stands out, it stands a good chance of being put into the "initial interview pile."

If you can't respond immediately, wait two or three days so your resume doesn't arrive with the big pile of other responses. Once again, your goal is to increase your chances of your resume not being passed over.

When you are trying to land an interview through a recommendation from friends or colleagues; cold calls; letters; executive search firms; recruiters; headhunters, employment agencies; people you met at job fairs; through other networking events; or any aspect of the hidden job market, the timing of sending a resume is essential. In these cases, you want the people receiving your information to remember that someone said it was coming, so send it as soon as possible. This is not the time to procras-

tinate. If you do, you might lose the opportunity to set up that all-important meeting.

Persistence is the word to remember when trying to get an interview. If you are responding to an advertisement and you don't hear back within a week or two, call to see what is happening. If after you call the first time you don't hear back after another week or so (unless you've been specifically given a time frame), call back again. Don't be obnoxious and don't be a pain, but call.

If you're shy, you're going to have to get over it. Write a script ahead of time to help you. Don't read directly from the script, but practice so it becomes second nature. For example: "Hello, this is Donna Johnson. I replied to an advertisement you placed in the newspaper for the hospital grant writer. I was wondering who I could speak with to find out about the status of the position?"

When you get to the correct person, you might have to reiterate your purpose in calling. Then you might ask, "Do you know when interviewing is starting? Will all applicants be notified one way or the other? Is it possible to tell me whether I'm on the list to be contacted?" Don't be afraid to try to get as much information as possible, once again making sure you are being pleasant.

You want to be friendly with the secretary or receptionist. These people are on the inside and can provide you with a wealth of information.

Be aware that there is a way that you can get your resume looked at, obtain an interview, and beat the competition out of the dream job you want. Remember that we discussed the hidden job market? We know that some jobs are not advertised. Following this theory, all you have to do is contact a company and land the job you want *before* it is advertised.

"How?" you ask.

Take a chance. Make a call or write a letter and ask. You might even stop in and talk to the human resources department or one of the department heads. There is nothing that says you have to wait to see an ad in the paper. Call up and ask to speak to the human resources department or hiring manager. Once again, write out a script ahead of time so you know exactly what you want to say. Ask for the hiring manager or human resources department. Ask about job openings. Make sure you have an idea of what you want to do and convey it to the person you are talking to.

If you are told there are no openings or that the company or organization doesn't speak to people regarding employment unsolicited, be pleasant yet persistent. Ask if you can forward a resume to keep on file. In many cases, they will agree just to get you off the phone. Ask for the name of the person to direct your resume to; then ask for the address to send it *and* the fax number. Thank the person you spoke with and make sure you get his or her name.

Now here's a neat trick. Fax your resume. Send it with a cover letter that states that a hard copy will be coming via mail. Why fax it?

Did you know that when you fax documents to a company they generally are delivered directly to the desk of the person you are sending it to? They don't go through the mailroom where they might be dumped into a general inbox. They don't sit around for a day. They are generally delivered immediately.

Now that your resume is in the hands of the powers that be, it's your job to call up, make sure they got it, and try as hard as you can to set up an interview. The individual's secretary might try to put you off. Don't be deterred. Thank her or him and say you understand his or her posi-

tion. Say you're going to call in a week or so after the boss has had a chance to review your material. Send your information out in hard copy immediately. Wait a week or so and call back. Remember that persistence pays off.

Sometimes you might reach someone who tells you that "if I weren't so busy, I would be glad to meet with you." They might tell you when their workload lightens or a project is done, they will schedule an interview. You could say thank you and let it go. Or you could tell them that you understand that they're busy. All you are asking for is 10 minutes and not a minute longer. You'll even bring a stopwatch and coffee if they want. Guarantee them that 10 minutes after you get in the door, you will stand up to leave.

If you're convincing, you might land an interview. If you do, remember to *bring* that stopwatch. Introduce yourself, put the stopwatch down on the desk in front of you, and present your skills. It's essential that you practice this before you get there. Give the highlights of your resume and how hiring you would benefit the company. When your time is up, thank the person you are meeting with for their time, give them your resume, any supporting materials you have brought with you, and your business card. Then leave. If you are asked to stay, by all means, stay and continue the meeting. One way or the other, write a note thanking them for their time.

If you have sold yourself or your idea for a position in the company, someone may just get back to you. Once again, feel free to call in a week or two to follow up.

The Interview Process

You got the call. You landed an interview. Now what? The interview is an integral part of getting the job you want. There are a number of

Tip from the Coach

While the following occurred when I was first trying to enter the music business, I think the concept illustrates how persistence can pay off in any industry. At that time, I met and got to know a young man who was a comedian. He wasn't a very good comedian, but he said he was a comedian and did have a good number of jobs and bookings, so I guess he was a comedian.

During this time, I was trying to land interviews with everyone I could so I could get my own dream job in the music industry.

I made a contact with a booking agent with whom I called and developed a business relationship. Every week I'd call, and every week he would tell me to call him back. It wasn't going anywhere, but at least someone was taking my calls. This went on for about three or four months.

One day when I called, the owner got on the phone and said, "Do you know Joe Black?" (Not his real name.) "He said he has worked up in your area."

"Yes, he works as a comedian," I said.

"What do you know about him?" he asked.

"He's very nice," I answered.

"But what do you know about him?" the agent asked again. "Is he any good?"

"Well, he's not a great comedian, but he seems to keep getting jobs. He's booking himself," I replied.

"That's interesting," he said. "He has called me over 25 times looking for a job as an agent. What do you think?"

I was wondering why he was asking my opinion, because I had yet to get into his office myself. "If he can book himself, he can probably do a great job for your agency," I said. "You have great clients. I bet he would do a great job."

"Thanks," he said, "I might just do that."

"What about me?" I asked.

"I still can't think of where you might fit in," he said. "Why don't you give me a call in a couple of weeks."

I waited a couple of weeks, called back, and asked to speak to the owner.

"Hello," he said. "Guess who's standing next to me?"

He had hired Joe Black the comedian to work as an agent in his office.

"He had no experience, outside of booking himself," the agent said. "But I figured if he was as persistent making calls for our clients as he was trying to get a job, he'd work out for us. Why don't you come in and talk when you have a chance. I don't have anything, but maybe I can give you some ideas."

I immediately said that I had been planning a trip to the booking agent's city the next week. We set up an appointment.

Did the agent ever have a job for me? No, but while in his office, he introduced me to some of the clients he was booking, who introduced me to some other people, who later turned out to be clients of mine when I opened up my public relations company.

No matter what industry you want a job in, the moral of the story is the same: Networking and persistence always pay off.

different types of interviews. Depending on the company and the job, you might be asked to go on one or more interviews, ranging from initial or screening interviews to interviews with department heads or supervisors you will be working with.

Things to Bring

Once you get the call for an interview, what's your next step? Let's start with what you should bring with you to the interview.

◎ Copies of your resume
  ▫ While they probably have a copy of your resume, they might have misplaced it or you might want to refer to it.
◎ Letters of reference
  ▫ Even though people have given you their letters of reference, make sure you let them know you are using them.
◎ References
  ▫ When interviewing for jobs, you often need to fill in job applications that ask for both professional and personal references. Ask before you use people as references. Make sure they are prepared to give you a good reference. Then when you go for an interview, call the people on your reference list and give them the heads-up on your job-hunting activities.
◎ A portfolio of your work
  ▫ Refer to Chapter 6 to learn how to develop your professional portfolio.
◎ Business cards
  ▫ Refer to Chapter 6 to learn more about business cards.
◎ Other supporting materials

You want to look as professional as possible, so don't throw your materials into a paper bag or a sloppy knapsack. A professional-looking briefcase or portfolio is the best way to hold your information. If you don't have that, at the very least, put your information into a large envelope or folder to carry into the interview.

Your Interviewing Wardrobe

You've landed an interview, but what do you wear? That depends to a great extent on the specific job for which you're interviewing. However, the rule of thumb is to dress for the job you want.

That doesn't mean that if you're pursuing a career where you will be wearing a uniform when working as a nurse or lab technician that you want to go to the interview in a uniform. It means that you want to dress professionally so interviewers will see you as a professional.

Let's start with a list of what not to wear:

◎ sneakers
◎ flip-flops
◎ sandals
◎ micro-miniskirts or dresses
◎ very tight or very low dresses or tops
◎ jeans of any kind
◎ midriff tops
◎ skin-tight pants or leggings
◎ very baggy pants
◎ sweatshirts
◎ work-out clothes
◎ T-shirts
◎ heavy perfume, men's cologne, or aftershave lotion
◎ very heavy makeup
◎ flashy jewelry (this includes nose rings, lip rings, and other flamboyant piercings)

Now let's talk about what you should wear:

Men
◎ dark suit
◎ dark sports jacket, button down shirt, tie, and trousers
◎ clean, polished shoes

Women

◎ suit

◎ dress with jacket

◎ skirt with blouse and jacket

◎ pumps or other closed-toe shoes

◎ hose

Arriving On Time

Timing is everything in an interview. Whatever you do, don't be late. If you can't get to an interview on time, chances are you won't get to a job on time. On the other hand, you don't want to be an hour early either.

Try to time your arrival so you get there about 15 minutes before your scheduled time. Walk in and tell the receptionist your name and who your appointment is with. When you are directed to go into the interview, walk in, smile sincerely, and shake hands with the interviewer or interviewers and sit down. Look around the office. Does the interviewer have a photo on the desk of children? Is there any personalization in the office? Does it look like the interviewer is into golf, or fishing, or basketball or some other hobby? Do you have something in common? You might say something like:

"What beautiful children."

"Is golf one of your passions too?"

"Do you go deep sea fishing?"

"Those are amazing orchids. How long have you had them?"

★ Tip from the Top

If you have an extreme emergency and absolutely must be late, call and try to reschedule your appointment. Do not see if you can get there late and come up with an excuse when you get there.

"What an incredible antique desk. Do you collect antique furniture?"

Try to make the interviewer comfortable with you before his or her questions begin.

Interview Environments

In most cases, interviews are held in office environments. If you are asked if you want coffee, tea, soda, or any type of food, my advice is to abstain. This is not the time you want to spill coffee, inadvertently make a weird noise drinking soda, or get sugar from a donut on your fingers when you need to shake hands.

In some cases, however, you may be interviewed over a meal. Whether it is breakfast, lunch, or dinner, in these cases it is usually best to order something simple and light. This is not the time to order anything that can slurp, slide, or otherwise mess you up. Soups, messy sauces, lobster, fried chicken, ribs, or anything that you have to eat with your hands would be a bad choice. Nothing can ruin your confidence during an interview worse than a big blob of sauce dropping on your shirt, except if you cut into something and it splashes on your interviewer's suit. Eating should be your last priority. Use this time to present your attributes, tell your story, and ask intelligent questions.

This is also not the time to order an alcoholic beverage. Even if the interviewer orders a drink, abstain. You want to be at the top of your game. If, however, the interviewer orders dessert and coffee or tea, do so as well. That way he or she isn't eating alone and you have a few more minutes to make yourself shine.

In some cases, a company may invite you to participate in a meal interview to see how you will act in social situations. They might want to check out your table manners, whether you keep your elbows on the table, or talk with your

⭐ Words from the Wise

Never ask for a doggie bag at an interview meal. I don't care how good the meal is, how much you have left over, or how much you've had it drummed into your head that you shouldn't waste food. I don't care if the interviewer asks for a doggie bag. In case you're missing the message, do not ask for a doggie bag. I've seen it happen, and I've heard interviewers talking about it in a negative manner weeks later.

⭐ The Inside Scoop

If you have been invited to a meal interview, generally the interviewer will pay the tab and tip. At the end of the meal, when you are leaving, thank the person who paid the check and tell him or her how much you enjoyed the meal and the company.

mouth full. They might want to see whether you drink to excess or how you make conversation. They might want to know if you will embarrass them, if you can handle pressure, or how you interact with others. They might want you to get comfortable so they can see the true you. If you are prepared ahead of time, you will do fine. Just remember that this isn't a social meal. You are being scrutinized. Be on your toes.

During the meal, pepper the conversation with questions about the company and the job. Don't be afraid to say you're excited about the possibility of working with them, you think you would be an asset to the company, and you hope they agree. Make eye contact with those at the table.

When the interviewer stands up after the meal, the interview is generally over. Stand up, thank the interviewer or interviewers for the meal, tell them you look forward to hearing from them, shake everyone's hand, and leave.

Many companies today pre-interview or do partial interviews on the phone. This might be to pre-screen people without bringing them into the office. It also might come about if the employer is interested in a candidate and that individual lives in a different geographic location.

Whatever the reason, be prepared. If the company has scheduled a phone interview ahead of time, make sure your "space" is prepared so you can do your best.

Here are some ideas.

◎ Have your phone in a quiet location. People yelling, a loud television, or music in the background is not helpful in this situation.

◎ Have a pad of paper and a few pens to write down the name of the people you are speaking to, take notes, and jot down questions as you think of them.

◎ Have a copy of your resume near you. Your interviewer may refer to information on your resume. If it's close, you won't have to fumble for words.

◎ Prepare questions to ask in case you are asked if you have any questions.

◎ Prepare answers for questions that you might be asked. For example: "Why do you want to work for us?" "What can you bring to the hospital, facility, organization, company, and so on?"

⭐ Tip from the Coach

Everyone has their own opinions on politics and religion. During an interview, stay clear of conversations involving either subject.

"What type of experience do you have?" "Why are you the best candidate?" "Where do you see yourself in five years?" "Why did you leave your last job?" "Did you get along with your last boss?" "What are you best at?" "What is your greatest strength?" "What is your greatest weakness?"

Preparing for these questions is essential. While I can't guarantee what an interviewer might ask, I can pretty much guarantee that he or she probably will ask at least one of those questions or at least something similar.

Other Types of Interview Scenarios

When you think of an interviewing situation, you generally think of the one-on-one scenario where the interviewer is on one side of the desk and you are on the other. At some time during your career, you may be faced with some other types of interviews. Two of the more common ones you may run into are group interviews and panel interviews. What's the difference?

A group interview is a situation where a company brings a group of people together to tell them about the company and job opportunities. There may be open discussions and a question-and-answer period. During this time, individual one-on-one interviews may be scheduled.

Companies use these types of situations not only to bring a group of potential employees to-

---

★ The Inside Scoop

I frequently receive calls from individuals who are distraught after going on interviews. It seems that while they prepared for answering every question they can possibly think an interviewer might ask about the job they are applying for, they hadn't prepared for the unexpected.

"I prepared for answering every question," a man told me. "And then the interviewer threw me for a loop. He started asking me all kinds of questions that had nothing to do with the job I was applying for. I just couldn't come up with answers that made sense."

"What did he ask?" I questioned.

"He asked me what my favorite book was when I was a child. He asked me what I wanted to be when I was little. He asked me what my greatest strength was in my last job. Then he asked me what my biggest mistake was in my last job. I couldn't think of anything to say that made any type of sense."

Interviewers often come up with questions like this for a variety of reasons. They may want to see how you react to non-traditional questions. They may want to see how well rounded you are. Or they might just be thinking about something at the time they are interviewing you and the questions pop out of their mouth.

If this has happened to you, instead of beating yourself up about not coming up with what you consider a *good* answer, prepare for next time. Know there generally isn't any right or wrong answer. When an interviewer asks you a question, it's okay to compose yourself and take a moment to think about the best answer for you.

★ Words from the Wise

In your effort to tell people about your accomplishments, try not to monopolize the conversation talking solely about *you*. Before you go to an interview, especially a meal interview, read up on the news of the day in case someone at the table asks your opinion about the day's happenings. You want to appear as well rounded as possible.

gether but to screen potential employees. What do you need to know? Remember that while this may not be the traditional interview setting you are used to, this is still an interview.

From the minute you walk in the door in these settings, the employer is watching your demeanor and your body language. He or she is listening to what you say and any questions you might ask. He or she is watching you to see how you interact with others and how you might fit into the company.

How can you increase your chances of being asked to a one-on-one interview?

◎ Actively participate in conversations and activities.
◎ Be a leader, not a follower.
◎ Ask meaningful questions.

Panel Interviews

In a panel interview, you are interviewed by a group of people at the same time. While you might run into this type of interview at any time in your career, they are most often utilized for higher-level positions. You might, for example, go through a panel interview if you are pursuing a position as a physician, a physician executive, or the executive director of a hospital. You might also go through a panel interview if you are pursuing a job as a lab manager, director of sales for a pharmaceutical company, or director of nursing.

Why do employers use panel interviews? Every member of the panel brings something different to the table. Everyone has a different set of skills and experience. Many employers feel that a panel can increase the chance of finding the perfect applicant for the job. It also is sometimes easier to bring everyone involved together for one interview instead of scheduling separate interviews.

> ### ⭐ Tip from the Coach
>
> If the thought of participating in a panel interview stresses you out, think of it this way. You have more than one chance to impress interviewers. While one member of the panel may not be impressed by your credentials, another may think you are the perfect candidate and after the interview be your cheerleader.

The panel interview will rarely be the first interview you go through. Generally, after going on one or more one-on-one interviews, if you become one of the finalists, you will be asked to attend a panel interview.

Who is there? It can be any mixture of people, depending on the job. If you are pursuing a job as the executive director of a not-for-profit hospital, for example, the panel might include the human resources director, the chief of staff, and the board of directors. If you are interviewing for a job in research, the interview panel might include the HR director, supervisors, and other individuals on the research team with whom you might be working.

How can you succeed in a panel interview? Start by relaxing. Looking *or* feeling stressed will not help in this situation. When you walk into the interview, smile sincerely and make sure you firmly shake each person's hand. You want each person to feel equally important.

Prepare ahead of time. Know what is on your resume or CV. Sounds simple, but believe it or not, when you're on the hot seat, it is very easy to get confused. You want to be able to answer every question about your background without skipping a beat.

Research the company. Have some questions prepared so you can show a true interest in the position for which you are interviewing.

<table>
<tr><td>

★ **Tip from the Top**

Always prepare a response for the beginning of the interview when someone on interview panel says "Tell us about yourself." Have a long and short version of your response. Don't say, "I don't know what to tell you." Or "Where should I start?" Begin with your short version and ask if they would like you to go into more detail.

</td></tr>
</table>

Instead of referring to notes you have written, try to have your questions seem part of the conversation.

One of the important things to remember when participating in a panel interview is to make eye contact with everyone. Start by looking at the person who asks you the question. As you're answering, glance at the other people sitting around the table, making contact with each of them. You want everyone there to feel that you are talking to them.

Interview Questions

What might you be asked? You will probably be asked a slew of general questions and then, depending on the job, some questions specific to your skills and talent.

◎ Why should we hire you?
  ⊡ This is a common question. Think about the answers ahead of time. Practice saying them out loud so you feel comfortable. For example, "I believe I would be an asset to the company (hospital, office, and so on). I have the qualifications. I'm a team player, and this is the type of career I really want to pursue. I'm a hard worker and a quick study. I

have a positive attitude, and I'll help you achieve your goals."

You can then go on to explain one or two specifics. For example, "In my current position, I've developed a publicity plan that has generated 10 front-page articles as well as a number of feature stories for our company just this year alone. I would love the opportunity and challenge to work with a health care organization like yours, to do an even bigger, more exciting campaign."

◎ What makes you more qualified than other candidates?
  ⊡ Another common question. How about saying something like, "I believe my experience first working as an intern and then in a paid summer position while in college gave me a fuller understanding of the inner workings of health care administration. As an intern, I rotated through a number of departments in the administrative segment of a hospital, and last summer I worked in the health and wellness department. I brought my portfolio so you can see some of the projects I worked on. You've indicated today two of the challenges your facility is facing in bringing new your health and wellness program to the attention of the community and coordinating special events. Last summer I was the coordinator for our local Rotary Club's health fair in conjunction with the hospital. The event brought in hundreds of people who were

tested for everything from vision and hearing to cholesterol, breast cancer, and prostate cancer. As part of the program, I was in charge of developing the educational programs and finding speakers. I have copies of some letters from a number of people who attended the event as well as newspaper clippings that I'll leave for you to review later. You can see some of the other work I've done in my portfolio."

◎ Where do you see yourself in five years?

▫ Do not say, "Sitting in your chair" or "In your chair." People in every business are paranoid that someone is going to take their job, so don't even joke about it. Instead, think about the question ahead of time. It's meant to find out what your aspirations are and if you have direction?

One answer might be, "I hope to be a successful member of the administrative team at this hospital. I was born in this hospital, my mom volunteered on the hospital auxiliary when I was growing up, and my grandmother was a resident in the skilled nursing unit. This is a wonderful facility that is an asset to the community. I would love to think that I could have a long career here."

◎ What are your strengths?

▫ Be confident but not cocky when answering this one. Toot your horn, but don't be boastful. Practice ahead of time speaking what your greatest strengths, talents, and skills are. "I'm passionate about what I do. I love working at something I'm passionate about. That's one of the main reasons I applied for this position. I also have great organizational skills, I'm a people person, and I'm a really good communicator. I pride myself on being able to solve problems efficiently."

◎ Where are your weaknesses?

▫ We all have weaknesses. This is not the time to share them. Be creative. "My greatest weakness is also one of my strengths. I'm a workaholic. I don't like leaving a project undone. I have a hard time understanding how someone cannot do a great job when they love what they do."

◎ Why did you leave your last job?

▫ Be careful answering this one. If you were fired, simply say you were let go. Don't go into the politics. Don't say anything bad about your former job, company, or boss. If you were laid off, simply say you were laid off or, if it's true, that you were one of the newer employees and unfortunately that's how the layoff process worked. You might add that you were very sorry to leave because you really enjoyed working there, but on the positive side, you are free to apply for this position. If you quit, simply say the job was not challenging and you wanted to work in a position where you could create a career.

Never lie. I've mentioned it before and I'm going to reiterate it. People move around in the health care industry all the time. You can never tell when your former boss knows the person interviewing you. In the same vein, never say anything during an interview that is derogatory about anyone or any other company, facility, or organization. The boss you had yesterday might end up moving over to your new company and being your new boss. It is not unheard of in the industry.

◎ Why do you want to work in the health care industry? (Depending on the specific area of the industry, the question might be, "Why do you want to work in patient care?" "Why do you want to work as a nurse in a school instead of a hospital?" "Why do you want to work in emergency care?" "Why do you want to work with the elderly?")

◎ What do you think is the biggest medical problem in the country at this time?

◎ If you had to pick the most important advancement in medicine of all time, what would it be?

◎ When did you decide you wanted to work in medicine?

   ▫ Think about questions like this ahead of time and come up with answers. There is no right or wrong answer for these types of questions. You just want to be able to come up with answers without saying, "Uh… let me think. Well—I'm not sure."

◎ Are you a team player?

   ▫ Companies want you to be a team player, so the answer is, "Yes, it's one of my strengths."

◎ Do you need supervision?

   ▫ You want to appear as confident and capable as possible. Depending on the specific job and responsibilities, you might say, "I work well with limited supervision." Or "No, once I know my responsibilities, I have always been able to fulfill them."

◎ Are you free to travel?

   ▫ You might be required to travel for some jobs. A pharmaceutical salesperson may need to go on the road. So might a sales rep for medical equipment. If you're asked, be honest. If the job you are applying for requires travel and that is a problem, now is the time to straighten it out. If you're not sure what type of travel the position entails, ask. You might ask how often travel will be required and if it is scheduled ahead of time.

◎ Will working overtime, nights, or on weekends be a problem?

   ▫ The answer they are looking for is *no*. If it won't be a problem, a good answer here might be, "If a project requires it, it won't be a problem, and of course I'll be available." Or, "Of course, I'm always available for emergencies." Don't be afraid to ask how much overtime is anticipated or what situations would require working nights or weekends.

◎ Are you available to work all shifts?

   ▫ The answer they are looking for is "*Yes,* I can work all shifts." Once again, however, if you can't work the night shift because you're a single parent and you have no one to watch your children, don't say you can when you can't.

◎ Do you get along well with others?

▫ The answer they are looking for is "Yes, I'm a real people person." Do not give any stories about times where you didn't. Do not say anything like "I get along better with women" or "I relate better to men." Even if it's true, don't make any type of comment that can come back to haunt you.

◎ Every now and then, you get a weird question or a question that you just don't expect. If you could be a car, what type of car would you be and why? If you were an animal, what animal would you be? If you could have dinner with anyone alive or dead, who would it be? These questions generally are just meant to throw you off balance and see how you react.

▫ Stay calm and focused. Be creative but try not to come up with any answer that is too weird.

▫ An interviewer might ask what was the last book you read, what newspapers you read, what television shows are your favorites, or what your favorite movie of all time is.

▫ Be honest, but try not to say things like, "I don't have time to read." "I don't like reading," or "I watch the Playboy channel every chance I get." You want to appear well rounded.

◎ What type of salary are you looking for?

▫ This is going to be discussed in detail, but what you should know now is that this is an important matter. You don't want to get locked into a number, before you know exactly what you will be responsible for. You might say something to the effect of, "I'm looking for a fair salary for the job. I

Tip from the Top

Try not to discuss salary at the beginning of the interview. Instead wait until you hear all the particulars about the job and you have given them a chance to see how great you are.

---

really would like to know more about the responsibilities before I come up with a range. What is the range, by the way?" You might turn the tables and say something like, "I was interested in knowing what the salary range was for this position." This turns the question back to the interviewer.

What They Can't Ask You

There are questions it is illegal for interviewers to ask. For example, they aren't permitted to ask you anything about your age, unless they are making sure you are over 18. They aren't supposed to ask you about marriage, children, or relationships. Interviewers are not supposed to ask you about your race, color, religion, national origin, or sexual preference. If an interviewer does ask an illegal question, in most cases it is not on purpose. He or she just might not know that it shouldn't be asked.

Your demeanor in responding to such questions can affect the direction of the interview. If you don't mind answering, then by all means do so. If answering bothers you, try to point the questions in another direction, like back to your skills and talents. If you are unable to do so, simply indicate in a non-threatening, non-confrontational manner that those types of questions are not supposed to be asked in interviews.

What You Might Want to Ask

Just because you're the one being interviewed doesn't mean you shouldn't ask questions. You want to appear confident. You want to portray someone who can fit in with others comfortably. You want to ask great questions. Depending on the specific job, here are some ideas.

◎ What happened to the last person who held this job? Was he or she promoted or did he or she leave the organization?
  ▫ You want to know whose shoes you're filling.
◎ Does the company promote from within as a rule or look outside?
  ▫ This is important because companies that promote from within are good companies to build a career with.
◎ Is there a lot of longevity of employees here?
  ▫ Employees who stay for a length of time generally are happy with the company.
◎ Is there a lot of laughing in the workplace? Are people happy here?
  ▫ If there is, it means it is a less stressed environment.
◎ How will I be evaluated? Are there periodic reviews?
  ▫ You want to know how and when you will know if you are doing well in your supervisor's eyes.
◎ How do you measure success on the job? By that, I mean how can I do a great job for you?
  ▫ You want to know what your employer expects from employees.
◎ What are the options for advancement in this position?
  ▫ This illustrates that you are interested in staying with the company.
◎ Whom will I report to? What will my general responsibilities be?
  ▫ You want to know what your work experience and duties will be like.

Feel free to ask any questions you want answered. While it is perfectly acceptable to ask questions, don't chatter on incessantly. You want to give the interviewer time to ask you questions and see how you shine.

It's normal to be nervous during an interview. Relax as much as you can. If you go in prepared and answer the questions you're asked, you should do fine. Somewhere during the interview if things are going well, salary will come up.

Salary and Compensation

No matter how much you want a job, unless you are doing an internship, the good news is you're not going to be working for free. Compensation may be discussed in a general manner during your interview or may be discussed in full. A lot has to do with the specific job. One way or another, salary will generally come up sometime during your interview. Unless your interviewer brings up salary at the beginning of an interview, you should not. If you feel an interview is close to ending and another interview has not been scheduled, feel free to bring up salary when asked if you have any questions.

A simple question such as "What is the salary range for the job?" will usually start the ball rolling. Depending on the specific job, your interviewer may tell you exactly what the salary and benefits are or may just give you a range. In many cases, salary and compensation packages are only ironed out after the actual job offer is made.

Keep in mind that many jobs in the health care industry, especially in hospitals and other health care facilities, may be unionized. That means that minimum earnings (as well as working conditions) are negotiated and set by the union.

Let's say you are offered a job and a compensation package. What do you do if you're not happy with the salary? What about the benefits? Can you negotiate? You certainly can try. Sometimes you can negotiate better terms as far as salary, sometimes better benefits, and sometimes both. A lot of it depends on how much they want you, how much of an asset you will be, and what they can afford.

When negotiating, speak in a calm, well-modulated voice. Do not make threats. State your case and see if you can meet in the middle. If you can't negotiate a higher salary, perhaps you can negotiate extra vacation days. Depending on the company and specific job, compensation may include salary, vacation days, sick days, health insurance, stock options, pension plans, or a variety of other things. When negotiating, look at the whole package.

You might do some research ahead of time to see what similar types of jobs are paying. Information on compensation may also have been in the original advertisement you answered. General salary ranges on many jobs in the health care industry may also be located in one of my other books, *Career Opportunities In The Health Care Industry*.

Over the years, I have seen many people so desperate to get the job of their dreams that, once offered the job, they will take it for almost anything. Often, when questioned about salary, they ask for salary requirements far below what might have been offered. Whatever you do, don't undersell yourself.

Accepting a job offer below your perceived salary "comfort level" often results in you resent-ing your company, coworkers, and, even worse, whittles away at your self-worth. This can be especially difficult when working in the health care industry, where patient care is essential.

It is perfectly acceptable to ask for a day or two to consider an offer. Simply say something like "I appreciate your confidence in me. I'd like to think about it over night if that's okay with you. Can I give you a call tomorrow afternoon?"

Things to Remember

To give yourself every advantage in acing the interview, there are a few things you should know. First of all, practice ahead of time. Ask friends or family members for their help in setting up practice interviews. You want to get comfortable answering questions without sounding like you're reading from a script.

Many people go on real "practice interviews." In essence, this involves going on interviews for jobs you might not want in order to get experience in interview situations. Some people think that it isn't right to waste an interviewer's time. On the other hand, you can never tell when you might be offered a job that you originally didn't plan on taking but that turns out to be something you want.

Here are some other things to remember to help you land an offer.

◎ If you don't have confidence in yourself, neither will anyone else. No matter how nervous you are, project a confident and positive attitude.
◎ The one who looks and sounds most qualified has the best chance of getting the job. Don't answer questions in monosyllables. Explain your answers using relevant experiences. What does that mean? If you're asked if you have good organizational skills, for example,

you might say something like, "Yes, I have great organizational skills. When I interned in the volunteer office of the hospital, I developed a system for organizing the names and information of all the people who had volunteered over the last few years. After I gathered the information, I input it into a spreadsheet and we used it to make sure we always had volunteer coverage. I have a letter in my portfolio from my supervisor discussing how the system helped with the volunteer coverage."

Use your experiences in both your work and personal life to reinforce your skills, talents, and abilities when answering questions.

◎ Try to develop a rapport with your interviewer. If your interviewer likes you, he or she will often overlook less than perfect skills because you seem like a better candidate.

◎ Smile and make sure you have good posture. It makes you look more successful.

◎ Be attentive. Listen to what the interviewer is saying. If he or she asks a question that you don't understand, politely ask for an explanation.

◎ Be pleasant and positive. People will want to be around you.

◎ Turn off your cell phone and beeper *before* you go into the interview.

◎ When you see the interview coming to a close, make sure you ask when a decision will be made and if you will be contacted either way.

◎ When the interview comes to a close, stand up, thank the interviewer, shake his or her hand, and then leave.

Here are some things you should not do:

◎ Don't smoke before you go into your interview.

◎ Don't chew gum during your interview.

◎ Don't be late.

◎ Don't talk negatively about past bosses, jobs, or companies.

◎ Don't say "ain't," "heh," "uh-huh," "don't know," "got me," or other similar things. It doesn't sound professional and suggests that you have poor communication skills.

◎ Don't wear heavy perfume or cologne before going on an interview. You can never tell if the interviewer is allergic to various odors.

◎ Don't interrupt the interviewer.

◎ While you certainly can ask questions, don't try to dominate the conversation to try to look smart.

◎ Don't drop names.

◎ Don't swear, curse, or use off-color language.

Thank-You Notes

It's always a good idea to send a note thanking the person who interviewed you for his or her time. Think a thank-you note is useless? Think again. Take a look at some of the things a thank-you note can do for you.

A thank-you note after an interview can:

◎ Show that you are courteous and well mannered.

◎ Show that you are professional.

◎ Give you one more shot at reminding the interviewer who you were.

◎ Show that you are truly interested in the job.

◎ Illustrate that you have written communication skills.

◎ Give you a chance to briefly discuss something that you thought was important yet forgot to bring up during the interview.

◎ Help you stand out from other job applicants who didn't send a thank-you note.

Try to send thank-you notes within 24 hours of your interview. You can hand-write or type them. While it's acceptable to e-mail or fax them, I suggest mailing.

What should the letter say? It can simply say thank you or it can be longer. For example:

Dear Mr. Benson:

Thanks for taking the time to interview me yesterday for the director of fundraising and development position at your hospital. As I indicated during our meeting, I am sure the experience I gained handling the fund-raising for Community Hospital as their assistant director will transfer over well.

I feel that I would be a good match for the job and an asset to the Green Valley Hospital. I look forward to hearing from you and hope that I am able to help with the push to create a successful fund-raising campaign for Green Valley!

Thanks once again.

Sincerely yours,
George Driver

Or:

Dear Ms Berger:

While I was excited when I heard there was a position as a pharmacist open at Spring Valley pharmacy, I was absolutely thrilled about the possibilities after speaking to you. Thank you so much for taking the time not only to interview me but to explain all the intricacies of your pharmacy. You made me feel like I would fit right in.

This was just the type of position I had been hoping to find and I would welcome the oppor-

tunity to become part of the team.

I look forward to hearing from you about your choice of candidates for the position and am truly hoping that it's me.

Thanks again.

Sincerely,
Anthony Buckman

Waiting for an Answer

You've gone through the interview for the job you want. You've done everything you can do. Now what? Unfortunately, now you have to wait for an answer. Are you the candidate who was chosen? Hopefully you are!

If you haven't heard back in a week or so (unless you were given a specific date when an applicant would be chosen), call and ask the status of the job. If you are told that they haven't made a decision, ask when a good time to call back would be.

If you are told that a decision has been made and it's not you, thank them and say how you appreciated the consideration. Request that your resume be kept on file for the future. You might just get a call before you know it. If the organization is a large one, such as a hospital or other health care facility, ask if there are other positions available and how you should go about applying for them if you are interested.

If your phone rings and you got the job, congratulations! Once you get the call telling you that you are the candidate they want, depending on the situation, they will either make an offer on the phone or you will have to go in to the company to discuss your compensation package. If an offer is made on the phone, as we previously discussed, you have every right to ask if you can think about it and get back to them in 24 hours. If you are satisfied with the offer as it is, you can accept it.

Depending on the job, you may be required to sign an employment contract. Read the agreement thoroughly and make sure that you are comfortable signing it. If there is anything you don't understand, ask. Don't just sign without reading. You want to know what you are agreeing to.

Interviewing for jobs is a skill. Practice until you feel comfortable answering every type of question and being in a variety of situations. The more prepared you are ahead of time, the better you'll usually do. The more you do it, the more comfortable you'll be going through the process.

While we've been discussing interviewing for positions in general, it's important to remember that many jobs in health care deal directly with patients instead of the business or administrative segment of the industry. These include careers in medicine and dentistry, allied health, and other areas of patient care. It is especially important when interviewing for these positions to demonstrate that you have both compassion and empathy. You want to demonstrate that you have a good bedside manner. You want your interviewer to recognize that you *know* how to deal with patients and you can and will help them feel as comfortable as possible.

Mastering the art of interviewing can make a huge difference in your interview. Remember the intangible essentials that can help you win the job:

Tip from the Coach

Take every interview seriously. Don't waste any opportunity to sell yourself.

◎ enthusiasm
◎ excitement
◎ interest
◎ confidence

Enthusiasm is key when interviewing for a job. You want to be enthusiastic at the interview.

"But I don't want them to think I'm desperate," people always tell me.

My response is always the same. You don't want to appear desperate, but you don't want there to be a question in your interviewer's mind that you want the job.

What else? Yes, you want to be excited about the possibility of working at the job for which you are interviewing.

Anything else? You definitely want to appear interested. What does that mean? You want your interviewer to know without a shadow of a doubt that you are interested not only in the job but in the concept of working at that particular job.

And finally, you want to appear confident. As we have already discussed, if you don't believe you're the best, neither will anyone else.

9

MARKETING YOURSELF FOR SUCCESS

What Marketing Can Do for You

Here's a question. Do you know what Bayer Aspirin, Kleenex Tissues, Coca-Cola, Pepsi, Dr. Pepper, McDonalds, Burger King, Wendy's, Disney World, Las Vegas, the Rolling Stones, and every other successful corporation and person have in common? It's the same thing that hot trends, major sports events, blockbuster movies, top television shows, hot CDs, mega superstar athletes, and even hot new toys have in common. Do you know what it is yet?

Here's the answer: Every one of them utilizes marketing. Do you want to know the inside track on becoming successful and getting what you want no matter what segment of the health care industry you're interested in pursuing? It's simple: All you have to do is use marketing yourself.

Many people think that marketing techniques are reserved for businesses or products. They don't think about marketing when it comes to themselves. Here's something to think about. From the moment you begin your career until you ultimately retire, you are a product. It doesn't matter what direction your career is going or what area you want to pursue.

There are thousands of people in this world who want to work in the health care industry.

Some want to be doctors, nurses, dentists, or chiropractors. Others want to be pharmacists, pharmacy technicians, physical therapists, music therapists, arts therapists. lab technicians, technologists, or radiologists. Some want to work in medical writing, journalism, or communications. Some want to work in the retail or wholesale segment of the industry. Still others want to purse a career on the administration or business end of the health care industry.

Some make it, and some don't. Is it education? Thousands of people are highly educated but don't get the jobs they want. Is it talent? A lot of it has to do with talent, but that is not everything. Thousands of talented individuals haven't made it either. Is it skills? Thousands of people are skilled yet don't make it too. So if it isn't just education, talent, or skills, what is the answer? What is the key to success?

Like it or not, a lot of it has to do with luck and being in the right place at the right time. Some of it may be related to working hard and having a strong passion. One of the factors, however, which appears to be related to success is how one individual sets him or herself apart from another in the way he or she was marketed or conversely marketed themselves.

Here's something you should know. When a pharmaceutical company wants to turn a new drug into one that is asked for by patients, they develop and implement a successful marketing plan. When major corporations want to turn a new product into a hot commodity they develop and implement a successful marketing plan. Whatever segment of the health care industry in which you want to work and succeed, marketing can help *you* become one of the hottest commodities around too.

While most people can understand how marketing can help stars and big companies, they never think about the possibility of marketing themselves to benefit their career.

When I give seminars on succeeding in various industries and we start discussing this area, there are always a number of attendees who inevitably ask, "Does this relate to me?" How can marketing help me? I just want to work in the administrative or business end of the industry." Or, "I want to work in a lab? What is marketing going to do for my career? Why do I have to market myself?"

Here's the answer in a nutshell. If you aren't marketing yourself and someone else is, they will have an advantage over you. One of the tricks to success is taking advantage of every opportunity. Marketing yourself is an opportunity you just can't afford to miss.

What is marketing? On the most basic level, marketing is finding markets and avenues to sell products or services. In this case, you are the product. The buyers are employers if you are looking for a traditional job or perhaps patients if you are a physician, dentist, or other medical professional.

To be successful, you not only want to be the product, you want to be the *brand*. Look at Nabisco, Kelloggs, McDonalds, Coke, Pepsi and Disney. Look at Orange County Choppers,

Martha Stewart, NASCAR, *American Idol*, and Michael Jordan.

Look at Donald Trump. One of the people most successful in branding, Trump, a master marketer, believes so strongly in this concept that he successfully branded himself. While he made his mark in real estate, in addition to his successful television show, Trump has a successful line of hotels, casinos, clothing, water, ice-cream, books, seminars, and even Trump University. He continues to illustrate to people how he can fill *their needs*. Then he finds new needs he can fill. If you're savvy, you can do the same.

If you know or can determine what you can do for an employer or what can help them, you can market yourself to illustrate how you can fill those needs. If you can sell and market yourself effectively, you can succeed in your career; you can push yourself to the next level and you can get what you want.

Is there a secret to this? No, there really isn't a secret, but it does take some work. In the end, however, the payoff will be worth it.

Do you want to be the one who gets the job? Marketing can help. Want to make yourself visible so potential employers will see you as desirable? Marketing can help. Do you want to set yourself apart from other job candidates? Guess what? Marketing can help. It can also distinguish you from other employees. If you have marketed yourself effectively, when promotions, raises, or in-house openings are on the horizon, your name will come up. Marketing can give you credibility and open the door to new opportunities.

If you're pursuing a career as a physician, dentist, chiropractor or other medical professional, marketing is just as important if not more. Of course, you need the knowledge, skills and talent. But that's not all. Do you want to stand out from every other physician in your field? Do you want to set yourself apart from other dentists? You know what you have to do? Market yourself!

Do you want to become more visible? Get the attention of the media? Do you want to get the attention of recruiters, headhunters, industry insiders and other important people? Do you want to open up the door to new opportunities? Do you want to catch the eye of board members or human resources of health care facilities who want you to be part of their team? Market yourself!

"Okay," you're saying. "I get it. I need to market myself. But how?"

That's what we're going to talk about now. To begin with, understand that in order to market yourself effectively, you are going to have to do what every good marketer does. You're going to have to develop your product, perform market research, and assess the product and the marketplace.

Are there going to be differences between marketing yourself for a career in the business or administration segments of the industry and a career in medicine or allied health? Yes, of course there are going to be some differences, but in general, you're going to use a lot of the same techniques.

Read over this section and see which techniques and ideas will work best for you. As long as you are marketing yourself in a positive manner, you are on the right track.

The Five Ps of Marketing and How They Relate to Your Career

There are five Ps to marketing whether you're marketing your career, a medical practice, a hot new restaurant, a new product, or anything else. They are *product*, *price*, *positioning*, *promotion*,

and *packaging*. Let's look at how these Ps relate to your career.

◎ *Product*: In this case, as we just mentioned, the product is you. "Me," you say. "How am I a product?" *You* are a package complete with your physical self, skills, ideas, and talents.

◎ *Price*: Price is the compensation you receive for your work. As you are aware, there can be a huge range of possible earnings for any one job. One of your goals in marketing yourself is to sell your talents, skills, and anything else you have to offer for the best possible compensation.

◎ *Positioning*: What positioning means in this context is developing and creating innovative methods to fill the needs of one or more employers or potential clients or patients. It also means differentiating yourself and/or your talent and skills from other competitors. Depending on your career area, this might mean differentiating yourself from other employees, physicians, dentists, administrators, journalists, marketing people, and so on.

◎ *Promotion*: Promotion is the promotion and implementation of methods that make you visible in a positive manner.

◎ *Packaging*: Packaging is the way you present yourself.

Putting Together Your Package

Now that we know how the Five Ps of marketing are related to your career, let's discuss a little more about putting together your package.

The more you know about your product (*you*), the easier it is to market and sell it. It's

---

Tip from the Coach

While you can't tell a book by its cover, it's human nature to at least look at the book with an interesting cover first. You might put it back after looking at it, but you at least gave it a first shot. That is why it is so important to package yourself as well as you possibly can.

---

also essential to know as much as possible about the markets to which you are trying to sell. What do you have to offer that a potential buyer (employer) needs? If you can illustrate to a market (employer) that you are the package that can fill their needs, you stand a good chance to turn the market into a buyer.

Assess what you have to offer as well as what you think an employer needs. We've already discussed self assessment in a prior chapter. Now review your skills and your talents to help you determine how they can be used to fill the needs of your target markets.

While all the Ps of marketing are important, packaging is one of the easiest to change. It's something you have control over.

How important is packaging? Very! Good packaging can make a product more appealing, more enticing, and make *you* want it. Not convinced? Think about the last time you went to the store. Did you reach for the name brand products more often then the bargain brand?

Not convinced? How many times have you been in a bakery or restaurant and chosen the beautifully decorated deserts over the simple un-iced cake? Packaging can make a difference—a big difference—in your career. If you package yourself effectively, people will want your package.

Want to know a secret? Many job candidates in every industry are passed over before they get very far in the process because they simply don't understand how to package themselves. What does this mean to you?

It means that if you can grasp the concept, you're ahead of the game. In a competitive world, this one thing can give you the edge. Knowing that a marketing campaign utilizes packaging to help sell products means that you will want to package yourself as well as you can. You want potential employers, recruiters, headhunters, patients, and others to see you in the most positive manner possible. You want to illustrate that you have what it takes to fill *their* needs.

So what does your personal package include?

The Inside Scoop

A number of years ago I met a man who I was told was brilliant. He was excellent at getting grants and bringing in huge amounts of monies to the facility where he worked. He knew all about the rules and regulations in the health care industry and was successful in developing and creating a business plan for the facility. Unfortunately, the man was also a slob. His shirt was never tucked into his pants. He had no table manners and dropped food over his clothing when he ate. When he went to industry meetings, people from other facilities always spoke about him in a disparaging manner prefacing their statements with, what a shame it was because he was so bright and so good at his job. While well-meaning colleagues told him he should clean up his act, he never really took any positive actions. When new management came into the facility, the man was let go. No matter how good you are at your job, packaging continues to matter throughout your career.

People base their first impression of you largely on your appearance. Whether you are going for an interview for a hot job or currently working and trying to move up the ladder of success, appearance is always important.

It might seem elementary, but let's go over the elements of your appearance. Personal grooming is essential. What does that mean?

- ◎ Your hair should be clean and neatly styled.
- ◎ You should be showered with no body odor.
- ◎ Your nails should be clean. If you polish them, make sure that your polish isn't chipped.
- ◎ If you are a man, you should be freshly shaved and mustaches and beards should be neatly styled.
- ◎ If you are a woman, your makeup should look natural and not overdone.
- ◎ Your breath should be clean and fresh.

Good grooming is important no matter what segment of the industry you are pursuing.

Now let's discuss your attire. Whether you're going on interviews, in a networking situation, or already on the job, it's important to dress appropriately. What's appropriate? Good question.

Appropriateness to a great extent depends on what area of the industry you're involved

---

★ Words from the Wise

Strong perfume, cologne, and after-shave often make people *not* want to be near you. Many people are allergic to strong odors. Many just can't stand the smell. This is especially important if you work around patients. You don't want to be known as the one who wears that stinky stuff. If you wear scents, go light.

---

and your specific job. If you're working in the business end of the industry, you want to look professional.

Always dress to impress. Employers want to see that you will not only fit in, but that you will not embarrass them when representing the company. So what should you do? What should you wear?

If you are going on an interview, dress professionally. If you're a man, you can never go wrong in a suit and tie or a pair of dress slacks with a sports jacket, dress shirt, and tie. Women might wear a suit, a professional looking dress, a skirt and jacket, or a skirt and blouse. Once you're hired, learn the company dress policy. It's okay to ask. No matter what the policy is observe what everyone else is wearing. If the policy is casual and everyone is still dressed in business attire, dress in business attire.

"But I'll be wearing a uniform on the job," you say. "What do I wear on the interview?"

★ Tip from the Top

Make sure you have mints or breath strips with you when you go to interviews. Nothing can turn off an interviewer faster than someone breathing funky breath in their face.

★ Words from a Pro

Even if you are interviewing for an entry-level job, dress professionally. You want your interviewer to see that you are looking for a *career* not just a job.

The Inside Scoop

It's always easier to make yourself look more casual than it is to make yourself appear dressed more professionally. If in doubt about what to wear, err on the side of looking professional.

Even if you will be wearing a uniform on the job, you still want to dress professionally when you go on an interview.

"But I'm going for an entry-level job in the lab," you say. "Why would I get dressed up?"

The answer is simple. You want to make a good impression. You want to look like you care and you want to look like you're serious about your career. You want to look professional.

You might also want to think about your image when you're *not* working. Why is this important? If you project an unprofessional image of the job, it can possibly affect your career in a negative manner.

Communication Skills

Your communication skills, both verbal and written, are yet another part of your package. What you say and how you say it can mean the difference between success and failure in getting a job or succeeding at one you already have. You want to sound articulate, polished, strong, and confident.

Do you ever wonder how others hear you? Consider using a tape recorder, recording yourself speaking, and then playing it back.

Is this scary? It can be if you never heard yourself. Here's what to remember. No matter what you think you sound like, it probably isn't that bad. You are probably your own worst critic.

When you play back your voice, listen to your speech pattern. You might, for example, find that you are constantly saying "uh" or "uh-huh." You might find that your voice sounds nasal or high pitched or that you talk to quickly. If you're not happy with the way you sound, there are exercises you can do to practice to change your pitch, modulation, and speech pattern.

There are even methods to change your accent, if you have one. Accents generally are acquired by being around others who speak in a certain way. Can someone tell you're from New York City, Boston, Alabama, South Carolina, or England just by talking to you?

Do you need to change your accent? Only if *you* feel it's a hindrance to your career. If, for example, you are an aspiring television or radio medical reporter, you might feel a very heavy accent might limit your career. If you are a physician or pharmacist, you also want to make sure your patients can understand you. This is something you have to decide for yourself; no one else can make this decision.

If you do feel you need to change your accent, look for a speech therapist, speech coach, or vocal coach.

Because you can't take words back into your mouth after you say them, here are some *don'ts* to follow when speaking.

Tip from the Top

Here's a tip for career advancement. Check out what the higher-ups are wearing and emulate them. If you dress like you're already successful, not only will you feel more successful, but you will set yourself apart in a positive way in your superior's eyes.

◎ Don't use off-color language.
◎ Don't swear or curse.
◎ Don't tell jokes or stories that have either sexual, political, ethnic, or racial undertones or innuendoes.
◎ Don't interrupt others when they are speaking.
◎ Don't use poor grammar or slang.

We've discussed your verbal communication skills; now let's discuss the importance of your written communication skills. Here's the deal. Whatever your career choice in health care, you need at least basic written communication skills. You need to be able to compose simple letters, memos, and reports. If you are uncomfortable with your writing skills, either pick up a book to help improve them or consider taking a basic writing class at a local school or college.

Your body language can tell people a lot about you. The way you carry yourself can show others how you feel about yourself. We've all seen people in passing that were hunched over or who looked uninterested or just looked like they didn't care. Would you want one of them working for *you?* Generally, neither do most employers.

What does your body language illustrate? Does it show that you are confident? That you are happy to be where you are? Do you make eye contact when you're speaking to someone? Are you smiling? What about your demeanor? Common courtesy is mandatory in your life and your career. Polite expressions such as "please," "thank you," "excuse me," and "pardon me" will not go unnoticed.

Your personality traits are another part of your package. No one wants to be around a whiner, a sad sack, or people who complain constantly. You want to illustrate that you are calm, happy, well balanced, and have a positive attitude. This is especially important in the health care industry.

You want to show that you can deal effectively with others, are a team player, and can deal with problems and stress effectively. You might be surprised to know that in many cases employers will lean toward hiring someone with a bubbly positive and energetic personality over one with better skills who seems negative and less well balanced. And that's not only on the business end of the industry; it's in all segments of the industry.

Last but not least in your package are your skills and talents. These are the things that make *you* special. What's the difference between skills and talents?

Skills can be learned or acquired. Talents are things that you are born with and can be embellished. Your personal package includes both.

What you must do is package the product so the buyer wants it. In this case, as we have discussed, the product is you and the buyer might be a potential employer, recruiter, head hunter, patient, and so on. Now you know what goes into your package, and you're going to work on putting together your best possible package. What's next?

Marketing Yourself like a Pro to Make Yourself Visible

How can you market yourself? If you're like many people, you might be embarrassed to promote yourself, embarrassed to talk about your accomplishments, and embarrassed to bring them to the attention of others. This feeling probably comes from childhood when you were taught "it wasn't nice to brag."

It's time to change your thinking. It's time to toot your own horn! Done correctly, you won't be bragging. Done correctly, you are simply taking a step to make yourself visible. Want to know the payoff? You can move your career in a positive direction quicker. Career success can be yours, but you need to work at it.

Visibility is important in every aspect of business, and the health care industry is no exception. Whether you want to make it in the business or administration segment of the industry, in medicine or allied health, in the retail or wholesale area, education, health and wellness, or in any of the other segments of the health care industry, visibility can help you attain your goals. What can visibility do for you?

To start with, it can help set you apart from others who might have similar skills and talents.

How can you make yourself visible?

◎ Tell people what you are doing.
◎ Tell people what you are *trying* to do.

Tip from the Coach

Be positive about yourself and don't be self-deprecating, even in a joking manner. The truth is, when you're self-deprecating, you will start believing, it and so will the people with whom you are speaking.

Words from the Wise

If you are currently employed, make sure you check out any press releases or articles you want to send out regarding your company or company operation with management *prior* to mailing. For example, if you are working as a emergency room nurse in a hospital, you might want to give your supervisor the courtesy of letting them know you are going to be writing an article on emergency room procedures.

On the other hand, if you are sending out a press release on your expertise as a gourmet chef and just stating in that release you are an emergency room nurse, it probably isn't necessary.

◎ Share your dreams.
◎ Live your dreams.
◎ Send out press releases.
◎ Toot your own horn.
◎ Make it happen.

When you make yourself visible, you will gain visibility in the workplace, the community, the media, and more. This is essential to get what you want and what you deserve in your career, whether it's the brand new job you want in health care or a promotion pushing you up the career ladder.

We will discuss how you can you tell people what you're doing without bragging later, but first let's discuss when it's appropriate to toot your own horn. Here are some situations:

◎ when you get a new job
◎ when you get a promotion
◎ when you get a good review
◎ when you are giving a speech
◎ when you are giving a presentation

◎ when you are going to be (or have already appeared) on television or radio
◎ when you have a major accomplishment
◎ when you receive an honor or an award
◎ when you chair an event
◎ when you graduate from school, college, or a training program
◎ when you obtain professional certification
◎ when you work with a not-for-profit or charity organization on a project (as a volunteer)

And the list goes on. The idea isn't only to make people aware of your accomplishments, but to make yourself visible in a positive manner. These are the reasons you would toot your own horn, but how do you do it? Well, you could shout your news from a rooftop or walk around with a sign, but that probably wouldn't be very effective.

One of the best ways to get the most bang for your buck is by utilizing the media.

"I don't have money for an ad," you say. Well, here's the good news. You don't have to take out an ad. You can use publicity. Newspapers, magazines, and periodicals *need* stories to fill their pages. Similarly, television and radio need to fill airspace as well. If you do it right, your story can be one of the ones filling that space and it will cost you next to nothing.

Tip from the Top

A press release is not an ad. Ads cost money. There is no charge to send press releases to the media. Press releases are used by the media to develop stories or are edited slightly or published as is.

The Inside Scoop

Press releases and news releases are the same thing. The phrases are used interchangeably.

How do you get your news to the media? The easiest way is by sending out press or news releases.

There are also many books, classes, seminars, and workshops that can help you learn how to develop and write effective press releases.

To get you started, you should know that news releases are composed of answering the five Ws. These are:

◎ Who
  ▫ Who are you writing about?
◎ What
  ▫ What is happening or has happened?
◎ When
  ▫ When did it happen or is it happening?
◎ Where
  ▫ Where is it happening or has it happened?
◎ Why
  ▫ Why is it happening or why is it noteworthy or relevant?

While it would be nice for everyone to have their own personal press agent or publicist this is not generally the case. Until you have one, you are going to have to be your own publicist. To market yourself, you'll have to find opportunities to issue press releases, develop them, and then send them out. You want your name to be visible in a positive manner as often as possible.

Let's look at a possible scenario. Let's say Mike Poole is an assistant director of marketing at a hospital. The hospital is one of three in a 45-mile radius. The hospitals are all vying for the same patients.

Poole was watching television one night when he heard a story that noted that many of the students in the local high school had poor written communication skills.

He knew how important written communications skills were. He thought about that story for a bit, decided to do something about it, and came up with a plan of action.

Poole first talked to his supervisor, the director of marketing, and then the hospital CEO. After getting the go ahead he spoke to the editor of one of the local newspapers about the possibility of the paper and the school partnering with the hospital. His idea was to give students who wanted to participate a chance to learn how to write better. He developed a pilot program where he would give weekly workshops to interested students on various aspects of writing. To make the program interesting, Poole suggested bringing the participants to the hospital and giving them the opportunity to interview some of the administrators, physicians, nurses, and lab personnel and then report about their experiences in a special section in the paper.

Poole's administrator loved the idea as did the newspaper. Together they brought it to the school. Poole became the coordinator of the project, which resulted in feature stories in not only the newspaper but also other media both in the immediate area and outlying areas. He also spoke to a number of the civic groups in the area about the program and how important it was to learn good communications skills.

In this scenario, Poole was gaining visibility in a number ways. Not only would the CEO

Tip from the Coach

Contacts are an important part of your career. Once you make them, don't risk losing your relationships. Stay in contact by periodically sending e-mails, cards, and letters and making period calls and arranging to meet for lunch, coffee, or just to get together and talk.

---

see him in a different light, but he would be gaining visibility in the community from people who might not have not known him, including the CEO's of the other area health care facilities. Additionally Poole was making important contacts with the media. Because he was dealing with them on a different level than that of a traditional hospital marketing professional, he would also stand out in a positive manner from the other marketing people they dealt with on a daily basis.

Think it can't happen this way? Well, it can! While you might not live this exact scenario, you can potentially create your own scenario with a similar outcome if you are creative and think outside of the box.

Whatever career area you aspire to, from medicine to allied health to business or administration to education to sales; get creative; use your imagination and come up with your own scenario.

Here's an example of a press release that Mike or the paper might send out to further market the project. Note that in marketing the project, the press release is also helping market Mike Poole.

What does this press release do? In addition to publicizing Pool's radio appearance, it gets his name in the news. It gets his message out. It

NEWS FROM THE *TIMES NEWS*

P.O. Box 222
Some City, NY 11111
Media: For additional information, contact:
Mike Poole, 333-333-3333
For Immediate Release:

Write-Right Program Coordinator on Life Lessons

Mike Poole of Some City, New York, will be a guest on WCTE's popular talk show, *New Ideas on Tuesday,* October 18 at 8:00 p.m. He will be discussing a pilot program he is coordinating called Write-Right involving helping high school students improve their written communications skills.

Poole, the assistant director of marketing at Community Hospital in Some City heard a report noting that over 60 percent of the student population at Some City High had less than minimum written communication skills. What that meant was they couldn't write an essay, they couldn't write a report, and they could barely write a letter.

Poole, a graduate of State University with a double major in health care administration and marketing has been working at Community Hospital for three years. Poole was recently promoted to his current position after beginning his career at the hospital first as a publication coordinator and then moving into the marketing department.

"If you think about it, writing skills are important in every job. When I heard the statistics on how many kids had less than average skills, I had to do something. We came up with this unique idea because it not only helps the young people improve their skills, it helps them learn more about the career opportunities in the health care industry."

Knowing how important written communications skills are in his life, when Poole heard the report, he knew he wanted to do something. Before long, he had developed a plan of action, spoken to his supervisor, Thomas Ewing, the hospital's director of marketing, and William Smith, Community Hospital's CEO. Once he got the go ahead, he went to *Times News* publisher Susan Wynan and the Some City School with the pilot program.

Poole and a number of other members of the Community Hospital's marketing and public relations team give weekly workshops to interested students on various aspects of writing. Participants take part in writing exercises and then have their work critiqued.

Poole has arranged to have participants visit the hospital and meet employees, giving each student the opportunity to interview administrators, physicians, nursing staff, laboratory personnel, dieticians, pharmacists, and more. They will then write articles about the experience in a special section in the paper.

Over 100 students have already signed up to participate in the new Write-Right program, which is being held after school hours as an extracurricular activity.

"I'm excited to see such a positive reaction to the program," noted Poole. "I can't wait to see how it progresses."

The Inside Scoop

Always be ready for the media. Keep stock paragraphs on your computer so you can turn out press releases quickly when needed. As a matter of fact, you might want to keep stock press releases and bios on hand so you're always ready when the media calls.

Words from the Wise

Remember that just because you send a press release doesn't mean it will get into the publication. Small local publications are likely to eventually use your press releases. Larger publications are more discriminatory. Do not call up media and insist that they use your release. This will make you look like an amateur and they will probably ignore your releases from that day forward.

exposes his career accomplishments, and helps keep him in the pubic eye in a positive way. By Poole using this avenue to market himself, he his putting himself in a different light from those who are not doing so.

"Well, that's a nice story," I can hear you saying. "But in the real world, does that kind of thing happen?"

You might not hear about it all the time, but those situations do happen and they can happen to you. The key here is that in order for them to occur, as we just mentioned, you have to think out of the box.

Make sure your press releases look professional by printing them on press or news release stationery. This can easily be created on your computer. Have the words "News" or "News From" or something to that effect someplace on the stationery so the media is aware it is a press release. Also make sure to include your contact information. This is essential in case the media wants to call to ask questions about your release. In many instances, the media just

uses the press release as a beginning for an article. Once you pique their interest, they use the press release as background and write their own story.

You've developed a press release. Now what? Whether it's about getting a promotion, being

Words from a Pro

Many of the stories you read in newspapers and magazines or hear on the radio or television are the direct result of press releases. Don't make the mistake of not sending out press releases because you *think* the media won't be interested.

Call up each media outlet and ask whom press releases should be directed to. Sometimes it may just be "News Editor," "Health Editor," or "Business Editor." Sometimes it will be a specific person. Get their contact information. Put together a database consisting of the name of the publication or station, contact name or names, address, phone and fax numbers, e-mail, and any other pertinent information. You might for example, find out the publication's deadline. The deadline is the day you need to get the information to the publication so that your news can be considered for the next issue.

Voice of Experience

It's difficult to proofread your own press releases to catch errors. Always have someone else read them not only for errors but to ensure that your releases make sense.

> ## ⭐ Tip from the Top
>
> If you're e-mailing press releases, find out what format they accept *ahead* of time. If you're sending out printed press releases, you might also call to find out what font is preferred. Many smaller publications just scan your release in and certain fonts scan better.

named employee of the month or anything else, developing and writing a great press release is just the first step. Once that's done, you have to get the releases to the media.

How do you do this? You have a few options. You can print the press releases and then send or fax them to the media or you can e-mail them. Either way it's essential to put together a media list so you can reach the correct people. Look around your area. Get the names of your local media. Then find regional media. If your stories warrant it, national or trade media should also be included. Don't forget any Web or online publications.

Becoming an Expert

Want another idea to make yourself visible? Become an expert. You probably already are an expert in one or more areas either in or out of your area of the health care industry. Now it's time for you to exploit it.

Many people are used to the things they know well. They don't give enough credence to being great at them. It's time to forget that type of thinking!

One of the wonderful things about being an expert in any given area is that people will seek you out. Everyone knows how to do something better than others. What you have to do is figure out what it is.

"Okay," you say. "You're right. Let's say I'm a gourmet chef. But what does that have to do with health care?"

Well, it might have nothing to do with health care on the surface. However, if it can help you gain some positive attention and visibility, it will give you another avenue to get your story out. This will help you achieve the career success you desire. So with that in mind, it has everything to do with it.

Let's begin by determining where your expertise is. Sit down with a piece of paper and spend some time thinking about what you can do better than anyone else in or out of the health care industry. What subject or area do you know more about than most? Do you volunteer in an interesting area? Are you a gourmet chef? Can you teach almost anyone how to pitch a ball? Can you teach senior citizens how to use a computer? Can you spell words backwards?

Need some help? Can't think of what you're expertise is? Here are some ideas to get you started.

- ◎ Are you a gourmet cook?
- ◎ Do you bake the best brownies?
- ◎ Are you a sports trivia expert?
- ◎ Are you a master gardener?
- ◎ Do you design jewelry?
- ◎ Can you speak more than one language fluently?
- ◎ Do you love to shop?
- ◎ Do you know how to coordinate just the right outfit?
- ◎ Do you know how to write great songs?
- ◎ Can you put together events with ease?
- ◎ Do you know how to write great press releases?
- ◎ Do you know how to pack a suitcase better than most people?

- Are you an expert organizer?
- Do you know how to arrange flowers?
- Are you an expert in building things?
- Are you a great fund-raiser?
- Have you set a world record doing something?
- Do you volunteer teaching people to read?
- Do you know about helping children with special needs?
- Do you volunteer reading books for the blind?
- Do you have special skills or talents that others don't?

Are you getting the idea? You can be an expert in almost any area. It's the way in which you exploit it that can make a difference in your career.

You want to get your name out there. You want to draw positive attention to yourself. You want others to know what you can do. That way you can market yourself in the areas in which you are interested.

Find ways to get your name and your story out there. How? Developing and sending out press releases is one way, but what else can you do?

You can become known for your expertise by talking about it. How? Most areas have civic or other not-for-profit groups that hold meetings. These groups often look for people to speak at their meetings. You can contact the president of the board or the executive director to find out who sets up the meeting speakers. In some areas, the chamber of commerce also puts together speaker lists.

You might be asking yourself, "Unless I'm a rocket scientist, why would any group want to hear me speak about anything? What would anyone want to know about me knowing how to pack a suitcase?" or "Why would anyone be interested in my organizing ability?"

Here's the answer: They might not, *unless* you tailor your presentations to their needs. If you create a presentation from which others can learn something useful or interesting, they usually will. For example, if you're speaking to a group of business people, you might do a presentation about "The Stress Free Bag…Packing Easily For Business Trips," "Organizing your Career… Organize Your Life," "Helping Children Feel Good About Themselves Through Sports," or "Using Cooking to Build Teamwork." Depending on your audience, you might do presentations on "Using Complimentary Medicine," "How to Choose a Physician," "How to Be a Better Patient," and so on. Whatever your subject matter is when you speak in front of a group, whether it be 20 or 2,000 people, you will gain visibility.

When you are introduced, the master of ceremonies or emcee of the event will often mention information about your background to the audience. Make sure you always have a short paragraph or two with you to make it easy for the emcee to present the information *you* want to convey.

For example, based on information you provide, the emcee might introduce you like this: "Good evening ladies and gentlemen. Our dinner speaker today is Andrea Clark. Some of you might know her from her weekly columns on health and wellness in the *Times Standard*. Others of you might have met her at one of Green Hospital's health fairs where she is the health and wellness coordinator. Tonight, she will be here talking to you about how being more organized can help make you healthier and help cut your stress levels. Andrea will be speaking about how you can make your life easier by organizing things. Please join me in welcoming Andrea Clark."

As you can see, Andrea is getting exposure, which can help her get visibility as the health and wellness coordinator at the hospital in which she works. Someone at the luncheon may enjoy her presentation and know someone who is looking for a full-time position as a health reporter. Someone from a more prestigious facility may be looking for a health and wellness coordinator or even director of a health and wellness program. One way or another, Andrea is getting noticed.

Here's another example of how an emcee might introduce a guest.

"Good evening folks. Our dinner speaker is Bernard James. Bernard just graduated from State University in May with a communications degree and, I'm glad to say, decided to come back to the area. Tonight, he'll be speaking about how to motivate volunteers.

Many of you might remember Bernard from last summer when he was the chairperson of Green Regional Hospital's Golf Tournament and auction where he helped raise over $200,000. Let's give a warm welcome to Bernard James."

As you can see, Bernard is getting exposure, which will be an asset to his career. People at his presentation are aware that he can take charge of an event, coordinate it and successfully bring it to fruition. In many cases, his appearance in front of the group may also be covered by the media.

Why is all this important? It gives Bernard exposure. It helps him network, and if the presentation is covered by the media, even if it is just a mention, Bernard has something to use in his career portfolio. Not only that, one of the people in the audience or reading about the presentation might know of just the opening Bernard might fill. The important thing to remember is to use every opportunity as an opportunity.

On a local level, you will generally get no fee for most of these types of presentations. The benefit of increased visibility, however, will usually be well worth it. When you are scheduled to do a presentation, make sure you send out press releases announcing your speech. If it was a noteworthy event, you might also send out a release after the event as well. Many organizations will also call the media to promote the occasion. Sometimes the media will call you for an interview before the event. Take advantage of every opportunity.

It's exciting once you start getting publicity. Take advantage of this too. Keep clippings of all the stories from the print media. Make copies. If you have appeared or have been interviewed on television or radio, get clips. Keep these for your portfolio. Every amount of positive exposure will help set you apart from others and help you market yourself to career success.

I can almost hear some of you saying, "Oh, no! I'm not getting up to speak in public."

Here's the deal. If you don't feel comfortable speaking in public, you don't have to. These ideas are meant to be a springboard to get you thinking outside of the box. Use any of them to get you started and then find ways you *are* comfortable in marketing yourself.

★ Words from a Pro

The media works on very tight deadlines. If they call you, get back to them immediately or you might lose out.

> ### ⭐ Tip from the Coach
>
> If you aren't comfortable speaking in front of large groups, consider joining Toastmasters or the Dale Carnegie Institute. Both will help you gain experience in a nurturing and safe environment.

More Strategies to Market and Promote Yourself

If you aren't comfortable speaking in public, how about writing an article on your area of expertise instead?

What about writing articles or columns on a given subject? The idea once again is to keep your name in the public's eye in a positive manner. While it's helpful to write about something in your career area, it is not essential.

For example, you might write an article on what life is like as a new doctor or a day in the life of a nurse. You might write an article on collecting quilts or cookbooks. You might write articles on organizing your office, your schedule or your life. You might write an article on stress management or laughter or humor. If you can tailor the articles in some manner to your career area, all the better. If not, that's okay as well.

If you look at similar types of articles or stories in newspapers, you will notice that if the article is not written by a staff reporter, after the article there generally is a line or two about the author. For example, "Jane Larkin is a physical therapist at Summers Memorial Hospital."

How do you get your articles in print? Call the editor of the publication you are interested in writing for and ask! Tell them what you want to do, and offer to send your background sheet, resume, or bio and a sample. Small or local publications might not pay very much if at all. Don't get hung up on money. You are not doing this for cash. You are doing it to get your name and your story before the public.

Don't forget to tell media editors about your expertise. You can call them or send a short note. Ask that they put you on their list of experts for your specific area of expertise. Then when they are doing a story on something that relates to your subject area, it will be easy to get in touch with you.

Remember that if you don't make the call or write the note, no one will know what you have to offer. You have to sometimes be assertive (in a nice way) to get things moving.

If you are a good writer, enjoy writing, are already working in some area of health care, and want to move up the career ladder, think about offering to put together a periodical column for your company's newsletter.

If they don't have one, offer to put one together. Why? It will bring you visibility. You will have opportunities to meet and converse with higher-ups that you might not otherwise speak with.

Consider teaching a class, giving a workshop, or facilitating a seminar in your area of expertise. Everyone wants to learn how to do something new and you might be just the person to give them that chance. Every opportunity for you is an opportunity to become visible and move your career forward. Can you give someone the basics of writing a press release or doing publicity? Offer to teach a class at a local college or school. Can you easily explain how to understand what you see when watching a game on television? Offer to teach a workshop? Do you think you can illustrate the basics of putting together a fund-raiser? Suggest a workshop! What a great way to get your name out!

⭐ **The Inside Scoop**

Don't get caught up in the theory that if you help someone do something or learn how to do something, it will in some way take away opportunities from you. Help others when you can.

There are a plethora of possibilities. You just need to use your imagination.

What can your expertise do for you? It will get your name out there. It will give you credibility and it will give you visibility. Of course, when you're at meetings or speaking to the media, it's up to you to network. Tell people what you do. Tell people what you want to do. Give out cards. This technique works effectively no matter what area of the health care industry in which you want to succeed. As a matter of fact, this technique can help you succeed in any venture.

Join professional associations and volunteer to be on committees or to chair events that they sponsor. Similarly, join civic groups and not-for-profit organizations volunteering to work on one or two of their projects.

"I don't have time," you say.

Make time. Volunteering, especially when you chair a committee or work on a project is one of the best ways to get your name out there, obtain visibility, and network.

The radio and television talk show circuit is yet another means to generate important visibility. Offer to be a guest on radio, cable, and television station news, variety, and information shows.

"Who would want me?" you ask.

You can never tell. If you don't ask, no one will even know you exist in many instances. Check out the programming to see where you might fit. Then send your bio, resume or CV with a letter to the producer indicating that you're available to speak in a specific subject area. Pitch an idea. A producer just might take you up on it.

Here's a sample pitch letter to get you started.

Lisa Nester-Producer
WGAT Radio
Talk Tonight Show
P.O. Box 3333
Anytown, NY 44444

Dear Ms Nester:

How many of your listeners are looking for a career? How many are looking for something to do where they can make a difference? I'm betting there are many!

As far back as I can remember, I have wanted to work in the health care industry. I wanted to make a difference. I know that it is a dream many have. I got lucky. My dream is coming true.

Five years ago, I graduated from college and became a registered nurse. While I've worked in a number of different areas within the hospital, I now work in the emergency room and find the challenges very rewarding.

Unfortunately, all too often, in the past few years, I've been seeing young people come in to the ER in critical condition because they have been driving while under the influence of alcohol or drugs. Some make it...others do not.

It is now my mission to help educate young people on the seriousness of these actions.

I would love to share some of my stories with your listeners. I regularly listen to your program and believe that the subject matter fits well into your show's format.

I have included my background sheet for your review. Please let me know if you require additional information.

I look forward to hearing from you.

Sincerely,
Gina Hastings

Wait a week or so after sending the letter. If you don't hear back, call the producer and ask if he or she is interested. If there is no interest, say thank you, and request that your background sheet be kept on file.

Remember that people talk to each other, so every person you speak in front of, who reads an article about you, who hears you on radio, or sees you on television has the potential of speaking to other people who might then speak to others.

As we've discussed, networking is one of the best ways to get a job, get a promotion and advance your career. Even if your expertise is in something totally unrelated to the health care industry, just getting your name out, can help boost your career.

If your expertise happens to be something related to the health care industry, that's even better. What might that be? That depends which part of the health care industry you are pursuing. You might have expertise in alternative health. You might be an expert in cosmetic dentistry. You might be an expert in fitness or nutrition.

You might be an expert in ways to deal with the emotions of cancer. You might have expertise in applying make-up or styling wigs for cancer patients. You might be an expert in dealing with sibling rivalry. Or you might have expertise in geriatrics. The possibilities are endless.

What else? You might be an expert in dealing with volunteers or handling publicity for not-for-profits. Whatever your expertise, exploit it and it will help your career move forward.

More Ways to Market Yourself

Here's another idea that can get you noticed: a feature story in a newspaper or magazine. How do you get one of these? Well, everyone wants a story about them or their product or service so you have to develop an angle to catch their attention. Then contact a few editors and see if you can get one of them to bite. Before you call anyone, however, think out your strategy. What is your angle? Why are *you* the person someone should talk to or do a story on? Why would the story be interesting or unique or entertaining to the reader?

How do you develop an angle? Come up with something unique that you do or are planning to do. What is the unique part of your package? Were you the one that was so afraid to speak in high school that you skipped the class where you had to give a report…yet today you are the spokesperson for a large pharmaceutical company? Were you the one who succeeded despite severe adversity? Do you have a human-interest story?

Send a letter with your idea and a background sheet, bio, CV, or resume. Wait a week and then call the editor you sent your information to. Ask if he or she received your information. (There is always a chance it is lost, if only on the reporter's desk.) If the answer is no, offer to send it again and start the process one more time. Sometimes you get lucky. Your angle might be just what an editor was looking for or he might need to fill in space with a story.

★ Tip from the Top

Many people lose out because they just don't follow up. They either feel like a nuisance or feel like they are being a pain. No matter how awkward and uncomfortable you feel, call and follow up on things you are working on. Be polite, but call to see what's happening.

Opening the Door to New Opportunities

If you keep on doing the same old thing, things might change on their own, but they probably won't. It's important when trying to create a more successful career to find ways to open up the door to new opportunities.

Start to look at events that occur as new opportunities to make other things happen. If you train yourself to think of how you can use opportunities to help you instead of hinder you, things often start looking up.

Do you want to be around negative people who think nothing is going right, people who think they are losers? Probably not. Well neither does anyone else. Market yourself as a winner, even if you are still a *winner in training.*

The old adage "misery loves company" is true. One problem people often have in their career and life is that they hang around other people who are depressed or think that they're not doing well. Remember that negative energy attracts negative results, so here's your choice. You can either stay with the negative energy, help change the negative energy, or move yourself near positive energy. Which choice do you want to make?

Work on developing *new* relationships with positive people. Cultivate new business relationships. When doing that, don't forget cultivating a business relationship with the media. How? Go to events where the media is present. Go to chamber of commerce meetings; not-for-profit organization events; charity functions, entertainment events, sports events, meetings, and other occasions.

Walk up, extend your hand and introduce yourself. Give out your business cards. Engage in conversation. If a reporter writes an interesting story about anything, drop him or her a note saying you enjoyed it. If a newscaster does something special, drop a note telling him or her. The media is just like the rest of us. They appreciate validation.

Don't just be a user. One of the best ways to develop a relationship with the media or anybody else is to be a resource. Help them when you can.

Want to close the door to opportunity? Whine, complain, and be a generally negative person who no one wants to be near. Want the doors of opportunity to fly open? Whatever level you are in, more doors will open if you're pleasant, enthusiastic, and professional.

Dreams can come true. They can either happen to you or happen to someone else. If you want it bad enough and market yourself effectively, you will be the winner.

It's essential in marketing yourself and your career to move out of your comfort zone even if it's just a little bit. Take baby steps if you need to, but learn to move out of your comfort zone. Find new places to go, new people to meet, and new things to do.

Words from the Wise

Many people go to networking events and social occasions where they meet people and make important contacts. They then proceed to "forget" whom they met. It's essential to keep track of business cards, names, people you meet and where you met them. In order to do this, after any event where you make contacts, make it a habit to write notes about whom you met, where you met them, and any other pertinent details. Do it quickly. While you think you can't possibly forget meeting someone important to your career, you would be surprised how easy it is to forget details.

And before you think that marketing will only help your career if you are at a higher level, think again. Marketing can help you at every level of your career no matter what area in the health care industry you are pursuing.

You can be the number one factor in creating your own success. Don't let yourself down! Market yourself and reap the rewards of a great career.

10

SUCCEEDING IN THE WORKPLACE

Learning As You Go

Congratulations. You got the job! Now what? Are you ready to succeed?

"Well," you say. "I guess so."

Did you know that there are things you can do which can help increase your chances of success? Things you can do which can turn your job into the career of your dreams?

"Can't I worry about that later?" you ask.

You don't need to worry about it at all. You need to take action. Lots of people have jobs. You don't just want a job. You want a great career! In order to succeed and move up the career ladder, you sometimes have to do a little extra, do more than is expected of you and put some effort into getting what you want.

No matter how it looks, there are very few overnight successes. Appearances can be very deceiving. While it may seem that some individuals might just appear to get their foot in the door one day and zoom to the top rung of the career ladder the next, it generally doesn't happen like that.

While there are exceptions, more than likely, the people you *think* are overnight successes have been working at it and preparing for their dream career for some time. Many of them were probably in the same position you are now.

What looks like someone who just became an overnight success, is generally a person who had a well thought out plan, did a lot of work, had some talent, a bit of luck and was at the right place at the right time.

Unfortunately, just getting your foot in the door is not enough. It's essential once you get in, to take positive actions to climb the ladder to success. If you don't take those actions, someone else will.

Let's begin by discussing some of those positive actions you might take. Now that you've got the job, what can you do to increase your chances of success and turn your job into the career of your dreams? Lots of people have jobs, but you don't just want a job. You want a great career! In order to move up the career ladder, you have to do more than is expected of you and put some extra effort into getting what you want.

Once you get your foot in the door, you're going to want to take steps to get to the top. You

---

★ Tip from the Coach

While success does sometimes just fly in the window, it always helps to at least open the window.

---

want to create your perfect career. Getting a job is a job in itself. However, just because you've been hired doesn't mean your work is done. It's essential once you get in to learn as you go.

If you look at some of the most successful people, you'll see that they continue the learning process throughout their life. If you want to succeed, you will want to do the same.

Learning is a necessary skill for personal and career growth and advancement. Many people feel that your ability to learn is linked to your success in life. This doesn't necessarily mean going back to school or taking traditional classes although sometimes that's a good idea. In many cases, it means life learning.

What is life learning? It's learning that occurs through life experiences. It's learning that occurs when you talk to people, watch others do things, work, experience things, go places, watch television, listen to the radio, hear others talking, or almost anything else. Every experience you have is a potential learning experience.

Not only that, but almost everyone you talk to can be a teacher. If you're open to that concept, you can usually learn something from almost everyone with whom you come in contact.

"What do you mean?" you ask.

Look for opportunities. Be interested. Everything you learn might not be fascinating, but

---

Tip from the Coach

Don't assume that because someone is under you on the career ladder they know less than you or you are above them. Career progression does not always follow traditional paths. Treat supervisors, colleagues, and subordinates all with the same respect.

---

it might be helpful; maybe not today or tomorrow, but it might be in the future. Sometimes you might learn something related to your career. Sometimes it might not be related at all. Use what you can. File the rest away in your mind until needed.

How do you learn all these things? Observe what people say or do in passing. Sometimes you might see that others have a skill you want to master. Don't be afraid to ask how to do something. Most people are flattered when someone recognizes they're good at something and asks for their help.

Challenge yourself to learn something new everyday. Not only will it help improve your total package, but it will make you feel better about yourself. Whether it's a new word, new skill, new way to do something, or even a new way to deal better with people, continue to learn as you go.

How else can you continue to learn? Take advantage of internships, formal and informal education, training programs, and volunteer opportunities.

Many organizations in and out of the health care industry have formal volunteer programs. If yours does, take advantage of it.

"I'm not working for nothing," you say.

That's right. You're not working for nothing. You're volunteering and the payoff can

---

Voice of Experience

Instead of presuming that a friend, colleague, superior, or subordinate won't show you how to do something, tell you how to do something, or teach you something, just ask. Most people will be more than happy to oblige.

be priceless for many reasons, one of which is knowledge.

What can you learn volunteering? The possibilities are endless. You might learn a new skill or a better way to get along with others. You might learn how to coordinate events, run organizations or publicize programs. You might learn new techniques, different procedures or find methods others use which you might be able to utilize in your career. You might learn almost anything...if you're out there. And as a bonus, if you volunteer effectively, you might obtain some important visibility.

Don't discount books as a learning tool. As the saying goes, reading is fundamental. Are you an administrative assistant in the marketing office of a hospital but yearn to work in fundraising? Look for a book. Read more about it. See if it's a career area you want to pursue. Interested in learning more about doing publicity? Find a book. Need help in improving your correspondence and letter writing skills? Check out some books for ideas.

Do you think you might want to be a nurse? What about a physical therapist? Want to know more? Find a book and read about the careers and their requirements. The more you read, the more you'll know. Books often hold the answers to many of your questions. They give you the opportunity to explore opportunities.

Trade journals offer numerous possibilities as well. They'll keep you up to date on industry

trends in your career area. They will also let you know about industry problems and solutions. What else can you find in the trades? Advertisements for job openings, notices for trade events, and current news. Check out the appendix in the back of the book for more information on trades for the specific area of the industry in which you aspire to succeed.

If you're not prepared to buy a subscription yet, there are some other options you might want to explore. To begin with, you often can locate the trade in which you're interested in your local library. If your library doesn't have the periodical you are looking for, try your local community college or university.

If you are already working in the industry, these trades may also be available in your workplace. For example, hospitals or other health care facilities often subscribe to many of the trades related to health care, physicians, allied health, etc.

National bookstore chains such as Borders or Barnes and Noble may also often carry some of the more popular trade publications. Be sure to check out the online versions of trade publications. While many require subscriptions to access some areas, they still often carry the latest news and job openings in the free section.

How about workshops, seminars, and other courses? In addition to learning new skills, there are a number of added benefits to going to these. First of all, you will have the opportunity to meet other people interested in the same subject area as you. You will also expand your network. If you're attending classes or seminars in physical therapy, for example, you'll be able to network with others interested in that area. If you are attending a seminar in health care marketing, you will have the opportunity to network with others interested in that area. Similarly, if you are attending a seminar in alternative or complimentary care methods, you will be networking with people interested in those areas.

Instructors, facilitators, and even other students in the class are all potential contacts who might be instrumental in your career. Classes, seminars and workshops also help stimulate your creativity.

"But I'm not in a creative type of career," you say. "How creative do I need to be working in health care?"

Well, if you are working in the business or administrative end of the industry, creativity is essential. Even if you have a career in medicine or one of the allied health fields, being able to think creatively or finding ways to think outside of the box is extremely useful.

"But," you say, "I'm busy enough without doing extra work. Is this really necessary? Do I have to take classes?"

No one is going to make you do anything, but you should be aware that they can help take your career to a new level. Classes, workshops and seminars will help give you new ideas and help you to look at things from a different perspective.

Additionally, if your career is in medicine or one of the allied health fields, you will want to take courses to keep up with changes and advances in your industry. In certain areas, you will also be required to take continuing education to remain certified.

Tip from the Top

Be sure to keep up with continuing education you may be required to take to keep any certification or licenses you might have. If you aren't sure what you need, talk to your supervisor or contact the trade association related to your career area.

Whether you are taking workshops, seminars or classes, learning new techniques or honing skills the results will help you in your quest to be the best at what you do. If you continue to navigate your way through formal and informal learning experiences throughout your life and career, you will be rewarded with success and satisfaction.

Workplace Politics

To succeed in your career in the health care industry, it is essential to learn how to deal effectively with some of the challenging situations you'll encounter. Workplace politics are a part of life. And depending what area of the health care industry you are pursuing, the *workplace* can be almost anyplace.

The real trick to dealing with workplace politics is trying to stay out of them. No matter which side you take in an office dispute, you're going to be wrong. You can never tell who the *winner* or *loser* will be, so try to stay neutral and just worry about doing your job. Is this easy? No. But for your own sake, you have to try.

Will keeping out of it work all the time? Probably not, and therein lies the problem. There's an old adage that says the workplace is a jungle. Unfortunately, that's sometimes true.

If you think you're going to encounter politics only in the office, think again. As we just

---

Words from the Wise

In some situations, having additional education or training may help you get a better job, a new promotion, or even higher compensation. It will also open up more opportunities.

mentioned, in the health care industry, the *work-place* can be almost anyplace. It can be in a doctor's office, any part of a hospital or health care facility, a pharmacy, or a lab. It can even be in the community in which you work.

What all this means is that no matter what part of the health care industry you are working in, you often may have additional challenges. In many cases, workplace politics will be expanded to every area of your life, from your personal relationships to your family to work. With this in mind, let's learn more about them.

Why are there are politics in the workplace? Much of it comes from jealousy. Someone might think you have a better chance at a promotion or are better at your job than they are at theirs. Someone might think you slighted them. Believe it or not, someone just might not like you. In any business setting there are people who vie for more recognition, feel the need to prove themselves right all the time, or who just want to get ahead. There really is nothing you can do about workplace politics, except to stay out of them to the best of your ability.

In certain parts of the health care industry, feelings of jealousy sometimes escalate. There are many reasons for this. Someone may feel they are more talented than you in their area of the industry. A physician may feel, for example, that he or she is a more talented surgeon than his colleague.

Often jealousy surfaces when someone doesn't understand why *you* got the job or the promotion and he or she did not. Some may not understand why you are a department head and they can't get a promotion. Others may not understand why you get the prime shifts and they are still on the night shift.

Sometimes people may want to protect themselves from feeling like a failure or may just be frustrated with their career (or lack of it).

Words from the Wise

We've all heard of someone who when others refer to them they say, "You know, he (or she) is such a nice man (or woman). He (or she) never says a bad word about anyone." These people stay out of office politics. They stay out of office squabbles and they stay out of trouble in the workplace. If you can keep this in mind and try to follow their lead, you will be ahead of the game. It may not be easy, but before you decide to speak about someone, remember that office politics and gossip can be problematic.

In these situations, many lash out and talk about others. Real or not, these words can hurt. Worse than that, your words can come back to haunt you…big time.

Office Gossip

Gossip is a common form of office politics. Anyone who has held a job has probably seen it, and perhaps even participated in it in some form. Have you? Forget the moral or ethical issues. Gossip can hurt your career.

Here's a good rule of thumb. Never, ever say anything about anyone that you wouldn't mind them hearing and knowing it came from you. If you think you can believe someone who says, "Oh, you can tell me, it's confidential," you're wrong.

"But she's my best friend," you say. "I trust her with my life."

It doesn't matter. Your friend might be perfectly trustworthy, but trust is not always the problem. Sometimes people slip and repeat things during a conversation. Other times, a person might tell someone else whom they trust what you said and ask him or her to keep it confidential, but then that person tells another person and so it goes down the line. Eventually, the person telling the story doesn't even know it's supposed to be confidential and might even mention it to a good friend or colleague of the person everyone has been gossiping about.

The reason people gossip is because it makes them feel like part of a group. It can make you feel like you're smarter or know something other people don't. Most of the time, however, you don't even know if what you're gossiping about is true, yet once a gossip session get started, it's difficult to stop.

Most people are good at heart. After gossiping about someone else, they often feel badly. It might just be a twinge of conscience, but it's there. Is it worth it? No. Worse than that, it's safe to assume that if you are gossiping about others, they are gossiping about you.

How do you rise above this? Keep your distance. People generally respect that you don't want to be involved. Don't start any gossip, and if someone starts gossiping around you, just don't get involved.

How do you handle the conversation?

Suppose someone says to you, "Did you hear that the Dr. Hughes got so drunk, that he fell over at the party?"

You respond, "No. Have you tasted that great new flavored coffee at the coffee shop?"

They might want to keep the conversation going and say, "Yeah, it's great. You should have seen Dr. Hughes. I don't know how he can show his face around here."

All you have to do is either change the subject again or say, "I made a decision a long time ago, not to get involved in gossip. It can only get me in trouble."

Every now and then, you hear through the grapevine that people are gossiping about you. It's not a good feeling, but you might have to deal with it. What do you do? You have a few options.

- ◎ You can ignore it.
- ◎ You can confront the person or people who are gossiping about you.
- ◎ You can start gossiping about the person or people gossiping about you.

What's your best choice? Well, it's definitely not gossiping about the person who is gossiping about you. Ignoring the gossip might be your best choice, except that suppressing your feelings of betrayal and anger can be stressful. So how about confronting the person or people who are gossiping about you? If you're certain about who has been spreading the gossip and you can do this calmly and professionally, it often resolves the situation.

Whatever you do, don't have a public confrontation and don't confront a group. Instead, wait until the person is alone. Calmly approach him or her and say something like this: "Jim, I didn't want to bring this up in front of anyone else because I didn't want to embarrass you, but I've heard that you've been talking to others in the hospital about the way I'm performing my job and discussing my personal life. I've always had respect for you so I really questioned the people who told me it was happening. I'd just like to know if it's true."

At this point, Jim probably will be embarrassed and claim that he doesn't know what you're talking about. He might ask you who mentioned it. Don't give out any names. It's better to let him start questioning the trust of all the people he's been talking to. While he might tell a couple of people you confronted him on the gossip subject, Jim will probably find someone else to gossip about in the future and keep you out of it.

In certain parts of the health care industry, gossip may often lead to bigger problems. Depending on your work environment, you might be privy to private stories about other medical personnel or patients. You might for example, hear that a nurse got drunk and missed her shift even though she said she had the flu or you might hear about some personal problems the chief of staff at the hospital is experiencing. You might be privy to contract negotiations of a staff member, know someone is being hired or someone is being terminated.

You might know some details about a patient that, if they got out, might be potentially embarrassing.

Here's the deal. Office gossip is bad enough, but gossip may get back to patients or even to the media and can get totally blown out of proportion. Gossiping about what happens in the office, (hospital, medical office, lab, etc.) about what you hear, or what you know (even if it is true) can ruin your career, especially if it leads to embarrassment for powerful people.

It is also essential to remember that no matter what portion of the health care industry you are working, information regarding patients is expected to be confidential. There are no ifs, ands or buts about it.

Talking about patients, gossiping about them or sharing information in any way is not only wrong, in many cases it is against the law. With new HIPPA (Health Insurance Portability and Accountability Act) guidelines and privacy rules, information cannot be given out to anyone other than the patient without his or her express written permission. Gossiping about patient's medical conditions can be very serious.

"But I wasn't talking about a patient's medical condition," you say. "I was simply discussing how difficult they were being."

The patient might have been worried about their illness or how their family was going to

Words from a Pro

Do you like to be around negative people? Probably not. Well, neither does anyone else.

We all have bad days when we complain and whine that nothing is going right. The problem comes when it occurs constantly. If you want to succeed in your career, try to limit the negativity, at least around your colleagues. While they say misery loves company, in reality after a while people won't want to be around you. Eventually, they'll start to avoid you.

On the other hand, most people like to be around positive people who make them smile and laugh. If you can do this, you'll have an edge over others.

deal with it or how to pay for the services they were receiving. There might have been any number of reasons a patient might have been difficult. While compassion and empathy are good traits to have in any industry, they are especially important in health care. Additionally, let's go back to our original rule of thumb. You will find it easier to succeed in your career if you never, ever say anything about anyone that you wouldn't mind them hearing and knowing it came from you.

It's essential to your success in the industry not to spread rumors in the hospital, office, etc. or out. Don't talk about the inside information you have whether it's good or bad. Don't be surprised if friends and family pump you for information. It's human nature to want to hear about things other people know. Learn to simply say, "Sorry, that's confidential."

Money, Money, Money

How upset would you be if you found out that a coworker who had a job similar to yours was making more money than you? Probably pretty upset. How distressed would you be if you knew another individual with the same education, skills, and talents as you was making more money than you?

Whether it's what you're earning, your coworker is making, or someone else is making, money is often a problem in the workplace. Why? Because everyone wants to earn more. No matter how much money people are paid, in most situations, they don't think they are getting enough.

Here's the deal. If you know you're making more than someone else, keep it to yourself. If you're making less than someone else, keep it to yourself. No matter what your earnings are, keep it to yourself.

Don't discuss your earnings with coworkers, other physicians, administrators, nurses, or anyone else. The only people in the workplace you should discuss your earnings with are the human resources department or your supervisor.

Why would one person be earning more than another in a similar position? There might be a number of reasons. Compensation for many positions is negotiated, and the person might be a better negotiator. He or she might have more experience, more education, other credentials, seniority, or different skills.

In certain situations, the individual or his or her specialty might be more sought out than others. Certain physicians may, for example, specialize in an area of medicine that health care facilities or medical groups have a desperate need for. This need may result in the ability of that physician to command higher compensation than other physicians working in the same facility.

"But it's frustrating," you say.

Tip from the Coach

It's very easy to start comparing your earnings with those of others who are making more and start feeling sorry for yourself. Try not to compare yourself, your job or your earnings to anyone else. Instead of concentrating on what "they're making," try to concentrate on how you can get "there."

I understand, but being frustrated won't help. Worry about your own job. Don't waste time comparing yourself to your coworkers, colleagues, or others in a position you consider similar. Definitely, don't whine about it in your workplace. It will get on people's nerves.

What can you do? Make sure you are visible in a positive way. Make sure you're doing a great job. If you're already doing a great job, try to do a better job. Keep notes on projects you've successfully completed, ideas you've suggested which are being used and things you are doing to make the company better. Then, when it's time for a job review, you'll have the ammunition to not only ask for, but get the compensation you deserve.

Dealing with Colleagues

Whatever area of the health care industry you choose to work, you're going to be dealing with others. Whether they are superiors, subordinates, or colleagues, the way you deal with people you work with will affect your opportunities, your chances of success, and your future.

Many people treat colleagues and superiors well yet treat subordinates with less respect. One of the interesting things about the health care industry, like other industries is that career progression doesn't always follow a normal pattern. What that means is that with the right set of circumstances someone might jump a number of rungs up the career ladder quicker than expected. The result could be someone who is a subordinate might technically become either a colleague or even a superior. It's essential to treat everyone with whom you come in contact, with dignity and respect. Aside from being common courtesy, you can never tell when the person making you coffee today will be making a decision about your future tomorrow.

Want to know a secret about dealing effectively with people? If you can sincerely make every person you come in contact with feel special, you will have it made. How do you do this? There are a number of ways.

When someone does or says something intelligent or comes up with a good idea, mention it to them. For example, "That was a great idea you had at the meeting, Katrina. You always come up with interesting ways to solve problems."

Sometimes you might want to send a short note instead. For example,

> Mark,
>
> While I'm sure you're ecstatic that the press conference is over, I hope you know how impressed everyone was with the event. You handled the coordination like a seasoned pro. No one would ever have guessed that this was the first time you ever put a press conference together.
>
> Everything was perfect. But the real coup was getting the story about the hospital's new pediatric wing on every major television station in the area. You did a great job. I'm glad we're on the same team.
>
> Evan

If another employee does something noteworthy, write a note. If a colleague receives an award or an honor, write a note. It doesn't make

you any less talented or skilled and your words can not only make someone else's day but help you build a good relationship with a colleague.

Everyone likes a cheerleader. At home, you hopefully have your family. In your personal life, you have friends. If you can be a cheerleader to others in the workplace, it often helps to excel yourself.

Never be phony and always be sincere. Look for little things that people do or say as well. "That's a great tie, John." "Nice suit, Amy. You always look so put together." "The ER was so busy this morning. We are really lucky to have you coordinating things down there."

Notice that while you're complimenting others, you're not supposed to be self deprecating. You don't want to make yourself look bad, you want others to look good. So, for example, you wouldn't say, "Nice suit, Amy. You always look so put together. I couldn't coordinate a suit and blouse if I tried," or "Great job on the press conference. I never could have coordinated an event like that," or "The ER was so busy this morning. We are really lucky to have you coordinating things down there. If they left the ER solely in my hands, we still would be there."

The idea is to build people up so they feel good about themselves. When you can do that, people like to be around you, they gain self-confidence, and they pass it on to others. One of them might be you. Best of all, you will start to look like a leader. This is a very important

---

⭐ Tip from the Coach

In an attempt to build themselves up, many try to tear others down. Unfortunately, it usually has the opposite effect.

image to be building when you're attempting to move up the career ladder.

Dealing with Your Superiors

While you are ultimately in charge of your career, superiors are the people who can help either move it along or hold it back. Depending on what area of the health care industry in which you are involved, your superior might be a supervisor, boss, a director, department head, physician, pharmacist, and so on. Try to develop a good working relationship with your superiors whoever they are in your career. A good boss can help you succeed in your present job as well as in your future career.

One of the mistakes many people make in the workplace is looking at their bosses as the enemy. They get a mind set of *us* against *them*. Worse than that is they sit around and boss-bash with other colleagues.

Want to better your chances of success at your job? Make your boss look good. How do you do that?

◎ Don't boss-bash.
◎ Speak positively about your boss to others.
◎ Do your work.
◎ Cooperate in the workplace.
◎ If you see something that needs to be done, offer to do it.
◎ Volunteer to help with projects which aren't done.
◎ Ask if he or she needs help.

"But what if my boss is a jerk?" you ask. It's still in your best interest to make him or her look good. Believe it or not, it will make you look good.

While we're on the subject, let's discuss bad bosses. With any luck, your boss will be a great person who loves his or her job. But, every now and then you just might run into a bad boss.

He or she might be a jerk, a fool, an idiot,

"I could do a better job than him or her," you say. Well you might be able to, but not if you can't learn to deal with people so you still have a job. In many cases, your boss has already proven him or herself to the organization and is therefore more of a commodity than you are at this point. So just how do you deal with a bad boss and come out on top?

Let's first go over a list of *don'ts.*

◎ Don't be confrontational. This will usually only infuriate your boss.
◎ Don't shout or curse. Even if you're right, you will look wrong.
◎ Don't talk about your boss to coworkers. You can never tell who is whose best friend or who is telling your boss exactly what you're saying.
◎ Don't send e-mails to people from your office about things your boss does or says.
◎ Don't talk about your boss to clients or patients. It's not good business and it's not really ethical.
◎ Don't—I repeat don't—cry in your workplace. No matter how mad your boss makes you, no matter what mistake you made, no matter what nasty or obnoxious thing someone says about you, keep your composure until you're alone. If you have to, bite your lip, pinch yourself, or do whatever you have to do to keep the tears under control.

Now let's go over a list of *do's* which might help.

◎ Do a good job. It's hard to argue with someone who has done what they are supposed to do.

◎ Be at work when you are scheduled to be there and always be on time.

◎ Attend all scheduled meetings.

◎ Keep a paper trail. Keep notes when your boss asks you to do things and when you've done them. Keep notes regarding calls which have been made, dates, times, and so on. Keep a running list of projects you've completed successfully. Do this as a matter of course. Keep it to yourself. When you need something to jog your memory, you can refer to it.

◎ Wait until there is no time constraint to finish something and there is no emergency and ask your supervisor if you can speak to him or her. Then say you'd like to clear the air. Ask what suggestions he or she can give you to do a better job.

   ▫ You might say, "Robert, I just wanted to clear the air. We're on the same team and if there is something I can be doing to do a better job, just let me know. I'll be glad to try to implement it." Or you might say something like, "Dr. Jones, you didn't seem happy with the way I assisted you during the tooth extraction this morning. Can you give me suggestions how I can make it easier for you during the procedure? I want to make the procedures as easy for you to perform as possible."

◎ Think long and hard before you decide to leave yourself. If your supervisor is as much of a jerk as you think, perhaps he or she will find a new job or be promoted.

★ Words from the Wise

Do not put anything in e-mail that you wouldn't mind someone else reading. No matter what anyone tells you, e-mail is not confidential. Furthermore, be aware that in many situations your e-mails, private or business, may be classified as company property. This means management may have the right to access your e-mail.

No matter what type of boss you have, learning to communicate with him or her is essential. Everyone has a different communicating style and it's up to you to determine what his or hers is.

Does your boss like to communicate through e-mail? Some organizations today communicate almost totally through e-mail. Everything from the daily "Good morning" until "See you tomorrow" and everything in between will be in your inbox. If this is the way it is at your office, get used to it. E-mail will be your communication style. The good thing about it is you pretty much have a record of everything.

Other bosses communicate mainly on paper. He or she may give you direction, tell you what's happening, or ask for things via typed or handwritten notes. Sometimes communications may be in formal memos, other times informal or even on sticky notes.

★ Tip from the Top

Check out your organization's policy on private e-mail and Internet usage. Be aware that in many situations, private e-mails are not allowed, nor is surfing the Web for personal reasons.

Tip from the Top

If you carry a personal cell phone, set it to the vibrate mode while in the office. Getting constant calls from friends in the office, even on your cell phone, is inappropriate. While we're on the subject, never take a call on your personal cell phone during a business meeting.

A great deal of business is also done by phone. Good phone etiquette is essential. Whether you're on a business phone in the office, your cell phone on the road, or your home phone speaking to the office, the phone is a major communications tool. Learn how to use it effectively.

It's important to realize that you have a choice in your career. You can sit there and hope things happen or you can make them happen. You can either be passive or pro-active. To succeed in your career, being pro-active is usually a better choice.

You can go to work and let your supervisor tell you what to do or you can do that little bit extra, share your dreams and aspirations and work towards your goals. No matter what segment of the industry you are pursuing, supervisors can help you make it happen.

Dealing With Patients

If you're dealing with patients, treating people respectfully is extremely important. Let's take a moment to discuss what is commonly known as bedside manner. Exactly what is bedside manner? In regard to the health care industry, bedside manner means the entire way a physician or other medical personnel treat a patient.

It's not uncommon when asking patients what they like about a certain physician to hear that they like that he or she has a good bedside manner. Conversely, when asked what people don't like about physicians, their answer is often that the doctor has no bedside manner.

Someone who has a good bedside manner will be compassionate, empathic, reassuring, and comforting. A good bedside manner uses soft skills including the attitude that the individual has towards his or her patient. It encompasses the individual's tone and body language. A physician with a good bedside manner is not short with patients and knows that they might be frightened, in pain, or not understand exactly what is happening.

What is essential to remember is that whether you're a doctor, nurse, lab tech, therapist or any other individual dealing with patients, a good bedside manner is crucial to your career.

Why? There are a number of reasons, beginning with the fact that a good bedside manner is helpful to patients, making them feel more comfortable. The more comfortable patients feel, the better. Health care professionals with a good bedside manner also have better communications with patients increasing positive interactions on both sides.

It is also important to realize that patients have a choice in health care. They can go to any number of physicians, health care facilities, dentists, therapists, pharmacies, etc. As a result, employers in the health care industry are beginning to be more aware of the satisfaction level of patients and clients. Medical personnel who have a good bedside manner, in essence, are providing good customer service. Employees who provide that service have a better chance at career advancement, both through promotion and better compensation.

In an effort to help medical personnel develop a better bedside manner, many hospitals and health care facilities now are creating programs to help teach these soft skills.

How can you improve your bedside manner? There are a number of ways. Here are a few that might help.

- ◎ Treat patients as you would want to be treated if you were the patient yourself.
- ◎ No matter what the situation, how busy you are, or how overworked you are, be courteous to patients and their families.
- ◎ Ask patients what they would prefer you call them. Do they want you to call them by their first name or would they prefer to be called Mr. Jones, Mrs. Smith, or Miss Ames. While this seems like a small thing, it gives the patient a bit of control in a situation where they might not have any other.
- ◎ Make eye contact when you can.
- ◎ Smile. It will make patients feel more comfortable.
- ◎ Be friendly.
- ◎ Be respectful.
- ◎ Be sensitive.
- ◎ Remember that each patient has feelings.
- ◎ Remember that even though examining a patient may be part of your job, it can feel invasive to him or her. You might, for example, say something like, "I'll be examining you now if that's okay with you."
- ◎ Have good communications. Ask the patient if he or she has any questions and then answer them fully.
- ◎ Listen to the patient. See if there are things he or she may want to ask, but be uncomfortable asking.
- ◎ Try to make the patient feel that you care.

> ⭐ **Words from the Wise**
>
> Studies have suggested that medical personnel who have a good bedside manner and developed a good relationship with their patients are less apt to be sued by those patients.

Ethics, Morals, and More

We all have our own set of ethics and morals. They help guide us on what we think is right and wrong. In your career, you may be faced with situations where a person or group of people wants you to do something you know or feel is wrong. In return for doing it, you may be promised financial gain or career advancement.

Would you do it? "Well," you might say. "That depends on what I'd have to do and what I'd get." Here's the deal. No matter what anyone wants you to do, if you know it's wrong, even if you only think it *might* be wrong, it probably is a bad idea.

"But they told me no one would know," you say. Hmm…most people are not that good at keeping secrets, and if *they* get caught, you're going down too. If you're just getting started in your career, you might be looking at ending it for a few dollars. If you're already into your career, are you really prepared to lose everything you worked that hard to get.

"But they told me if I did this or did that, they'd remember me when promotions came up," you say. How do you know someone isn't testing you to see what your morals are? And exactly what are you planning on doing after you do whatever the person asked you to do and he or she doesn't give you the promotion? Report them? Probably not.

It's important to realize that people move around in this industry. They move from job to job and location to location. It is not unheard of to hear that someone took a job on the other side of town or the other side of the country.

What this means is that while every supervisor you have may not know every other supervisor, there is a chance that some of them may know other people in the industry. With this in mind, do you really want to take a chance doing something stupid? Probably not.

And forget getting caught. Do you want to build a great career on unethical activities? Once again, the answer is probably not.

How do you get out of doing something you don't want to do? You might simply say something like, "My dream was to work in health care. I am not about to mess it up for something like this." Or "I've worked so hard to get where I am now, I really don't want to lose what I have." What about, "No can do. Sorry." How about, "Sorry, I'm not comfortable with that."

But what do you do if a supervisor wants you to do something unethical? How do you handle that? You can try any of the lines above, but if your job is on the line you have a bigger problem to deal with. In cases like this, document as much as you can. Then, if you have no other choice go to human resources, a higher supervisor or someone you think can help.

"What do I do if I see something going on around me," you say? What if I'm not involved but I see a supervisor or coworker stealing or doing something to that effect? Then what? "

This is a tough one as well. No one likes a tattle-tale, but if something major is going on, you have a decision to make.

Do you say something? Bring it to the attention of a higher up? Mention it to the alleged thief or wrong doer? Or just make sure you're not involved and say nothing?

Hopefully at the time, you'll make the right choice. It generally will depend on the position you hold, your responsibilities, and the alleged crime. It's a difficult decision. If you decide to say something, be very sure that you are absolutely, positively positive about your information.

What do I do if I see someone not treating a patient correctly? Or stealing drugs? What then?

In cases like this, you need to make a choice as well. If you think someone is mistreating a patient, it is your responsibility to say something. If you see someone stealing drugs or not giving patients their prescribed medications correctly, you will probably want to say something as well.

Accountability

No one is perfect. We all make mistakes. No matter how careful anyone is, things happen. Accept the fact that sometime in your career you are going to make one too. In many cases, it's not the mistake itself that causes the problem, but the way we deal with it.

The best way to deal with it is to take responsibility, apologize, try to fix it and go on. Be sincere. Simply say something like, "I'm sorry, I made a mistake. I'm going to try to fix it and will make sure it doesn't happen again." With that said, it's very difficult for anyone to argue with you.

If on the other hand you start explaining mitigating circumstances, blame your coworkers, your secretary, your boss, or make excuses, others generally go on the defensive. Similarly, when you're wrong, just admit it and go on. People will respect you, you'll look more professional and you'll have a lot less turmoil in your life.

For example, "I was wrong about the marketing campaign. You were right. Good thing we're a team. "I am so sorry I was late today. I know we had a procedure scheduled. I'll make sure it doesn't happen again. Thanks for covering for me."

Okay, you're taking credit for your mistakes, but what happens if someone else makes a mistake and you're blamed or you're the one who looks like you're unprepared. Let's say for example, you are working in the fund-raising office of a health care facility and find that the name of a major benefactor has inadvertently been spelled wrong on an engraved plaque which is supposed to be presented at a luncheon in forty five minutes. What do you do? Blame the engraver? Blame your assistant? Blame your secretary?

The benefactor probably doesn't care or want to know if you have an incompetent staff. It's not his or her problem. The best thing to do in these types of situations is also to acknowledge the problem, apologize and see what you can do to fix it quickly. "I'm sorry. I should have triple-checked the spelling on your plaque before I brought it to the luncheon. I've already called the engraver to rectify the situation and asked him to make a new plaque. I personally will get you the new plaque with the correct spelling tomorrow. I hope you can forgive me." The result? What could have been a major faux pas is now just a minor inconvenience that no one will probably even remember a few weeks down the line.

In work as in life, many people's first thoughts when there is a problem is to cover themselves. So when things go wrong, most people are so busy reacting or coming up with excuses.

Here's something to remember. The most successful people don't come up with excuses. Instead, when something goes wrong, their first thoughts are how to fix the problem, mitigate

any damages, and get things back to normal. If you can do this, and remain cool in a crisis, it will enhance your position whether you are working in the business, administration, creative, or talent areas of the industry.

Time, Time Management, and Organization

Here's a question for you. What is one thing every person on the planet has the same amount? Do you know what it is?

Here's a hint. I have the same amount you have. Bill Gates has the same amount I have. Oprah Winfrey has the same amount Bill Gates has. William Shakespeare had the same amount Oprah Winfrey does. Do you know what it is yet?

Every person in this world, no matter who they are or what they do, has the same 24 hours a day. You can't get less and you can't get more, no matter what you do. It doesn't matter who you are or what your job is. You don't get more time during the day if you're young, old or in-between. You don't get more time if you're a millionaire or you're making minimum wage. You wouldn't even get more time if you were a Nobel Prize winner who had discovered a cure for cancer.

With all this in mind, it's important to manage your time wisely. That way you can fit more of what you need to fit into your day and get the most important things accomplished.

To start with, let's deal with your workday. Try to get in to work a little earlier than you're expected. It's easier to get the day started when you're not rushing. On occasion, you might also want to stay late. Why? Because when superiors see you bolting at 5 p.m. (or whenever your shift or day ends) it looks like your not really interested in your job.

If your career is in medicine or one of the allied health areas, getting to work a little earlier than needed is a good idea as well. You want to be relaxed before dealing with patients, not stressed because you got stuck in a traffic jam and started worrying that you were going to be late getting to the hospital or your office.

No matter what your career choice, in order to be successful, you will need to learn to prioritize your tasks. How do you know what's important?

If your boss needs it now, it's important. If it's dealing with a life or death situation, it's important. If a patient needs something and you can do it, it's important. If you promised to do something for someone, it's important. If something is happening today or tomorrow and you need to get a project done, it's important. If things absolutely *need* to get done now, they're important.

⭐ The Inside Scoop

The time period before everyone else gets in or after everyone has left the office or workplace is usually less formal and less stressed. This is true even in hospitals or other facilities where people work 24/7. If you make it a habit to come in right before the big brass comes in and leave either when they leave or just afterwards, you will generally become visible in a more positive manner to higher ups. More than that, however, you will often have the opportunity to ask a question, make a comment or offer a suggestion. If someone questions you about what you're doing at work so early, simply say something like, "Preparing for the day ahead," "Getting some project started before it gets busy," or "Finishing up a few things so I can devote tomorrow to new projects."

⭐ Words from the Wise

In prioritizing, don't forget that you must fit in the things you promised others you would do. Don't get so caught up in wanting to be liked or wanting to agree or even wanting to be great at your job, that you promise to do something you really don't have time to get done. Doing so will just put you under pressure.

Generally, what you need to do is determine what is most important and do it first. Then go over your list of things that need to get done and see what takes precedence next.

The more organized you are, the easier it will be for you to manage your time. Make lists of things you need to do. You might want to keep a master list and then a daily list of things you need to do. You might also want a third list of deadlines that need to be met.

It's important to remember that just making lists won't do it. Checking them on a consistent basis to make sure the things that you needed to do actually got done is the key.

Here's an example of the beginnings of a master list. Use it to get you started on yours.

◎ Call Jamie Burns to set up appointment.
◎ Get statistics from lab.
◎ Prepare report for department head meeting Thursday.
◎ Check class schedule for certification program.
◎ Confirm in-service meeting time.
◎ Meet with Jerry Brown, regarding intern program.
◎ Talk to Dr. Gleason regarding board meeting.
◎ Call to confirm next weeks interviews.
◎ Lunch with Sandy R, Monday, 1:00 p.m.

Writing things down is essential to being organized. Don't depend on your memory…or anyone else's. Whatever your job within the health care industry, it is sure to be filled with lot of details, things that need to get done and just plain stuff in general. The more successful you get, the busier you will be and more things you'll have to remember. Don't depend on others reminding you. Depend on yourself.

If you want, you can input information into your blackberry or another device. However, always keep a back-up.

Here's an idea if you want to be really organized. Keep a notebook with you, where you jot things down as they occur. Date each page so you have a reference point for later. Then make notes. Like what?

◎ The dates people called and the gist of the conversation.
◎ The dates you call people and the reason you called.
◎ Notes on meetings you attend. Then when someone says something like, "Gee, I don't remember whether we said May 9 or May 10," you have it.
◎ Names of people you meet.
◎ Things that happened during the day.

After you get used to keeping the notebook, it will become a valuable resource. You might, for example, remember someone calling you six months ago. "What was his name?" you ask yourself. "I wish I knew his name." Just look in your notebook.

"It seems like a lot of trouble," I hear you saying.

It is a little extra effort, but I can almost guarantee you that once you keep a notebook like this for a while, you won't be able to live without it. You won't be looking for little sheets of paper on which you have jotted down important numbers and then misplaced. You won't have to remember people's names, phone numbers, or what they said. You won't have to remember if you were supposed to call at 3:00 or 4:30. You'll have everything at your fingertips.

A Few Other Things

It's important to realize that while of course you want to succeed in your career, everything you do may not be successful. You might not get every job you apply for. You might not get every promotion you want. Every idea you have may not work out. Every project you do may not turn out perfectly. And every job may not be the one you had hoped it would be.

Things take time. Careers take time…especially great careers. None of these situations mean that you are a failure. What they mean simply is that you need to work on them a little bit more.

Be aware that success is often built on the back of little failures. If you ask most successful people about their road to success, many will tell you it wasn't always easy. As we discussed at the beginning of this chapter, no matter what it looks like, most people are not overnight successes.

While some may have it easier, others may have had one or more rejections or failures before they got where they were going. What you'll find, however, is those who are now successful didn't quit. After keeping at it and plugging away, they landed the jobs they aspired to, got the promotions, received good work reviews and got where they are today.

You might not get the promotion you wanted right away. You might not have the job of your dreams yet. That does not mean it won't happen. Keep plugging away and work at it and success will come to you.

Most successful people have a number of key traits in common. They have a willingness to take risks, a determination that cannot be undone, and an amazing amount of confidence in themselves and their ideas.

Can they fail? Sure. But they might also succeed and they usually do. What does this have to do with you? If you learn from the success of others, you can be successful too. If you emulate successful people, you too can be on the road to success.

Don't be so afraid of getting things right that you don't take a chance at doing it a better way; a different way; or a way that might work better. Don't get so comfortable that you're afraid to take a risk. Don't get so comfortable that you don't work toward getting a promotion or accepting a new job or new responsibilities. Be determined that you know what you want and how to get it, and you will.

If you want to succeed in your career and your life, I urge you to be confident and be willing to take a risk. Success can surprise you at any time.

Take advantage of opportunities that present themselves, but don't stop there. Create opportunities for yourself to help launch your career to a new level by using creativity and innovative ideas.

Know that you not only can *have* success in your career but *deserve* success, and if you work hard enough, you can achieve your goals and dreams.

11

SUCCEEDING IN YOUR CAREER AS A PHYSICIAN

We've discussed a myriad of things in this book that can help you in your quest for a great career in health care. We've talked about a variety of jobs and career options. We've discussed making your job into a career. We've discussed ways to get past the gatekeeper, some unique ways to obtain interviews and interviews tips. We've discussed developing resumes, cover letters and putting together action plans. We have talked about job search strategies and tools for success. We've discussed marketing yourself and balancing your career.

You might have picked up this book for many reasons. I'm assuming if you're still reading, you've decided you want to work in some segment of the health care industry. While we've talked about a number of different career areas of health care throughout the book, what I would like to do is take some time to focus first on those who are thinking about a career as a physician and then on those who are already physicians.

If medicine is not your field, you can skip over this chapter if you wish. However, while much of this information is specific to those becoming doctors or those who are already physi-

cians, even if medicine is not your career, you might find some of the information helpful in your career as well.

How Do You Know if a Career in Medicine Is for You?

Have you decided you want to become a physician? Has it been your life's calling for as long as you can remember? Some people know from the time they are quite young that they are going to be doctors when "they grow up." Others made the decision when they were in high school or in college. There are also some who make the decision *after* they are already in another career but realize a career in medicine is really their dream.

Many people make the decision to become a doctor after having an experience (either good or bad) with a doctor themselves. I remember asking a doctor why he chose a career in that field and he told me that he had grown up with a very ill mother and he didn't like the way the doctor treated her. He decided at that point to not only become a physician, but become a compassionate physician who treated people the way he wished his mom had been treated.

★ The Inside Scoop

I recently heard a speech by a physician who told the audience that her dream had been to work in medical research. After a few years of doing that, she realized that her real passion was working directly with patients in patient care and went back to med school to fulfill her goal and dream. Had she stopped and thought, "I already made my decision" instead of going after her dream, she would have not only shortchanged herself, but all the patients whom she helped over the years. It's never too late to go after your dreams.

Another physician told me he had been in an accident and a doctor just happened to see the accident and stopped and helped save his sister's life.

Many people go into medicine because they have a genuine desire to help others. Some have parents or other family members who were doctors and decide to follow in their footsteps. Whatever reason you have to go into medicine, know this. When you go into medicine and choose to become a doctor there is a tremendous commitment and that commitment goes on throughout your career. Becoming a doctor is a very personal decision. Everyone has their own reason why they decide to enter the field. If you haven't made your decision yet, read on.

I've often been asked by people making career choices if I thought medicine was the right choice for them; if I thought they would be good doctors. If you are wondering the same thing, you might want to ask yourself a few questions.

◎ Do I really *want* to become a doctor?
   ▫ This sounds like it should be easy to answer, but in many cases, people become doctors because someone else tells them it's a good idea or it is someone else's dream. In other cases, people decide to become a doctor for the wrong reasons. They might, for example, think that a career as a physician is a good choice because they have heard that doctors make a lot of money or doctors have a lot of prestige. These are not good reasons.

◎ Do I genuinely care about other people and their health?
   ▫ What this means is do you not only care, but want to help people attain better health, alleviate their pain, and make them feel better.

◎ Am I prepared to be around ill and infirm patients and people who may have problems?
   ▫ Once again, this sounds like a simple question, but on occasion I have talked to people who wanted to become doctors and wanted to help others, yet had major concerns about being around ill people.

◎ Do I want to know as much as possible about medicine, healing, and health? Am I interested in learning more than is required of me?
   ▫ Medicine is an every changing science. You are not *done* with your education and training just because you finished medical school. You will need to continue your education throughout your career.

◎ What are my core values?
   ▫ There are certain core values that good physicians should have. Are you responsible? Are you compassionate and caring? Do you have integrity?

The Inside Scoop

The University of Virginia began an interesting program in 1992 called "Mini-Med School" in 1992 to help give people a glimpse of what medical school was like. Taught by some of the same University of Virginia professors who teach at the med school, the seven-week, tuition-free program simulates what med school might be like, helps familiarize people with medical terminology, helps them learn about advances in medical research, and helps improve their knowledge of medicine. While no exams are given, the lectures given are similar to those given in the medical school. People of all ages from 14 to 85 and all walks of life have attended the program since it began, which has turned into one of the most popular non-credit courses.

Can you keep a confidence? Are you committed to your patients?

Now that you've answered those questions, have you decided that a career in medicine is for you? Have you decided that you want to be a physician? Have you decided that you're ready to make a major commitment?

If so, know that whatever area of medicine you choose, whether you decide to be a generalist or specialize you will truly be making a difference in the lives of patients. Let's talk a bit about the path you will take.

The Road to Becoming a Physician

Becoming a doctor takes a lot of time, a lot of education and a great deal of commitment. The earlier you start preparing, the better. If you're still in high school, start getting the background you will need by making sure you take classes in the math, science and English.

If you are sure (or pretty sure) of your career choice to go into medicine and you are getting ready to apply for college, you have a couple of choices. You might first get your bachelors degree and then go on to medical school or you might apply to a college that offers a program that combines college and medical school.

There are a few things to keep in mind when choosing the school and program in which you are interested. You first need to determine if you want to go to medical school and become a medical doctor or an osteopathic college and

Tip from the Top

To prepare for medical school, make sure you take a broad range of courses in math, science, English, and the humanities. Some of these might include:

Life Sciences:
- Biology
- Anatomy
- Physiology

Physical Sciences:
- Chemistry
- Physics

Social Sciences
- Psychology
- Sociology

Math
- Algebra

English
- Writing communications
- Verbal communication

Computer
- Basic computer competency
- Word processing
- Internet

become an osteopathic doctor. What are the differences? What are the similarities?

Medical School

◎ Medical doctors or MDs graduate from medical school. After graduation, they may specialize in a variety of fields.

◎ In order to get into medical school, individuals must complete at least three years of college before entering. Medical programs are four years long. There are also a number of colleges that offer a combined college and medical school program that lasts only six years.

◎ Individuals must take the Medical College Admission Test (MCAT).

◎ Selection criteria include exam scores, college grades, letters of recommendation, interviews, and participation in extracurricular activities.

◎ Individuals must take and pass an exam offered by the National Board of Medical Examiners while still in school.

◎ Additional training is required for individuals who want to specialize or be board certified in a specialty.

◎ This training takes up to five years in a residency program.

◎ Those aspiring to become board certified in a specialty must also take and pass another exam.

◎ Medical doctors must be licensed. Requirements include graduation from an accredited medical school, completing an internship and passing the licensing exam.

Osteopathic College

◎ Osteopathic doctors or DOs graduate from osteopathic college. After graduation, they may specialize in a variety of fields.

◎ In order to get into osteopathic college, individuals must complete at least three years of college. Osteopathic programs are four years long.

◎ Individuals must take an admissions exam prior to being accepted.

◎ Selection criteria include scores of the exam, college grades, letters of recommendation, interviews, and participation in extracurricular activities.

◎ While still in school, individuals must take and pass an exam offered by the National Board of Osteopathic Medical Examiners.

◎ After finishing osteopathic school, osteopathic doctors go through a 12-month rotating internship.

◎ Those who want to specialize or become board certified in a specialty need additional training that can take up to five years in a residency program.

◎ Osteopathic doctors who want to become board certified must also take and pass additional exams.

◎ Osteopathic doctors must be licensed. Requirements include graduating from an accredited osteopathic college, taking and passing the licensing exam and completing an internship.

Both medical doctors and osteopathic doctors both utilize all accepted forms of treatment when caring for patients. These might include drugs and surgery. The major difference is, however, that osteopathic doctors place an emphasis on the body's musculoskelatal system. DOs believe that a person requires the proper alignments of bones, muscles, ligaments and nerves in order to reach optimum health.

Getting into Medical or Osteopathic School

Getting into medical school is not easy. Competition is fierce. There are only 125 allopathic American medical schools in the entire country. Getting into Osteopathic College is even more difficult with only 23 Osteopathic Medical Colleges in this country.

What can you do to increase your chances of acceptance? There is an assortment of things you can do that may help, depending on the type of school to which you are applying.

If you are applying to medical school, you are going to want to get the most current copy of the book, *The Medical School Admission Requirements.* This is chock full of information on the medical schools in the country and advice on the process of applying. It will be a valuable resource.

While you probably have a pre-med advisor, look for a mentor too. He or she might be a physician or a professor who can help you through the application process, give you ideas and cheer you on.

We just discussed some of the things that medical schools and osteopathic colleges look for in an application. We know, for example, that college admissions committees look at your college GPA and especially your grades in the sciences and math. With that in mind, you want to make sure that you take college seriously, take the appropriate courses (such as course work in mathematics, biology, chemistry, physics, and so on, and English), and get the best grades possible. If you want to get into medical or osteopathy school, you cannot slack off.

We also know how important the MCATs are to your acceptance in the medical school of your choice. There are a number of seminars given throughout the country to help you prepare for these important tests. You can also take pre-tests so you can get a feel for the test before the actual exam.

A lot of people don't want to put the extra time and money into taking these seminars. However, the payoff can be tremendous. Just knowing you're prepared can help alleviate a lot of the anxiety most people get having to take this exam. Many who take these seminars find that they can substantially increase their scores. Increasing your score will often give you the edge you need to get into the college of your choice.

Another of the criteria that the committee at a medical or osteopathic school looks at are the extracurricular activities in which you have participated. What should you do?

Volunteering at a hospital or clinic is a good start. What else can you do? While all volunteer and extra-curricular activities are helpful, you might want to think outside the box. You want to demonstrate that you not only are involved in volunteer and extracurricular activities but that you go that extra mile. You want to stand out from the crowd.

You might start a program of some type that illustrates your leadership skills. For example, you might work with a local hospital or clinic on a new program teaching teen moms how to keep their babies healthy. You might work on a program teaching simple first aid to secondary school students.

People often ask if their extracurricular and volunteer activities need to be in medical settings. They don't all have to be, however, at least one of your volunteer efforts should be. Why? Basically, if you are volunteering in a medical setting, you are illustrating that you know what it's like to work in medicine, that you know what medicine entails, and that you have the motivation to help others.

Another factor to keep in mind is that you want to show a commitment to your volunteer efforts. What does that mean? Basically, it shows that you are dedicated to a project. Instead of hopping from one activity to another, be sure that you have at least one ongoing volunteer activity.

Earlier in this book, we discussed how important joining not-for-profit, civic, and community groups can be to your career. It is similarly important when applying to med school. As we also discussed, just being a member of a group is not enough. It is also helpful if you can get on the board of directors, chair a committee or participate in some extra manner.

When you apply to medical school or osteopathic college, you will be required to write an essay to accompany your application. A good, creative essay can help set you apart from other applicants, especially if the acceptance committee is on the fence. Take time writing your essay. In many cases, it can make the difference between acceptance and rejection.

How do you do it? Come up with a theme, develop it, and weave it throughout your story. Make your opening paragraph engaging so its grabs the attention of the reader. Tell your story in an interesting and compelling manner, lacing in information about you, your background, and interests.

What else? Proofread, proofread, proofread. And then, you know what: proofread it again. As it's often difficult to see your own mistakes, you might want to ask a trusted friend or family member to look it over too.

Letters of recommendation are another important part of your application as well. Who do you ask? Professors, employers, the president of a not-for-profit for which you volunteered, or others who know you well and will write an effective letter on your behalf. Remember to ask

people well in advance so they can take some time to write a thoughtful letter.

A big question for many individuals interested in applying to med school or osteopathic college is which is the best school? Where should they apply? There is no simple answer to this. You have to look at all the options and decide where you think you will do best, be happiest, and get the best education. Of course, just because you *want* to go to a specific medical or osteopathy school does not mean you will automatically be accepted. However, I can guarantee you that one way to definitely make sure you don't get accepted is by not applying.

Keep in mind when making your decision that all medical schools and osteopathic colleges are not the same. Each has its own culture, style of teaching, student life, and more.

In making your decision, you might want to consider a few things.

◎ The size of the school. There are good reasons to go to smaller schools and good reasons to go to bigger schools. Where will *you* be most comfortable?

◎ The geographic location of the school. Where in the country do you want to be? Which schools have the teaching style where you think you would most excel?

◎ Which schools have the curriculum in which you are interested?

The Inside Scoop

Many public osteopathic medical schools admit a certain percentage of students who are residents of the specific state in which the college is located.

◎ Which schools are most prestigious? Which ones do you think will accept you? Which ones do *you* want to attend?

The physical application process of applying to most medical schools is now easier than ever thanks to a not-for-profit centralized application processing service called the American Medical College Application Service. If you are a first-year applicant, all you have to do is send one completed application via e-mail to AMCAS, and AMCAS will then distribute them to the colleges of your choice. While there are fees involved, it makes the process a lot easier.

How many colleges should you apply to? That's a difficult question to answer. As we just mentioned, competition is keen getting into both medical school and osteopathic college. You should know that the more schools you apply to, the better your chances of getting accepted someplace.

Most applicants apply to a minimum of 10 schools. Some apply to 30 or more. Is it expensive? It can be, but you are investing in your future.

Tip from the Top

If you are still in high school and choosing a college, it's important to know that some medical schools are affiliated with undergraduate colleges and universities. In many cases, if you go through a college or university's undergraduate program and do well, you will be given preference over others if you apply to their medical school. Other schools have programs that guarantee you a seat in the medical school program if you finish college with a specific GPA. Choosing your undergraduate program tactically may very well help you get into med school down the line.

The Inside Scoop

The Medical College Admission Test, better known as the MCAT, is a standardized exam used by medical schools to assess a student's problem-solving, critical-thinking, and writing skills, knowledge of science concepts, and principles related to the study of medicine.

The MCAT is given in multiple-choice format via computer at testing sites throughout the country and abroad twice annually. It can be taken up to three times without getting special permission to take it again. The MCAT should be taken approximately 18 months before you want to enter medical school.

As most state schools give preference to state residents, always apply to your own state's medical schools. Then choose the private schools in which you are interested in applying.

To save money in applying to medical schools, remember to check each school's acceptance policy before you apply. Certain state medical schools, for example, do not accept out-of-state residents. Applying to them, therefore, if you are not a state resident would be a waste of time and money. How do you know which schools have which policies? This information is available in the *Medical School Admission Requirements* pamphlet published by the AAMC.

Once You're A Doctor

Let's now look at another scenario. In this scenario, we're going to move ahead in your career a bit. In this scenario, let us now imagine that you applied to medical school or osteopathic medical school, were accepted, and went through and graduated with flying colors and honors. You went through an internship. You got your license. Congratulations. You are a doctor! Now what?

Well…you're almost there. You must now choose a specialty and do a residency. What do you want to do? What has been your dream? Your passion?

Do you want to specialize or become a general or family practitioner? Do you want to be a pediatrician? A cardiologist? A neurosurgeon? Do you want to be an anesthesiologist? An internist? Do you want a career in oncology? What about ophthalmology? Do you want to be a plastic or cosmetic surgeon? Do you want a career in geriatrics?

After you choose your specialty, your next step will be getting additional training and experience in that particular area through a residency. What else? To succeed in your career, your best bet is to become board certified in your specialty. What does that mean?

Board certification means that you have completed additional approved training in your specialty and then taken and passed exams by the certification board in your specialty. It means that you have proved proficiency in your specialization.

Do you absolutely need board certification? No, certification is voluntary. You don't need it, but you want it. You might not become board certified immediately, but you will want to begin working toward certification as soon as possible. It will give you an edge over others in your field.

Now that you're licensed and have gone through a residency, you have some decisions to make. You are very lucky. As a licensed physician, you have a wide array of opportunities. What do you want to do? What direction do you want your career to take? Let's take some time to discuss your plans.

Do you want to work for someone else or do you want to work for yourself?

Do you want to start your own practice or do you want to join a medical group? Do you want to be on staff at a hospital or other health care facility? What about working at a clinic? Would you prefer to be on staff at a managed care group? Do you want to work as a locum tenens? Do you want to buy into a medical group practice? Do you have some other ideas?

What is your passion? Where do you think you can make the biggest difference? Do you want to be a small fish in a big sea or a big fish in a small sea? What's that mean? Do you want to practice in a small rural area, or would you prefer to practice in a large metropolitan area?

These are all important decisions. How do you make the right one? Start by knowing that whatever decision you make in most cases will be the right one. And if by any chance it isn't, most decisions are reversible. Let's say you decide you want to be on staff at a hospital in their emergency medicine department. After a year, you decide you really wish you had opened up your own practice. Guess what? It's not too late. You can always change your mind and go in a different direction in your career.

As we've discussed throughout this book, when you have a decision regarding your career, take some time and think about it. Get out some paper and a pen or pencil and start writing. What are the good points of each opportunity? What are the negative points?

If you are looking for a job instead of opening your own practice, you may have headhunters and recruiters contacting you with various opportunities. You may, for example, be contacted about positions in various hospitals and health care facilities throughout the country. You may be contacted about positions in clinics, managed care organizations, or as associates in medical group practices.

You might not be contacted by a headhunter or recruiter, or you might not want the jobs they tell you about. Instead, you might have to search out jobs. How? You can check out Web sites of hospitals and health care facilities. There are also a number of career/jobs sites that specialize in listing openings for physicians.

Many positions are advertised in the classified sections of newspapers or in special health care and medical sections. Openings are also advertised in trade magazines and publications. Most medical schools also have career placement offices for their alumni.

Most important, remember to network. These networking efforts often open up opportunities you might not otherwise know about. You might want to review the section in this book on networking to refresh your memory on some ideas to help with this process.

Why would you want to take a job instead of opening your own practice? There are a number of reasons. You will not have to worry about setting up a practice, which means you also won't have to worry about the finances needed to open a practice. Additionally, you will immediately be bringing in a salary. Depending on your skills, talents, education, and experience, you can negotiate an excellent compensation and benefits package.

Furthermore, if you *are* considering opening your own practice in the future, working for someone else will give you a chance to get your name known, build up your professional reputation, and increase the finances needed to open your own practice.

As an employee, you won't have to worry about any of the business aspects of running a medical practice, and you won't have to concern

yourself with marketing, finances, staffing, or malpractice insurance.

Why would you want to open up your own practice? For the same reason people want to open up any business themselves: It's theirs. What are some of the pros? When you open your own practice, you are in control. You decide how you want your office to run, what your policies are and what your corporate culture will be. You have the opportunity to build your practice. If you desire later, you also have the opportunity to sell your practice.

What are some of the cons or concerns of opening your own medical practice? It can be very expensive opening up a new medical practice. In addition to the physical office space, medical offices require a great deal of expensive medical equipment. Start-up costs and operating expenses can be steep. Unless you're independently wealthy, just won the mega jackpot lottery, or have some other major outside funding, you probably will need to look into financing to make your practice a reality.

You are responsible for finding, hiring, and training a quality office staff as well as paying them. You are also responsible for malpractice insurance, business insurance, liability, property, worker's compensation, and a host of other insurances to cover yourself, your office, and your employees. You are additionally responsible for making sure you have all necessary licenses and credentials as well as assuring that you are adhering to all federal, state, and local laws.

You are responsible for various professional services, including accounting and legal services. You are also responsible for billings and reimbursements, marketing, advertising, public relations, customer relations, and, most important, caring for patients.

Tip from the Top

When opening your medical practice, you may use a variety of business structures. Depending on your situation and the people involved, your corporate structure may be:

- Sole proprietorship
- Partnership
- Limited Partnership
- Corporation or Limited Liability Company (LLC)

Opening up your own practice can be one of the most important decisions in your career. Many physicians decide it is the right move. Others open up joint practices or become partners in medical groups.

Despite the concerns many have with opening a medical practice, many physicians feel it is the smartest move. While some physicians become sole practitioners, others go into joint practices or medical groups with other physicians. In this manner, physicians can share the advantages and disadvantages of a medical practice.

Getting Your Name and Practice Known

Whether you're a new doctor, a sole practitioner, or part of any type of medical group, one of the keys to your success is getting your name known. To make a practice as successful as possible, you need patients. While some physicians go by the theory that if you "build it they will come," this leaves a lot to chance.

You can be the most talented surgeon in the world, the best diagnostician, a life-saving cardiologist, the best pediatrician, and so on, but if no one knows about you, it will be difficult to build a practice.

Marketing

What's the solution? Marketing! Marketing can make a tremendous difference in the success of your practice. Depending on your situation, you may decide to retain a marketing professional or may try your hand at marketing yourself.

Marketing can encompass a lot of activities. These include advertising, publicity, public relations, promotions, and more. While we discussed marketing in an earlier chapter, let's discuss it a bit more here.

It's important to remember that in this case, you (as the practitioner) and your practice are the products. It's necessary in the process to determine what your marketing goals are. For example, your marketing goals may be to get your name known and attract new patients.

How do you do this? You might go with traditional advertising by placing ads in local newspapers and commercials on the radio and perhaps television. There are a number of problems with using advertising as your sole marketing strategy. The first problem is it can get very expensive. The second issue is that people don't always believe advertising.

Depending on where you are located geographically, advertising costs may be astronomical.

"Well," you say. "Not a problem. I'll put in one ad so everyone knows I'm here. It won't be that expensive."

Unfortunately, placing one advertisement in a paper and hoping that all potential patients see it and remember it doesn't generally work. For advertisements to be effective, they generally need to be repeated a number of times to stick in people's mind.

What the solution? Using advertising in conjunction with other marketing strategies. What else can you do?

What else can you do to build your practice? Make sure you are active in community affairs. Join community organizations. If you can't attend every meeting, ask your office manager to attend on your behalf. Call up local civic and not-for-profit groups and offer to speak at their meetings. Tailor your presentations to the group using your expertise.

Are you a cardiologist? Did the local rotary ask you to speak at their monthly meeting? Why not give a presentation on how making little changes in your diet and exercise can make you healthier. Are you a pediatrician? Offer to speak at the local PTA meeting about emergency first aid techniques.

What else can you do? Many local hospitals hold informational health fairs in their facility as well as in auxiliary locations such as shopping centers. Participating in these types of events will not only get your name out in the community but give potential patients a chance to meet you in a non-medical setting.

What else can you do? Consider contacting your local newspaper and asking if they would be interested in a weekly (or monthly) column. You might answer general health questions in the column or you might write a column about some aspect of health that would be of interest to readers of the publication. This will put your name and your specialty in the byline every time your column is published.

You might also contact a local radio or television station to see if they would be interested in a weekly (or monthly) show about health issues. You might even be able to work out a call in show where you would answer general questions.

"I work long hours. I'm busy with patients," I can hear you saying. "Is all this worth it?"

Yes, it is. Getting your name out to potential patients is what building a practice is all about.

Publicity

One way to get and keep your name and your practice in the public eye is to send out press releases. Press releases (also known as news releases) tell the who, what, when, where, and why of a story.

How do you write a press release? Developing and writing press releases are covered briefly in Chapter 9. You might also want to take a workshop on press releases or check out a few pointers in a book on the subject.

How do you know where to send your press releases? Become familiar with your local print and broadcast media. Then, depending on the content of your release, send it to the news editor, medical editor, health editor, and so on. Your best bet is getting the specific editors' names. Keep in mind that just because you send a release does not mean it will get in the newspaper. However, in many cases, newspapers need filler material for the pages of their publication, and your releases do get in.

When might you send a press release out to the media? There are a lot of different situations. Here are a few.

- When you open your practice
- When you or someone in the practice becomes board certified
- When you are someone in the practice gets an award or honor
- When you or someone in the practice obtains professional certification

---

★ Tip from the Coach

Contact your local health and medical editors and let them know you are available for comments or an interview when hot health topics hit the news.

- When you or someone in the practice had an article published in a journal
- When you or someone in your practice has done something noteworthy

Press releases are not advertising.

Press Kits Tell the Story

Press kits might be called media kits, promo kits, or press packs. A well-designed and conceived press kit can be an effective marketing tool in your career.

What's a press kit? Your press kit is a marketing piece; in some cases, it's even a sales pitch. Done right, it's a chance to shine, to set yourself apart, and to get noticed. It can also be used to give to community or civic groups or the media.

Physically, it's a binder or folder that contains your background material, promotional material, head shots, and publicity you have received. It also contains your curriculum vitae and articles you have written.

Press kits are handy to give to anyone who needs information you or your practice. These might include:

- the media
- reporters
- editors
- journalists
- TV and radio news producers
- others in the industry
- radio and television health and medicine contacts
- community and civic groups

How do you put together a press kit? Depending on where you are in your career and your financial resources, you can retain a publicist or publicity firm to handle the task, or you might just want to put one together yourself.

> ### Words from the Wise
> When compiling your press kit, make sure that your contact information is on each and every piece of your kit. If you have a Web site, add that to each piece as well.

What goes into a press kit? There are a variety of documents. You don't have to use each one every time. Tailor your press kit to the person to whom it's being sent. Here's a list to get you started.

- Curriculum Vitae
- Articles you have written
- Fact sheet (one-page sheet giving key information on you and/or your practice)
- Press releases
- Professional head shot
- Press clippings
- Reprints of articles and feature stories
- Topics for presentations for community or civic groups
- Business cards

Now that you have all the components of your press kit, what should you do with them? You have a few choices. Here are some to get you started:

- Go to the office supply store, purchase some attractive presentation folders, and put your information in them.
- Purchase plain presentation folders and design an attractive label to go on the front.
- Look for companies that specialize in designing and printing press kit presentation folders and other marketing pieces. These usually can be located on the Internet.
- Have a graphic artist design press kit folders for you and have them printed.

Whatever type of packaging you choose, be aware that you often only have one chance to make a first impression. When you make copies and reprints, make sure they are clean and crisp.

Photos should be done by a professional. These pictures will be the ones used in publicity and in the print media. Glossy black and whites are best for reproduction in newspapers. Once you get the photos you want to use, you can get them duplicated inexpensively.

Promotional Materials

Promotional materials include a variety of brochures, fact sheets, press kits, bios, cards, and so on. Brochures are a great way for people to learn more about you and your practice. Done correctly, they can be wonderful marketing pieces.

Do you need brochures printed professionally? My advice is to do the most professional brochure possible. While you should never judge a book by its cover, most people do. It almost is better not to have any brochure than to have one that looks shoddy.

What should be in your brochure? That depends. You definitely want the names of the practitioners in the group, along with their specialties. You also need the address, phone numbers, and Web site (if available) of the office. Some practitioners list their services. Others have mini bios of each physician.

You can use your brochures to send out to potential patients, give out to current patients, or bring to events such as health fairs or speaking engagements.

Some practitioners now are also using large four-color postcards to market and advertise their practices.

Find a good printer in your area and work with them in developing your printed pieces. Most have artists on site who will help you set up graphically pleasing printed pieces. These pieces will serve to represent you even when you are not there.

It's www—Your Personal Web Address

If you don't have a Web site yet, you're going to need one. Why? Because the Internet is where it's at today. Your competition probably has a

Web site, which means that you need one too! It's yet another of the key tools for your success and a marketing tool you and your practice really can't do without.

What can a Web site do for you? It can showcase you and your practice. Your name, the names of other physicians in your groups, credentials, specialties, and professional services are right there at the click of a mouse.

Current and potential patients can easily find your address, directions to your office, phone number, and insurance plans you accept. Whether you're trying to build your practice or market your professional services or want an easy way to communicate to patients about office news, a Web site can help.

Want to show patients your newly redone waiting room? Simply post a photo on your site? Want to show some new equipment? Post a picture.

"A Web site? How do I put together a Web site?" you ask.

You can develop a Web site yourself, but you don't have to. If you want to, that's fine. There are a number of easy-to-use Web site development programs and other options for you to explore.

You can also hire a professional Web site developer or company to develop and manage your site. Many Internet service providers (ISPs) offer similar services. You might even have an employee in your office who puts together and manages the site.

How complicated is the whole process? Once you decide you want a Web site, you have to find a host (the person or company from whom you will *rent* Web space). You also will need to decide the name of your domain, your www.com, and then get it registered. If you're not using a professional Web designer and you

don't want to do this on your own, your ISP usually can do this for you.

How do you decide what your domain name should be? Make it simple and make it recognizable. You want to be able to say, "Check us out at www.drjohnson.com," or "Just go to our Web site, www.yourheartdoctor.com." You want to make it easy to remember and easy for people to find you.

Once that's done, you (or someone else) needs to develop the content. What do you need on your site? The possibilities are endless. Here are some ideas to get started.

- Your name and specialty (for example, Dr. Anna Jones, OB/GYN)
- A biography (a little about you, your qualifications, education, and so on)
- News about what is happening in your professional life ("Dr. Thompson will be a guest on the AAA radio show *Health and You* on Monday May 9 at 10 a.m. Call up and ask him all your health-related questions.")
- Photo (A photo may help *introduce* you to potential patients.)
- Press releases
- Links to news stories which have appeared online
- Contact information
- E-mail information

And the list goes on.

What is your Web site going to look like? If you are using a professional Web site developer, he or she might give you some ideas. Also, surf the net and look at other sites until you find some you like. What do you like about each? Is it the design? The colors? The graphics?

What do you want your home page to look like? What about links? There are many questions you have to answer, but once you get started, it's not difficult.

Once you have your site up and running, use your Web address on everything. Emblazon it on your business cards, flyers, advertisements, stationery, and every other marketing and publicity piece.

Building Patient Loyalty

Patients have a choice in doctors. When given that choice, you want patients to think of you. One of the best ways to build a practice is to establish good patient communications. Make sure your patients know you value them. How can you do this? There are a number of things you might do.

You want to continually find ways to communicate with your patients. You might, for example, send thank-you letters to new patients after their first visit. You might make it a habit to send birthday cards to patients every year. You might have an open house every year on the anniversary of the date you opened the office and invite past and current patients as well as potential new patients.

You might also develop an interactive Web site. This gives patients a way to ask questions, leave comments about a problem or situation they have encountered, offer suggestions, and generally stay in touch.

You might also build an e-mail list to send out pertinent information, health tips, and so on. Be sure if you are building an e-mail list you assure your patients their information is secure and will not be sold. Some practitioners also use their Web sites to provide searchable information on various areas of medicine or health care.

It is essential in building patient loyalty to remember that customer service is vital. In case I haven't stressed it enough, excellent customer service is crucial to your success. In many cases, this may entail training all office staff to be patient, kind, compassionate, and understanding in every situation.

No matter what is going on during the day, no matter how busy it is or what crises are occurring, every employee in your office must be dedicated to making every patient feel that they are important and valued.

You are on your way to achieving your full potential in this very important career. You can and will make a difference in the health and lives of many people. Creating a career in medicine that provides long-term satisfaction takes more than luck. It takes planning and commitment. It takes someone like you.

12

SUCCESS IS YOURS FOR THE TAKING

Do You Have What It Takes?

Imagine being able to help people stay healthy, make them feel better, and save lives. Imagine working in an industry that really makes a difference. Imagine knowing you are not only living your dream; you are succeeding. If you are reading this book, you don't have to imagine one more second. You are closer than ever to your dream career in the health care industry.

This book was written for every single person who aspires to work and succeed in the health care industry in any capacity. If this is you, and you know who you are, I need to ask you a very important question: Do you have what it takes?

"What do you mean, do I have what it takes," you ask?

Do you have what it takes to be successful in this industry?

"I think so," you say.

You think so? That's not good enough. You have to know so! Because if you don't believe in yourself, no one else will.

"Okay," you say. "I get it. I *know* I can be successful."

That's good. That's the attitude you need to succeed!

With that out of the way, let's go over a couple of other facts that can help you in your quest for success. You have to remember that no matter what comes your way, you can't give up. Whatever you have to deal with at this point, when you achieve your goals, you most likely will feel it was worth it. There may be stumbling blocks. You may have to take detours. There may be times when you have to choose a fork in the road. But if you give up, it's over.

Here's another fact you should know. When you share your dreams and goals with others about working in the health care industry, there will always be some people who insist on telling you the statistics of the industry.

They may try to tell you how difficult it is to get into medical school, how many people apply, and how many don't get in. They may tell you how difficult it is to get through school once you do get in, how long the hours are.

They may tell you how stressful the industry is or about the high rate of burnout in health care workers. Some may tell you about the high incidence of needle-stick injuries in nurses and lab workers. Others may tell you about the possibilities of other illness or injuries you *might* sustain.

There might be people who quote statistics on everything from the closings of health care facilities to the high cost of medical malpractice insurance; statistics on burnout in shift workers to high stress levels of those working in health care administration, and the list will go on. As a matter of fact, it probably doesn't matter what area of the health care industry in which you are trying to create a career; there will be people who will try to make you feel as though if you go for your dreams, statistically you will stand absolutely *no* chance of success at all.

If you listen to those people and start believing them, you probably will become one of their statistics. If you pay attention to them, a career in any aspect of the health care industry probably isn't for you. I'm willing to bet that no matter what career you choose and in what industry, they will probably have something negative to say about it.

However, if you have gotten to this section of the book, I'm guessing you aren't going to let anyone influence you, and you are still going after your dream.

Here's something to think about. Let's look at a few analogies. Statistically, it's difficult for most people to lose weight, yet many people do. Statistically, most people who play the lottery don't win, yet there are always winners. Statistically, the chances of winning the Publishers Clearing House Sweepstakes aren't great, yet someone always wins. Will it be you? Not if you don't enter.

With those analogies in mind, I stand behind what I have said throughout this book. No matter what the statistics are, someone has to succeed. Why shouldn't it be you? Someone has to be at the top. Why shouldn't it be you? If you give up your dream, someone else will be there. You will be standing on the outside looking in and watching someone doing what you want. I don't think that's your dream.

Will it be easy? Not always. But the industry is full of people in the medical and allied health fields. The industry is full of people working in the business and administration of hospitals, health care facilities, urgi-centers, surgi-centers, medical groups, and private physician's offices; people working in various trade associations and organizations related to the medical and health care industry; and leagues, associations, and organizations. It's full of educators, teachers, and trainers. It's full of medical reporters, journalists, medical writers, and columnists. The industry is huge. It is jam packed with wonderful and fulfilling opportunities. Why shouldn't you live your dream and be part it?

Many are concerned that success is too dependant on other people. Many are concerned that there are too many variables. Will you get into medical school? Will you succeed in nursing school? Will the area of the medical industry in which you desire to work still be viable in 15 years? Will you get burned out? Will there be jobs? Will you have to move to a different geographic location? Will you be good enough? Will this? Will that? What happens if....? And the list goes on.

While it is true that others can affect your career, they can't stop it, unless you let it happen. You are in the driver's seat. You can make it happen! What I am saying in essence is the decision to keep on working toward your goal is yours. You have the power. Are you going to quit?

Here's what I want you to remember. Whether you are dreaming of success as a pediatrician or cardiologist; surgeon or homeopathic physician; operating room nurse or an ER nurse; social worker or mental health counselor; physical therapist or respiratory therapist;

veterinarian or veterinarian technician; medical reporter or medical writer; in the forefront of the industry, behind the scenes, or somewhere in between; know this: You *can* do it and do it successfully as long as you don't give up.

Throughout your journey, always keep your eye on the prize: the great career you are working toward in health care industry.

Sometimes your dream may change. That's okay. As long as you are following *your* dreams, not those of others, you usually are on the right road.

Whether you are interested in a career in medicine, allied health care, health care business or administration, or a different segment of the industry, your choices are huge. What is going to be your contribution to this important industry? Are you going to be a physician? How about a nurse? What about a psychiatrist? How about a dentist? A researcher? A radiologist? An optometrist? A dispensing optician? An EMT? A physician assistant?

What about a surgeon? A chiropractor? A nurse midwife? A dental hygienist? What about a nursing assistant? How about a social worker? A social services aide? Are you going to be a physical therapist? A music therapist? What about a dance therapist? How about a recreational therapist?

Are you going to work in geriatrics? Are you going to be a geriatric care manager? A geriatric assessment coordinator? How about a nursing home activities director? What about a geriatric social worker?

Are you going to be a dietician? A nutritional counselor? What about the director of food services as a hospital or health care facility?

Will you be a pharmacist in a hospital? A retail chain? How about a pharmacist in your own pharmacy?

Will you work in medical records? Will you be a medical records administrator? A medical records transcriptionist? Will you instead be working in the radiology department as a radiation therapy technologist? A nuclear medicine technologist? A diagnostic medical sonographer? How about in some other capacity? What will you be doing?

Will you be working as a surgical technologist? A cardiology technologist? An EEG technologist or an EKG technician? Will you instead be working in counseling as a mental health counselor? A substance abuse counselor? What about a rehabilitation counselor?

Are you going to be the one who teaches others how to become nurses? Doctors? Therapists? Are you going to be the one who teaches others how to care for others?

Are you going to be a veterinarian? A vet technician? Will you be making a difference in the health and lives of animals?

Will you be working at a pharmaceutical company? Will you be developing new drugs? Marketing them? Or will you be in the sales force?

Are you going to be the administrator of a large hospital? How about the human resources director that finds the personnel that can help make the hospital number one? What about the marketing director? The public relations director? How about the publications manager?

Are you going to be the executive director of a trade association in the health care industry? A grant writer? What about working in the administrative end of one of the professional league offices?

Are you going to be the labor relations attorney who negotiates with the hospital union? The publicist who helps keep a physician's name positively in the public eye? Are you going to be the one putting together major fund-raising events or the one promoting them?

Are you going to be the one sharing health care news with the public on television or radio? Or will you be writing about it as a health or medical journalist?

Are you going to be an athletic trainer or physical therapist helping athletes deal with injuries? What about a sports nutritionist helping athletes plan their meals?

Do you think you'll be working as a facility manager keeping a major health care facility in perfect running order?

What path do you want to follow? Where do you envision yourself? What do you see yourself doing? Seize your opportunity. It's there for you. Grab onto your dream to start the ball rolling.

Over the years, I've talked to many people who are extremely successful in a variety of careers. One of the most interesting things about them is that most were *not* surprised at all that they were successful. As a matter of fact, they expected it.

I know doctors who have told me that from the time they were youngsters they knew they would be physicians; one even knew what his office would look like. Twenty years later, amazingly enough, the doctor was working in an office that looked just as he had imagined years back.

Similarly, I've known nurses who always knew they would be in the nursing profession as well as dentists who knew they would work in the dental field. I even remember talking to a pharmacist who planned on owning his own pharmacy when he was 10 years old.

I wanted to share a couple of other stories on this subject. While they relate to people out-

---

⭐ **Words fromt the Wise**

Throughout all history, the great wise men and teachers, philosophers, and prophets have disagreed with one another on many different things. It is only on this one point that they are in complete and unanimous agreement. We become what we think about.

−Earl Nightingale

---

side the health care industry, it helps prove the point of just how important a positive focus can be.

I remember sitting backstage at a concert before a show talking to one of the singers in the act. We were discussing some of the other hot artists in the industry. The singer was telling me a story of another singer on the charts. "We knew he was going to be a star," he said about the other artist. "When he was still in school, he told everyone he was going to be a star, and that's all he talked about."

"Doesn't everyone say that?" I asked.

"Sometimes they do," he continued. "But what made him different was he was specific about what he was going to do and when. He told everyone he was going to have a hit record before he graduated. [He hadn't even recorded anything yet at that time.] He started acting like a star and then dressing the part of a star. He went on and on about it so much that he almost had to be a star to save face. Funny thing was, he did have a hit before he graduated and he did turn into a huge star."

A friend of mine has a daughter who is now a WNBA player. From the time she was a little girl, she knew she would be a pro basketball player and that was before the WNBA was in existence. Her father always knew she would go pro as well, and they often spoke about the possibilities.

When you hear stories like these, it helps prove the point of just how important a positive focus can be to your career. What's really interesting, however, is that in many cases, way before successful people plan their success, they expect it.

Is it the planning and the work that creates the reality, or is it the dream that puts them on the road to success? I think it's a combination.

And in case you're thinking that you're only supposed to expect success in the health care industry if you're career aspirations are those of a doctor, think again. You are supposed to expect success in whatever area of the industry you pursue. Every job is important.

Are you ready for success? Are you really ready?

Do you know what you're going to say when you're being interviewed as Employee of the Year? Can you imagine the feeling you will have as CEO when your health care facility gets not only accredited but top accolades?

Can you almost feel the excitement you will experience when you help a patient who hasn't been able to walk since an accident take his or her first steps?

Have you chosen the perfect suit you're going to wear when you get promoted to CEO of the facility? Can you almost see what you will be wearing when you sign an employment contract? Can you picture what your office will look like? Do you know what you're going to say?

If not, you should, at least in your mind. Why? Because if you claim something, you're often closer to making it happen.

Over the years, I have heard many similar stories from people who are very successful in their careers of choice. Was it they knew what they wanted to do and focused on it more than others? Was it they had a premonition and things just worked out? Were they just lucky? Were they more talented than others? Was it visualization? Or was it that a positive attitude helped create a positive situation? No one really knows. The only thing that seems evident is that those who expect to be successful usually have a better chance of achieving it. Those who have a positive attitude usually have a better chance of positive things happening.

We've covered visualization earlier in the book. Whether you believe this theory or not, one thing is for sure: It can't hurt. So start planning your party now for when you become Physician of the Year. Plan your acceptance speech for when you become Employee of the Year at the hospital in which you work.

Plan on what you will say when you win the Pulitzer Prize for finding a cure for cancer. Plan your own celebration for your promotion or for the career of which you've been dreaming. Plan for your own success, and then get ready for it to happen.

Creating a Career You Love

While working toward your perfect career, it's important to combine your goals with your life objectives. The trick to success in any industry is not only following your interests but following your heart. If you're working toward your dream, going that extra mile and doing that extra task won't be a chore.

And when you run into obstacles along the way, they won't be problems, just stepping stones to get where you're going.

By now, you have read some (if not all) of this book. You've learned that there are certain things you need to do to stack the deck in your favor, whether you want your success to be as an athlete or in the business segment of the industry.

You know how to develop your resume and/or a CV, captivating cover letters, career portfolios, business cards, and other tools. You know how to get past the gatekeeper. You know what to do in interviews and what not to do.

You know how important it is to help develop a good bedside manner and you know how essential it is to have a good attitude.

You know that it is crucial to read everything before you sign it so you can protect yourself and you know how important good communications skills are in the health care industry.

Tip from the Coach

Before writing my first book, I mentioned to a number of people that I wanted to write a book and was looking for a publisher. Their response was always the same. "It is very difficult to get a publisher. It's very hard to write a book. Don't get your hopes up."

While my book wasn't yet written, I had already seen it in my mind. I knew what it would look like; I knew what it was going to say.

I had a plan and told everyone the same story. I was going to send out queries to publishers whose names started with A and go through the alphabet until I reached Z and knew I would find a publisher. The book would be a reality no matter what anyone thought.

By the time I got to the Fs, I had sold my book idea. I wasn't surprised, because I not only knew it would happen; I expected it. That first book, *Career Opportunities In The Music Industry*, is now in its fifth edition. Shortly after that, I sold other book ideas and soon *Career Opportunities In Health Care* was published. The rest is history. More than 25 books later, my dream has turned into reality.

You know a bit about entrance exams, getting into med school, and becoming successful.

You've learned how to network and how to market yourself. You've learned some neat little tips and tricks to get your foot in the door. You've learned that you need to find ways to stand out from the crowd.

Most of all, you've learned that it's essential to create a career you love. You've learned that you don't ever want to settle and wonder "what if?"

Creating the career you want and love is not always the easiest thing in the world to accomplish, but it is definitely worth it. To help you focus in on what you want, you might find it helpful to create a personal mission statement.

Your Personal Mission Statement

There are many people who want a career in various areas of the health care industry. Some will make it and some will not. I want you to be the one who makes it. I want you to be the one who succeeds.

Throughout the book, I've tried to give you tips, tricks, and techniques that can help. I've tried to give you the inspiration and motivation to know you can do it. Here's one more thing that might make your journey easier.

Create your personal mission statement. Why? Because your mission statement can help you define your visions clearly. It will give you a path, a purpose, and something to follow. Most important, putting your mission statement in writing can help you bring your mission to fruition.

What's a mission statement? It's a statement declaring what your mission is in your life and your career. How do you do it? As with all the other exercises you've done, sit down, get comfortable, take out a pen and a piece of paper, and start writing. What is your mission?

Remember that your mission statement is for *you*. You're not writing it for your family, your friends, or your employer. It can be changed or modified at any time.

Think about it for a moment. What do you want to do? Where do you want be? What's the path you want to take? What are your dreams? What is your mission?

There is no one right way to write your mission statement. Some people like to write it in paragraph form. Others like to use bullets or numbers. It really doesn't matter as long as you get it down in writing. The main thing to remember is to make your statement a clear and concise declaration of your long-term mission.

Your mission statement might be one sentence, one paragraph, or even fill two or three pages. It's totally up to you. As long as your mission statement is clear, you're okay.

Here are some examples of simple mission statements.

◎ Physician
  ▫ My mission is to use my education, skills, and talent to become a top-notch cardiologist with a large roster of patients.

◎ Physician
  ▫ My mission is to use my education, skills, talent, and compassion to become a family practitioner in a clinic for people who would not otherwise be able to afford high-quality medical care.
  ▫ It is also my mission to become the director of a medical clinic for the uninsured and indigent population.

◎ Dentist
  ▫ My mission is to use my education, skills, and talents to become an oral surgeon.

◎ Nurse
  ▫ My mission is to go through the nursing program at my community college and then go on to get my B.A. in nursing. I want to work as a floor nurse in a large hospital.
  ▫ My mission also includes getting my master's in nursing and becoming a nursing supervisor.

◎ Physical therapist
  ▫ My mission is get my master's degree in physical therapy and get a job in a hospital or health care facility. I want to use my skills and specialize in working with children.

◎ Psychiatrist
  ▫ My mission is to use my skills and talents to specialize in dealing with eating disorders.

◎ Administrator of health care facility
  ▫ My mission is to develop my skills and talents to create a career as the CEO of a large teaching hospital.

◎ Physician/Health care administrator
  ▫ My mission is to first become a physician, then a physician executive, and eventually use my education, experience, and skills to help develop legislation and regulations in the health care industry. Eventually, my mission is to become a state commissioner of Health Care. In that way, I hope to be able to make positive changes within the industry.

◎ Marketing director
  ▫ My mission is to use my skills and talent to create a career as a successful marketing executive in a large health care facility. I want to be the director of marketing for one of the largest, most prestigious teaching hospitals in the country.

◎ Complimentary care coordinator
  ▫ My mission is to have a career in health and wellness, helping people learn about complimentary care and alternative treatments. I eventually would like to create a pilot program for health care facilities nationwide so patients can be better informed about complementary and alternative treatments. I also want to be named director of complimentary care in a large, prestigious facility.

◎ Health/Medical writer
  ▫ My mission is to be working for a world-class publication, writing about health, health care, and medicine.

◎ Fund-raising and development director
  ▫ My mission is to use my talents, skills and passions to create a career as a in fund-raising and development for not-for-profit health care facilities. I want a career as a fund-raising and development director in a large facility where I can create unique development programs.

What do you do with your mission statement? Use it! Review it to remember what you're working toward. Use it as motivation. Use it to help you move in the right direction.

You would be surprised how many successful people have their personal mission statement

---

> ### ★ Tip from the Coach
> Put your personal mission statement on Post-It Notes and stick them up all around to keep you focused.

hanging on their wall, taped to their computer, or in their pocket. I know individuals who keep a copy of their mission statement in their wallet, taped to their bathroom mirror, stuck on their computer monitor, or placed in the inside of a desk drawer or in another location where they can regularly glance at it.

Wherever you decide to place your mission statement, be sure to look at it daily so you can always keep your mission in mind. It makes it easier to keep focus on your ultimate goal.

Success Strategies

We have discussed marketing, promotion, and publicity. Used effectively, they can help your career tremendously. Here's what you have to remember! Don't wait for someone else to recognize your skills and talents; promote yourself. There are many keys to success. Self-promotion is an important one.

Don't toot your own horn in an annoying or obnoxious manner, but make sure people notice you. You want to stand out in a positive way. Don't keep your accomplishments a secret. Instead, claim them proudly.

We've all been taught to be modest. "Don't boast," your mother might have said as you were growing up. But if your goal is success in your career, sometimes you can just be too quiet for your own good.

Your ultimate challenge is to create buzz. You need to create spin. You need others to know what you've done and what you're doing in the future. Some people aren't willing or able to do what it takes. If you want to succeed, it's imperative that you get started. Buzz doesn't usually happen overnight, but every day you wait is another day you're behind in the job.

Begin to think like a publicist. Whatever segment of the health care industry you're working in, you need to promote yourself, or no one will know you exist. While others may help, the responsibility really is on *you* to make your career work and make your career successful.

No matter what segment of the industry you are in or what level you are at, continue to look for opportunities of all kinds. Search out opportunities to move ahead in your career and then grab hold of them.

Also, know that in your life and career, on occasion there may be doors that close. The trick here is not to let a door close without looking for the window of opportunity that is always there. If you see an opportunity, jump on it immediately.

Throughout the book, we've discussed the importance of networking. Once you become successful, it's important to continue to network. Just because you landed a new job as a health care administrator doesn't mean you don't want to meet other health care administrators. Just because you got a job handling the publicity for a health care facility doesn't mean you don't want to meet other executives in the industry. Just because you got a job as a health reporter doesn't mean you shouldn't know other reporters, writers, editors, and publishers.

If you've landed a new job, keep networking. Continue meeting people. Continue getting your name out there. You can never tell who knows whom and what someone might need. There are always new opportunities ahead, and if you don't keep networking, you might miss some of them. Keep nurturing your network and developing contacts.

And it's not only in the business or administration segment of the health care industry. If you are a doctor, nurse, therapist, technician, technologist, and so on, it is just as important to keep on networking; keep meeting people; continue making contacts. It is essential to the success of your career.

Don't be afraid to ask for help. If you know someone who can help in your career, ask. The worst they can say is no. The best that can happen is you might get some assistance. Of course, if you can help someone else, do that as well.

Always be prepared for success. It might be just around the corner. Whatever segment of the industry you are pursuing, continue honing your skills. Keep taking classes, seminars, and workshops. Keep up with trends, read trade publications, and make sure you know what is happening today.

Stay as fit and healthy as you can. Try to eat right, get sleep, exercise, and take care of yourself. After all your hard work, you don't want to succeed and be too sick or tired to enjoy it.

Whatever facet of the industry you're in, you are going to be selling yourself. You might be selling yourself to a medical school or nursing school. You might be selling yourself to a human resources manager in a hospital or other health care facility. You might be selling yourself to

---

⭐ The Inside Scoop

Don't procrastinate when an opportunity presents itself. Someone else is always on the lookout just like you, and you don't want to miss your chances.

partners in a medical group. You might be selling yourself to a hospital's board of directors. You might even be selling yourself to patients.

What else? You might be pitching your story for publicity or a variety of other situations. Take a lesson from others who have made it to the top and prepare ahead of time. That way, when you're in a situation where you need to say something, you'll be ready. Come up with a pitch and practice it until you're comfortable.

Always be positive. Attitude is essential to your life and your professional success. Here's the deal. We've discussed this before. People want to be around other people who are positive. If there is a choice between two people with similar talents and skills and you have a better outlook than anyone else, a more positive type of personality and passion, you're going to be chosen. You're going to get the job. You're going to succeed.

Change the way you look at situations, and the situations you look at will change. What's that mean? If you look at a situation as a problem, it will be a problem. If, on the other hand, you look at a situation as an opportunity, it becomes one.

If you look at the health care industry and all you see are the trials and tribulations of trying to succeed, all you will have are trials and tribulations. If, on the other hand, you look at the road to success in this industry as a wonderful and exciting journey, it will be.

Keeping Things Confidential

Privacy and confidentiality are crucial when working in the health care industry. This means that it is your responsibility to keep patient names and issues private and confidential.

In addition to being common decency, there are now rules, regulations, and laws in place spe-cifically prohibiting giving patient information to others without permission from the patient.

For example, HIPPA (Health Insurance Portability and Accountability Act) prohibits giving patient information to others without express written permission from the patient. This incidentally even includes discussing treatment with a patient's family unless you have been given prior written permission.

It's often difficult after a day of work not to want to go home and discuss a patient or their diagnosis or even what happened during the day. It may be difficult to treat a friend or acquaintance of a family member and then not tell them when you get home. This is unacceptable in the health care industry and must be avoided at all costs.

★ Tip from the Coach

They say it takes approximately 21 days to break one habit and form a new one. With that in mind, if there is any habit you have that bothers you, is detrimental to your career, or any part of your life, for that matter, know that you cannot only change it but can do so fairly quickly. If, for example, you find yourself speaking over others when they are talking, begin today by consciously making an effort to listen; then speak. You will find that if you continue to do that on a daily basis, soon it will become a habit.

Similarly, if you are told that you are negative at work, start today by consciously making an effort to be positive. Before you make a comment about something, stop, think about what you are saying, and try to put a positive spin on it. Continue doing this and a few weeks later you will find that not only will your attitude be perceived more positively; it will be more positive.

The ability to honor confidentiality regarding patients and patient care is crucial to anyone working in the health care industry.

Climbing the Career Ladder

Generally, whatever you want to do in life, you most likely are going to have to pay your dues. Whatever part of the health care industry you've chosen to pursue, most likely you're going to have to *pay your dues* as well. Now that you've accepted that fact, how do you climb the career ladder? How do you succeed?

How do you go, for example, from a job as a coordinator to a job as the assistant director of a department? How do you go from a job as an assistant director to the full-fledged director of a department? How do you go from writing health news for a local daily paper to becoming a successful health reporter for a major publication?

How do you go from a new resident to one of the most sought-after doctors in town? How do you go from a floor nurse to a nursing supervisor?

There are many things you're going to have to do, but they can be done. We've covered a lot of them. Work hard, keep a positive attitude, and act professionally at all times. Stay abreast of the business, network, and hone your skills and talents so you can backup your claims of accomplishments.

Look for a mentor who can help you move your career in the right direction and propel you to the top of your field. Join trade associations and unions. Read the trades, take seminars, classes, workshops, and take part in other learning opportunities. Continue your education when you can. Be the best at what you do. Keep your goal in mind.

Look at every opportunity with an open mind. When you're offered something, ask yourself:

◎ Is this what I want to be doing?
◎ Is this part of my dream?
◎ Is this part of my plan for success?
◎ Is this opportunity a stepping-stone to advancing my career?
◎ Will this experience be valuable to me?

Fortunately or unfortunately, job progression doesn't always follow the normal career path. A coordinator in the marketing department may get a break and end up director of the health promotion department. A celebrity may talk about a specific nutritionist in a newspaper article, and the nutritionist's client roster may expand quicker than usual. A medical procedure discussed in the media might catapult the career of a new physician who does the procedure. It all depends. If it can happen to someone else, it might happen to you. That is one of the greatest things about your career. You just never know what tomorrow might bring.

You never know when a chance meeting is going to land you a great job or someone passing through town might read about one of your accomplishments in a local newspaper and recruit you for a position in a larger or more prestigious facility. You never know who will tell a headhunter, recruiter, or human resources director about you and you will get a call. You really never know when success will come your way. It can happen at any time.

It should be noted that success means different things to different people. There are many successful people who work in the health care industry who are not well-known physicians, don't work in large prestigious hospitals, or are the directors of their departments, yet they are earning a living and doing what they love.

And it's like that in all aspects of the health care industry. There are thousands of individuals working in medicine and allied health careers in small rural or regional medical facilities and private physicians' offices. There are many working in hometown pharmacies and local health clinics.

There are facility directors of small health care facilities, who, while they aren't in charge of megafacilities, are earning very good livings doing their job just the same.

There are marketing professionals, publicists, fund-raisers, grant writers, patient advocates, accountants, attorneys, and so on who might not be working for large prestigious hospitals but are working in the health care industry just the same. That doesn't preclude them from having a successful career in the health care industry. To the contrary, one of the best things about working in the health care industry is that almost every job has an impact on others. Every job can make a difference, even if it's just a little one.

Risk Taking— Overcoming Your Fears

Everyone has a comfort zone from which they operate. What's a comfort zone? It's the area where you feel comfortable both physically and psychologically. Most of the time, you try to stay within this zone. It's predictable, it's safe, and you generally know what's coming.

Many people get jobs, stay in them for years, and then retire. They know what's expected of them. They know what they're going to be doing. They know what they're going to

> **Tip from the Coach**
>
> If you're starting to feel comfortable in your career or starting to feel bored, it's time to step out of your comfort zone and look for new challenges.

be getting. The problem is that it can get boring, there's little challenge, and your creativity can suffer.

Stepping out of your comfort zone is especially important to your career. Wanting to step out of your comfort zone is often easier said than done, but every now and then you're going to have to push yourself.

The key to career success in the health care industry as well as your own personal growth is the willingness to step outside of your comfort zone. Throughout your career, you're going to be faced with decisions. Each decision can affect your career. Be willing to take risks. Be willing to step out of your comfort zone.

Is it scary? Of course, but if you don't take risks, you stand the chance of your career stagnating. You take the chance of missing wonderful opportunities.

Should you take a promotion? Should you stay at the same job? Should you go to a different company? Should you go back to school? Should you move? Should you take a chance?

How do you make the right decision? Try to think about the pros and cons of your choices. Get the facts, think about them, and make your decision.

"What if I'm wrong?" you ask.

Here's the good news. Usually, you *will* make the right decision. If by chance you don't, it's generally not a life-and-death situation. If you stay at the same job and find you should have left, for example, all you need to do is look for a new job. If you change jobs and you're not happy, you can usually find a new job as well. Most things ultimately work out. Do the best you can and then go on.

If your career is stagnant, do something. Don't just stay where you are because of your fear of leaving your comfort zone and your fear of the unknown.

Some Final Thoughts

No matter where you are in your career, don't get stagnant. Always keep your career moving. Once you reach one of your goals, your journey isn't over. You have to keep moving on to the next one.

Keep working toward your goal. It can happen. Don't settle for less than what you want. Every goal you meet is another stepping-stone toward an even better career, no matter what segment of the industry you are pursuing.

While I would love to promise you that after reading this book you'll become a better diagnostician; the CEO of a large, prestigious hospital; the chief of staff; the director of nursing; the director of your department; the dean of a medical school; own your own pharmacy; or win the Nobel Peace Prize for discovering the cure for cancer (or the common cold), unfortunately I can't.

What I can tell you is that the advice in this book can help you move ahead and stack the deck in your favor in this industry. I've given you the information. You have to put it into action.

Tip from the Top

Try to treat everyone from subordinates to superiors to colleagues to patients the way you want to be treated—with respect and dignity.

Words from the Wise

Persevere. The reason most people fail is because they gave up one day too soon.
—Shelly Field

Numerous factors are essential to your success. You need to be prepared. There's no question that preparation is necessary. Talent is critical as well. Being in the right place at the right time is essential, and good luck doesn't hurt.

Perseverance is vital to success, no matter what you want to do, what area of the industry you want to enter, and what career level you want to achieve. Do you want to know why most people don't find their perfect job? It's because they gave up looking *before* they found it. Do you want to know why some people are on the brink of success yet probably won't get there? It's because they give up.

Do you want to know what single factor can increase your chances of success? It's perseverance! Don't give up.

Have fun reading this book. Use it to jump-start your career and inspire you to greater success and accomplishments. Draw on it to achieve your goals so you can have the career of your dreams. Use it so you don't have to look back and say, "I wish I had." Use it so you can say, "I'm glad I did."

I can't wait to hear about your success stories. Be sure to let us know how this book has helped your career by logging on to www.shellyfield.com. I would also love to hear about any of your own tips or techniques for succeeding in the health care industry. You can never tell. Your successes might be part of our next edition.

APPENDIX I

TRADE ASSOCIATIONS, UNIONS, AND OTHER ORGANIZATIONS

Trade associations, unions, and other organizations can be valuable resources for career guidance as well as professional support. This listing includes many of the organizations related to the health care and peripheral industries. Names, addresses, phone numbers, Web sites, and e-mail addresses (where available) have been included to make it easier for you to obtain information. Check out Web sites to learn more about organizations and what they offer.

Academy of Dispensing Audiologists (ADA)
Windsor Cove
Columbia, SC 29223
(803) 252-5646
info@audiologist.org
http://www.audiologist.org

Academy of General Dentistry
211 E. Chicago Avenue
Chicago, IL 60611
(312) 440-4300
http://www.agd.org

Academy of Surgical Research (ASR)
7500 Flying Cloud Drive
Eden Prairie, MN 55344

(952) 253-6240
director@surgicalresearch.org
http://www.surgicalresearch.org

Accreditation Review Committee on Education In Surgical Technology (ARC-ST)
c/o Paul Price
7108-C S Alton Way
Centennial, CO 80112
(303) 694-9262
pprice@arcst.org
http://www.arcst.org

Accrediting Bureau of Health Education Schools (ABHES)
7777 Leesburg Pike
Falls Church, VA 22043
(703) 917-9503
info@abhes.org
http://www.abhes.org

Alliance of Cardiovascular Professionals
4356 Benney Road
Virginia Beach, VA 23452
(757) 497-1225

peggymcelgunn@comcast.net
http://www.acp-online.org

American Academy of Ambulatory Care Nursing (AAACN)

East Holly Avenue
Pitman, NJ 08071
(856) 256-2350
aaacn@ajj.com
http://www.aaacn.org

American Academy of Anesthesiologist Assistants (AAAA)

P.O. Box 13978
Tallahassee, FL 32317
(850) 656-8848
info@anesthetist.org
http://www.anesthetist.org

American Academy of Cosmetic Surgery (AACS)

737 N. Michigan Avenue
Chicago, IL 60611
(312) 981-6760
http://www.cosmeticsurgery.org

American Academy of Nurse Practitioners (AANP)

National Administrative Office
PO Box 12846
Austin, TX 78711
(512) 442-4262
admin@aanp.org
http://www.aanp.org

American Academy of Pediatrics (AAP)

141 NW Point Boulevard
Elk Grove Village, IL 60007
(847) 434-4000
pubs@aap.org
http://www.aap.org

American Academy of Physician Assistants (AAPA)

950 N Washington Street
Alexandria, VA 22314
(703) 836-2272
aapa@aapa.org
http://www.aapa.org

American Aging Association (AAA)

c/o The Sally Balin Medical Center
110 Chesley Drive
Media, PA 19063
(610) 627-2626
ameraging@aol.com
http://www.americanaging.org

American Art Therapy Association (AATA)

1202 Allanson Road
Mundelein, IL 60060
(847) 949-6064
info@arttherapy.org
http://www.arttherapy.org

American Association For Clinical Chemistry (AACC)

2101 L Street, NW
Washington, DC 20037
(202) 857-0717
info@aacc.org
http://www.aacc.org

American Association for Medical Transcription (AAMT)

100 Sycamore Avenue
Modesto, CA 95354
(209) 527-9620
aamt@aamt.org
http://www.aamt.org

American Association for Respiratory Care (AARC)

9425 N MacArthur Boulevard

Irving, TX 75063
(972) 243-2272
info@aarc.org
http://www.aarc.org

American Association for Thoracic Surgery (AATS)
900 Cummings Center
Beverly, MA 01915
(978) 927-8330
aats@prri.com
http://www.aats.org

American Association of Cardiovascular and Pulmonary Rehabilitation (AACVPR)
401 N Michigan Avenue
Chicago, IL 60611
(312) 321-5146
aacvpr@smithbucklin.com
http://www.aacvpr.org

American Association of Critical Care Nurses (AACCN)
101 Columbia
Aliso Viejo, CA 92656
(949) 362-2000
aacninfo@aacn.org
http://www.aacn.org

American Association of Homes and Services For the Aging (AAHSA)
2519 Connecticut Avenue NW
Washington, DC 20008
(202) 783-2242
pubs@aahsa.org
http://www.aahsa.org

American Association of Medical Assistants (AAMA)
20 N. Wacker Drive

Chicago, IL 60606
(312) 899-1500
http://www.aama-ntl.org

American Association of Pharmaceutical Scientists (AAPS)
2107 Wilson Boulevard
Arlington, VA 22201
(703) 243-2800
aaps@aaps.org
http://www.aaps.org

American Association of Pharmacy Technicians (AAPT)
PO Box 1447
Greensboro, NC 27402
(336) 333-9356
aapt@pharmacytechnician.com
http://www.pharmacytechnician.com

American Association of Spinal Cord Injury Nurses (AACIN)
75-20 Astoria Boulevard.
East Elmhurst, NY 11370
(718) 803-3782
aascin@unitedspinal.org
http://www.aascin.org

American College Health Association (ACHA)
PO Box 28937
Baltimore, MD 21240
(410) 859-1500
pubs@acha.org
http://www.acha.org

American College of Apothecaries (ACA)
PO Box 341266
Memphis, TN 38184
(901) 383-8119

aca@acainfo.org
http://www.acainfo.org

American College of Cardiology (ACC)

c /o Heart House
9111 Old Georgetown Road
Bethesda, MD 20814
(301) 897-5400
exec@acc.org
http://www.acc.org

American College of Cardiovascular Administrators (ACCA)

c /o American Academy of Medical
Administrators
701 Lee Street
Des Plaines, IL 60016
(847) 759-8601
info@aameda.org
http://www.aameda.org

American College of Health Care Administrators (ACHCA)

300 N Lee Street
Alexandria, VA 22314
(703) 739-7900
mtn@achca.org
http://www.achca.org

American College of Healthcare Executives (ACHE)

1 North Franklin
Chicago, IL 60606
(312) 424-2800
geninfo@ache.org
http://www.ache.org

American College of Healthcare Information Administrators (ACHIA)

701 Lee Street
Des Plaines, IL 60016

(847) 759-8601
mckenney.1@osu.edu
http://www.aameda.org

American College of Nurse-Midwives (ACNM)

8403 Colesville Road
Silver Spring, MD 20910
(240) 485-1800
http://www.midwife.org

American College of Obstetricians and Gynecologists (ACOG)

409 12th Street. SW
PO Box 96920
Washington, DC 20090
(202) 638-5577
communications@acog.org
http://www.acog.org

American College of Osteopathic Obstetricians and Gynecologists (ACOOG)

900 Auburn Road
Pontiac, MI 48342
(248) 332-6360
http://www.acoog.com

American College of Osteopathic Pediatricians (ACOP)

PO Box 11086
Richmond, VA 23230
stewart@acopeds.org
http://www.acopeds.org

American College of Physicians-American Society of Internal Medicine

190 N Independence Mall W
Philadelphia, PA 19106
(215) 351-2600
http://www.acponline.org

American College of Veterinary Internal Medicine (ACVIM)

1997 Wadsworth Boulevard
Lakewood, CO 80214
(303) 231-9933
acvim@acvim.org
http://www.acvim.org

American Council On Pharmaceutical Education (ACPE)

20 N Clark Street
Chicago, IL 60602
(312) 664-3575
info@acpe-accredit.org
http://www.acpe-accredit.org/about/directions.asp

American Dance Therapy Association (ADTA)

2000 Century Plaza
10632 Little Patuxent Parkway.
Columbia, MD 21044
(410) 997-4040
info@adta.org
http://www.adta.org

American Dental Assistants Association (ADAA)

35 E Wacker Drive
Chicago, IL 60601
(312) 541-1550
lsepin@adaa1.com
http://www.dentalassistant.org

American Dental Association (ADA)

211 E Chicago Avenue
Chicago, IL 60611
(312) 440-2500
http://www.ada.org

American Dental Hygienists Association (ADHA)

444 N Michigan Avenue
Chicago, IL 60611
(312) 440-8911 (312) 440-8900
mail@adha.net
http://www.adha.org

American Diabetes Association (ADA)

1701 N Beauregard Street
Alexandria, VA 22311
(703) 549-1500
askada@diabetes.org
http://www.diabetes.org

American Dietetic Association (ADA)

120 S Riverside Plaza
Chicago, IL 60606-6995
(312) 899-0040
sales@eatright.org
http://www.eatright.org

American Federation of State, County and Municipal Employees (AFSCME)

1625 L. Street NW
Washington, DC 20036
(202) 429-1000
pubaffairs@afscme.org
http://www.afscmeorganizers.org

American Foundation for Pharmaceutical Education (AFPE)

1 Church Street
Rockville, MD 20850
(301) 738-2160
info@afpenet.org
http://www.afpenet.org

American Geriatrics Society (AGS)

350 5th Avenue
New York, NY 10118
(212) 308-1414
info.amger@americangeriatrics.org
http://www.americangeriatrics.org

American Gynecological and Obstetrical Society (AGOS)

University of Utah
50 N. Medical Dr.
Salt Lake City, UT 84132

American Health Care Association (AHCA)

1201 L Street NW
Washington, DC 20005
(202) 842-4444
http://www.ahca.org

American Heart Association (AHA)

7272 Greenville Avenue
Dallas, TX 75231
(214) 373-6300
pubcust@amhrt.org
http://www.amhrt.org

American Health Information Management Association (AMRA)

233 N. Michigan Avenue
Chicago, IL 60601
(312) 233-1100
info@ahima.org
http://www.ahima.org

American Hospital Association (AHA)

One N Franklin
Chicago, IL 60606
(312) 422-3800
storeservice@aha.org
http://www.ahaonlinestore.com

American Institute of Homeopathy (AIH)

801 N Fairfax Street
Alexandria, VA 22314
(888) 445-9988
aih@homeopathyusa.org
http://www.homeopathyusa.org

American Marketing Association (AMA)

311 S Wacker Drive
Chicago, IL 60606
(312) 542-9000
info@ama.org
http://www.marketingpower.com

American Medical Directors Association (AMDA)

10480 Little Patuxent Parkway
Columbia, MD 21044
(410) 740-9743
info@amda.com
http://www.amda.com

American Medical Technologists (AMT)

710 Higgins Road
Park Ridge, IL 60068
(847) 823-5169
mail@amt1.com
http://www.amt1.com

American Music Therapy Association (AMTA)

8455 Colesville Road
Silver Spring, MD 20910
(301) 589-3300
info@musictherapy.org
http://www.musictherapy.org

American Neurological Association (ANA)

5841 Cedar Lake Road
Minneapolis, MN 55416
(952) 545-6284
ana@llmsi.com
http://www.aneuroa.org

American Neuropsychiatric Association (ANA)

c/o Sandra Bornstein
700 Ackerman Road

Columbus, OH 43202
(614) 447-2077
anpa@osu.edu
http://www.anpaonline.org

American Nurses Association (ANA)

8515 Georgia Avenue
Silver Spring, MD 20910
(301) 628-5000
memberinfo@ana.org
http://www.nursingworld.org

American Occupational Therapy Association (AOTA)

4720 Montgomery Lane
PO Box 31220
Bethesda, MD 20824
(301) 652-2682 (301) 652-6611
aotapresident@aol.com
http://www.aota.org

American Osteopathic Academy of Sports Medicine (AGASM)

7600 Terrace Avenue
Middleton, WI 53562
(608) 831-4400
info@aoasm.org
http://www.aoasm.org

American Pediatric Surgical Association (APSA)

60 Revere Drive
Northbrook, IL 60062
(847) 480-9576
eapsa@eapsa.org
http://www.eapsa.org

American Pharmaceutical Association (APA)

2215 Constitution Avenue NW
Washington, DC 20037

(202) 628-4410
http://www.aphanet.org

American Physical Therapy Association (APTA)

1111 N Fairfax Street
Alexandria, VA 22314
(703) 706-3171
ptmas@apta.org
http://www.apta.org

American Physiological Society (APS)

9650 Rockville Pike
Bethesda, MD 20814
(301) 634-7164
webmaster@the-APS.org
http://www.the-APS.org

American Registry of Diagnostic Medical Sonographers (ARDMS)

51 Monroe Street, Plaza East One
Rockville, MD 20850
(301) 738-8401
administration@ardms.org
http://www.ardms.org

American Registry of Radiologic Technologists (ARRT)

1255 Northland Drive
St. Paul, MN 55120
(651) 687-0048
http://www.arrt.org

American Society for Clinical Laboratory Science (ASCLS)

6701 Democracy Boulevard
Bethesda, MD 20817
(301) 657-2768
ascls@ascls.org
http://www.ascls.org

American Society of Clinical Pathologists (ASCP)

2100 W Harrison
Chicago, IL 60612
(312) 738-1336
info@ascp.org
http://www.ascp.org

American Society of Colleges of Pharmacy (AACP)

2830 Summer Oaks Drive
Bartlett, TN 38134
(901) 383-8119
aca@acainfo.org

American Society of Electroneurodiagnostic Technologists (ASET)

426 W 42nd Street
Kansas City, MO 64111
(816) 931-1120
info@aset.org
http://www.aset.org

American Society of Health System Pharmacists (AASHP)

7272 Wisconsin Avenue
Bethesda, MD 20814
(301) 657-3000
membership@ashp.org
http://www.ashp.org

American Society of Hospital Pharmacists

7272 Wisconsin Avenue
Bethesda, MD 20814
(301) 657-3000
www@ashp.org
http://www.ashp.org

American Society of Radiologic Technologists (ASRT)

15000 Central Avenue SE
Albuquerque, NM 87123
(505) 298-4500
customerinfo@asrt.org
http://www.asrt.org

American Society on Aging (ASA)

833 Market Street
San Francisco, CA 94103
(415) 974-9600
info@asaging.org
http://www.asaging.org

American Speech Language Hearing Association

10801 Rockville Pike
Rockville, MD 20852
(800) 638-8255
actioncenter@asha.org
http://www.asha.org

American Surgical Association (ASA)

c/o Robert P. Jones, Jr.
900 Cummings Center
Beverly, MA 01915
(978) 927-8330
asa@prri.com
http://www.americansurgical.info

American Therapeutic Recreation Association (ATRA)

1414 Prince Street
Alexandria, VA 22314
(703) 683-9420
national@atra-tr.org
http://www.atra-tr.org/atra.htm

American Thoracic Society (ATS)

61 Broadway
New York, NY 10006
(212) 315-8600
nblack@thoracic.org
http://www.thoracic.org

Anxiety Disorders Association of America (ADAA)

8730 Georgia Avenue
Silver Spring, MD 20910
(240) 485-1001
anxdis@adaa.org
http://www.adaa.org

Association for Gerontology in Higher Education (AGHE)

1030 15th Street NW
Washington, DC 20005
(202) 289-9806
info@aghe.org
http://www.aghe.org

Association for Surgical Education (ASE)

SIU School of Medicine
Department of Surgery
PO Box 19655
Springfield, IL 62794
(217) 545-3835
membershipo@surgicaleducation.com
http://www.surgicaleducation.com

Association of Clinical Research Professionals (ACRP)

500 Montgomery Street
Alexandria, VA 22314
(703) 254-8100
office@acrpnet.org
http://www.acrpnet.org

Association of Clinical Scientists

PO Box 1287
Middlebury, VT 05753
(802) 462-2507
clinsci@sover.net
http://www.clinicalscience.org

Association of Fundraising Professionals (AFP)

1101 King Street
Alexandria, VA 22314
(703) 684-0410
mnilsen@afpnet.org
http://www.afpnet.org

Association of Jewish Aging Services (AJAS)

316 Pennsylvania Avenue, SE
Washington, DC 20003
(202) 543-7500
ajas@ajas.org
http://ajas.org

Association of Medical Illustrators (AMI)

245 1st Street
Cambridge, MA 02142
(617) 395-8186
hq@ami.org
http://www.ami.org

Association of Physician Assistant Programs (APAP)

950 N. Washington Street
Alexandria, VA 22314
(703) 548-5538
apap@aapa.org
http://www.apap.org

Association of Physician Assistants In Cardiovascular Surgery (APACVS)

PO Box 4834
Englewood, CO 80155
(303) 221-5651
carol@goddardassociates.com
http://www.apacvs.org

Association of Professors of Gynecology and Obstetrics (APGO)

2130 Priest Bridge Drive
Crofton, MD 21114
(410) 451-9560
djohnson@apgo.org
http://www.apgo.org

Association of Reproductive Health Professionals (ARHP)

2401 Pennsylvania Avenue NW
Washington, DC 20037
(202) 466-3825
arhp@arhp.org
http://www.arhp.org

Association of Surgical Technologists (AST)

7108-C S Alton Way
Centennial, CO 80112
(303) 694-9130
bteutsch@ast.org
http://www.ast.org

Association of University Programs In Health Administration (AUPHA)

2000 N 14th Street
Arlington, VA 22201
(703) 894-0940
aupha@aupha.org
http://www.aupha.org

Cardiology Association

800 Peakwood Drive
Houston, TX 77090
(281) 444-1742

Cardiovascular Credentialing International (CCI)

1500 Sunday Drive

Raleigh, NC 27607
(919) 861-4539
director@cci-online.org

College of Osteopathic Healthcare Executives (COHE)

1730 Rhode Island Avenue NW
Washington, DC 20036

Commission on Opticianry Accreditation (COA)

PO Box 3073
Merrifield, VA 22116
coa@coaccreditation.com

Committee on Accreditation for Respiratory Care (CARC)

1248 Harwood Road
Bedford, TX 76021
(817) 283-2835
info@coarc.com
http://www.coarc.com

Council for Advancement and Support of Education (CASE)

1307 New York Avenue NW
Washington, DC 20005
(202) 328-2273
memberservicecenter@case.org
http://www.case.org

Council on Social Work Education (CSWE)

1725 Duke Street
Alexandria, VA 22314
(703) 683-8080
orders@cswe.org
http://www.cswe.org

Cystic Fibrosis Foundation (CFF)

6931 Arlington Road

Bethesda, MD 20814
(301) 951-4422
info@cff.org
http://www.cff.org

Dental Assisting National Board (NANB)

676 N. St. Clair
Chicago, IL 60611
(312) 642-3368
danbmail@danb.org
http://www.danb.org

Direct Marketing Association (DMA)

1120 Avenue of the Americas
New York, NY 10036
(212) 768-7277
customerservice@the-dma.org
http://www.the-dma.org

Direct Marketing Educational Foundation (DMEF)

1120 Avenue of the Americas
New York, NY 10036
(212) 768-7277
president@the-dma.org
http://www.the-dma.org/dmef

Hospice Foundation of America (HFA)

2001 S Street NW
Washington, DC 20009
(800) 854-3402
david@hospicefoundation.org
http://www.hospicefoundation.org

Medical Group Management Association (MGMA)

104 Inverness Terrace East
Englewood, CO 80112
(303) 799-1111

infocenter@mgma.com
http://www.mgma.com

NAADAC The Association for Addiction Professionals (NAADAC)

901 N Washington Street, Suite 600
Alexandria, VA 22314 USA
(703) 741-7686
naadac@naadac.org
http://www.naadac.org

National Academy of Opticianry (NAO)

8401 Corporate Drive
Landover, MD 20785
(301) 577-4828
info@nao.org
http://www.nao.org

National Association for Human Development (NAHD)

1424 16th Street NW
PO Box 100
Washington, DC 20036
(202) 328-2191

National Association for Practical Nurse Education and Service (NAPNES)

PO Box 25647
Alexandria, VA 22313
(301) 588-2491
napnes@bellatlantic.net
http://www.napnes.org

National Association of Boards of Pharmacy (NABP)

700 Busse Highway
Park Ridge, IL 60068
(847) 698-6227
custserv@nabp.net
http://www.nabp.net

National Association of Emergency Medical Technicians (NAEMT)

PO Box 1400
Clinton, MS 39060
(601) 924-7744
info@naemt.org
http://www.naemt.org

National Association of Professional Geriatric Care Managers (PGCM)

1604 N Country Club Road
Tucson, AZ 85716-3102
(520) 881-8008
info@caremanager.org

National Association of Social Workers (NASW)

750 First Street NE
Washington, DC 20002
(202) 408-8600
press@naswdc.org
http://www.naswpress.org

National Association of Substance Abuse Trainers and Educators (NASATE)

6400 Press Drive
Southern University at New Orleans
New Orleans, LA 70126
(504) 286-5234
eharrell@suno.edu

National Board for Certified Counselors (NBCC)

3 Terrace Way
Greensboro, NC 27403
(336) 547-0607
nbcc@nbcc.org
http://www.nbcc.org

National Board for Respiratory Care (NBRC)

8310 Nieman Road
Lenexa, KS 66214
(913) 599-4200
nbrc-info@nbrc.org
http://www.nbrc.org

National Center for Homeopathy (NCH)

801 N Fairfax Street
Alexandria, VA 22314
(703) 548-7790
info@homeopathic.org
http://www.homeopathic.org

National Coalition of Arts Therapy Associations (NCATA)

c/o AMTA
8455 Colesville Road
Silver Spring, MD 20910
(201) 224-9146
amforrester@compuserve.com
http://www.nccata.org

National Council for Therapeutic Recreation Certification (NCTRC)

7 Elmwood Drive
New City, NY 10956
(845) 639-1439
nctrc@nctrc.org
http://www.nctrc.org

National Federation of Licensed Practical Nurses (NFLP)

605 Poole Drive
Garner, NC 27529
(919) 779-0046
cbarbour@mgmt4u.com
http://www.nflpn.org

National League for Nursing (NLN)

61 Broadway

New York, NY 10006
(212)363-5555
http://www.nln.org

National Student Nurses' Association (NSNA)

45 Main Street
Brooklyn, NY 11201
(718) 210-0705
nsna@nsna.org
http://www.nsna.org

National Therapeutic Recreation Society (NTRS)

22377 Belmont Ridge Road
Ashburn, VA 20148-4501
(703) 858-0784
ntrsnrpa@nrpa.org
http://www.nrpa.org

Opticians Association of America (OAA)

441 Carlisle Drive
Herndon, VA 20170
(703) 437-8780
oaa@opticians.org
http://www.opticians.org

Physician Assistant Education Program

300 North Washington Street
Alexandria, VA 2231
(703) 548-5538
info@PAEAonline.org
http://www.paeaonline.org

Public Relations Society of America (PRSA)

33 Maiden Lane
New York, NY 10038
(212) 460-1400
exec@prsa.org
http://www.prsa.org

Society for Cardiovascular Magnetic Resonance (SCMR)

c/o Tom Sims
19 Mantua Road
Mount Royal, NJ 08061
(856) 423-8955
hq@scmr.org
http://www.scmr.org

Society for Vascular Technology (SVT)

4601 Presidents Drive
Lanham, MD 20706
(301)459-7550
info@svtnet.org

Society of Air Force Physician Assistants (SAFPA)

c/o Teshia A. Birts
950 N Washington Street
Alexandria, VA 22314
safpa@aapa.org
http://www.aapa.org/safpa

Society of Cardiovascular Anesthesiologists (SCA)

2209 Dickens Road
PO Box 11086
Richmond, VA 23230
(804) 282-0084
sca@societyhq.com
http://www.scahq.org

Society of Critical Care Medicine (SCCM)

701 Lee Street
Des Plaines, IL 60016
(847) 827-6869
info@sccm.org
http://www.sccm.org

Society of Diagnostic Medical Sonography (SDMS)

2745 N Dallas Parkway
Plano, TX 75093
(214) 473-8057
ccowser@sdms.org
http://www.sdms.org

Society of Interventional Radiology (SIR)

10201 Lee Highway
Fairfax, VA 22030
(703) 691-1805
http://www.sirweb.org

Society of Invasive Cardiovascular Professionals (SICP)

PO Box 61606
Virginia Beach, VA 23466
(757) 497-3694
http://www.sicp.com

APPENDIX II

CAREER WEB SITES

The Internet is a premier resource for information, no matter what you need. Surfing the Web can help you locate almost anything you want from information to services and everything in between.

Throughout the appendices of this book, whenever possible, Web site addresses have been included to help you find information quicker. This listing contains an assortment of various general and sports-related career and job Web sites that may be of value to you in your career.

Use this list as a beginning. More sites are emerging every day. This listing is for your information. The author is not responsible for any site content. Inclusion or exclusion in this listing does not imply any one site is endorsed or recommended over another by the author.

Access Nurses
http://www.accessnurses.com

Advanced Practice Jobs
http://www.advancedpracticejobs.com

All Therapy Jobs
http://www.alltherapyjobs.com

Best Nurses.com
http://www.bestnursejobs.com

CampusRN.com
http://www.campusrn.com

Career Builder.com
http://www.careerbuilder.com

Dental Assistant Jobs
http://www.dentalassistantjobs.com

Diversity Health Works
http://www.diversityhealthworks.com

DocCafe.com
http://www.doccafe.com

EmploymentForPhysicians.com
http://www.employmentforphysicians.com

Happy Career
http://www.happycareer.com

Health CareerNet
http://www.healthcareernet.com

HealthCareerWeb.com
http://www.healthcareerweb.com

HealthCareSource
http://www.healthcaresource.com

HEALTHeCAREERS.COM (HECC)
http://www.healthecareers.com

HealthNetwork Usa
http://www.hnusa.com

HireHealth.com
http://www.hirehealth.com

hireRX
http://www.hirerx.com

Hospital Jobs Online
http://www.hospitaljobsonline.com

Hot Jobs.com
http://www.hotjobs.com

HSpeople.com
http://www.hspeople.com

Human Services Career Network
http://www.hscareers.com

Job Bank USA
http://www.jobbankusa.com/

Job.com
http://www.job.com

jobscience.com
http://jobs.jobscience.com

Jobs4MedicalAdmin
http://www.jobs4medicaladmin.com

JobsinTherapy
http://www.jobsintherapy.com

JobsStat.com
http://www.jobsstat.com

MedHunters.com
http://www.medhunters.com

Medical Job Street
http://www.medicaljobstreet.com

Medical Staff Recruiters
http://www.medicalstaffrecruiters.com

MedicalWorkforce.com
http://www.medicalworkforce.com

MediCenter.com
http://www.medicalcareercenters.com

MedZilla
http://www.medzilla.com

MDJobSite.com
http://www.mdjobsite.com

Monster.com
http://www.monster.com

Monster Healthcare
http://www.medsearch.com

MyNurseJobs
http://www.mynursejobs.com

The New Social Worker online
http://www.socialworker.com

Nurse-Recruiter.com
http://www.nurse-recruiter.com

Nurses123.com
http://www.nurses123.com

Nursetown.com
http://www.nursetown.com

NurseUniverse.com
http://www.nurseuniverse.com

nursing-jobs.com
http://www.nursing-jobs.com

Nursing Jobs
http://www.nursing-jobs.us

Nursing Spectrum
http://www.nursingspectrum.com

PharmaceuticalJobs-usa.com
http://www.pharmaceuticaljobs-usa.com

PharmaOpportunities
http://www.pharmaopportunities.com

PharmWeb
http://www.pharmweb.net

PhyJob.com
http://www.phyjob.com

PhysEmp.com: Physician Employment
http://www.physemp.com

PhysicianWork.com
http://www.physicianwork.com

podiatristjobs.com
http://www.podiatristjobs.com

Pohly's Net Guide: Healthcare Employment Resources
http://members.aol.com/pjpohly/links.htm

Recruitech
http://www.recruitech.com

The Scientist Careers
http://www.biomedscientistjobs.com

SocialService.com
http://www.socialservice.com

TherapyJobs.com
http://www.therapyjobs.com

WorkinHealthcare.net
http://www.workinhealthcare.net

Worldwide Medical Services
http://www.wwmedical.com

BIBLIOGRAPHY

A. Books

There are thousands of books on all aspects of medicine and health care. Sometimes just reading about someone else's success, inspire you, motivates you or just helps you to come up with ideas to help you attain your own dreams.

Books can be a treasure trove of information if you want to learn about a particular aspect of a career or gain more knowledge about how something in the industry works.

The books listed below are separated into general categories. Subjects often overlap. Use this listing as a beginning. Check out your local library, bookstore or online retailer for other books that might interest you about the industry.

Alternative Medicine

Boericke, William. *A Compend of the Principles of Homeopathy*. Whitefish, MT: Kessinger Publishing, 2004.

Kronwitter, Carol. *Women of Grace: Women Healers and Healing Practices*. Conover, WI: D & S Publications, 2001.

Dorling Kindersley Publishing Staff. *Encyclopedia of Homeopathy*. New York: Dorling Kindersley, 2006.

Institute of Medicine. *Complementary And Alternative Medicine in the United States*. Washington, DC: National Academies Press, 2005.

Schmukler, Alan. *Homeopathy*. Woodbury, MN: Llewellyn Publications, 2006.

Career Planning

Field, Shelly. *The Unofficial Guide to Hot Careers*. New York: Hungry Minds, 2000.

Field, Shelly. *Career Opportunities In Health Care*. New York: Facts On File, 2007.

Vault Editors. *Vault Guide to the Top Health Care Employers*. New York, 2007.

Dentistry

Aspatore Books Staff. *The Art and Science of Being a Dentist: Leading Dentists Reveal the Secrets to Professional and Personal Success*. Boston: Aspatore Books, 2003.

Gaylor, Linda. *The Administrative Dental Assistant*. Philadelphia: Elsevier Health Sciences Division, 2006.

Dietetics, Nutrition, and Food Service

Bowling, Tim. *Nutritional Support in Hospital for Adults and Children: A Handbook for Hospital Practice*. Abingdon, UK: Radcliffe Publishing, 2003.

Puckett, Ruby P. *Food Service Manual For Health Care Institutions*. Hoboken, NJ: John Wiley & Sons, 2004.

Whitney, Ellie. *Nutrition For Health and Health Care*. Pacific Grove, CA: Brooks/Cole, 2006.

Health Care

Gardner, Fiona, Jan Fook, and Sue White. *Critical Reflection in Health and Social Care*. New York: McGraw-Hill Education, 2006.

Health Care Administration

Aspatore Books Staff. *The Health Care Management Team: The Roles, Responsibilities, and Leadership Strategies of CEOs, CTOs, Marketing Executives, and HR Leaders*. Boston: Aspatore Books, 2006.

Behan, Pamela. *Solving the Health Care Problem: How Other Nations Have Succeeded and Why America Has Failed*. Albany: State University of New York Press, 2006.

Dunn, Ross, and Theo Haimann. *Haimann's Healthcare Management*. Chicago: Health Administration Press, 2006.

Hayward, Cynthia. *Healthcare Facility Planning: Thinking Strategically*. Chicago: Health Administration Press, 2005.

Kaufman, Kenneth. *Best Practice Financial Management: Six Key Concepts for Healthcare Leaders*. Chicago: Health Administration Press, 2006.

Stewart, Yaschica. *The Complete Guide to Planning, Starting, Operating, and Managing A Medical Staffing Agency*. Morrisville, NC: Lulu.com, 2005.

Health Care Education

Diekelmann, Nancy L. *Teaching the Practitioners of Care: New Pedagogies for the Health Professions*. Madison: University of Wisconsin Press, 2003.

Evans, Lois K. *Academic Nursing Practice: Helping to Shape the Future of Healthcare*. New York: Springer Publishing Company, 2004.

King, Cedric. *Bedside Manner: During the Time That Was Best Ever for Patient and Doctor Alike—Now Gone with the Summer Wind*. Philadelphia: Xlibris Corporation, 2003.

Health Care Management

Schermerhorn, John, R. *Health Care Management*. New York: John Wiley, 2007.

Shortell, Stephen M., and Arnold D. Kaluzny. *Health Care Management: Organization Design and Behavior*. Albany, NY: Thomson Delmar Learning, 2005.

Ginter, Peter M. *Strategic Management of Health Care Organizations*. Blackwell Publishing Professional, 2005.

Health Care Marketing, Public Relations, Planning, and Development

Aspatore Books Staff. *Maximizing Your Marketing Budget in the Health Care and Pharmaceutical Industries: The Over-Arching Issues You Need to Know*. Boston: Aspatore Books, 2006.

Berkowitz, Eric N. *Essentials of Health Care Marketing*. Sudbury, MA: Jones & Bartlett Publishers, 2006.

Field, Shelly. *Career Opportunities In Advertising and Public Relations*. New York: Facts On File, 2005.

Fortenberry, John L., Jr. *Marketing Tools for Healthcare Executives*. Oxford, MS: Oxford Crest, 2006.

Hartunian, Paul. *Power Publicity For Non-Profit Organizations*. Upper Montclair, NJ: Clifford Publishing, 2006.

Kemper, John. *Launching a Healthcare Capital Project: What Every Executive Should Know*. Chicago: Health Administration Press, 2004.

Liles, Jason. *Building a Successful Practice: A Step by Step Guide to Building and Marketing Your Own Profitable Healthcare Business*. Santa Rosa, CA: Heart to Heart Medical Center, 2004.

McGinly, William C. *Philanthropy and Health Care, No. 47: New Directions for Philanthropic*. Edison, NJ: John Wiley & Sons, 2006.

Murray, Katherine. *Fundraising For Dummies.* Edison, NJ: John Wiley and Sons, 2005.

How to Achieve Superior Marketing Results from Your Hospital's Newsletter. Montvale, NJ: Dowden Publishing Company, 2005.

Humor in Health Care

Schwartz, Enid A. *Humor in Healthcare: Laughter Prescription.* Western Schools, 2006.

Du Pre, Athena. *Humor and the Healing Arts: A Multimethod Analysis of Humor Use in Healthcare.* Lawrence Erlbaum Associates, Incorporated: Mahwah, NJ, 1997.

Q Fever Editors. *Q Fever! Medical Humor and Satire for Healthcare Professionals.* North Charlotte, SC: BookSurge, 2003.

Long-term Care

Berzoff, Joan. *Living with Dying: A Handbook for End-of-Life Healthcare Practitioners.* London, UK: Kegan Paul International, 2004.

Gerlach, Mary Jo, and Barbara Hegner. *Assisting In Long Term Care.* Albany, NY: Thomson Delmar Learning, 2006.

Medical Assisting

Fremgen, Bonnie. *Pearson's Comprehensive Medical Assisting.* East Rutherford, NJ: Prentice Hall PTR, 2006.

Koprucki, Victoria R. *Client Centered Care for Clinical Medical Assisting.* Albany, NY: Thomson Delmar Learning, 2006.

Medicine

Aronson, Neil. *That's My Bellybutton: Memoirs of a Pediatrician.* Philadelphia: Xlibris Corporation, 2006.

Association of American Medical Colleges. *Medical School Admission Requirements (MSAR) 2007-2008: The Most Authoritative Guide to U.S. and Canadian Medical Schools* (Medical School Admission Requirements, United States and Canada) 2006.

Danek, Jennifer, and Danek, Marita. *Becoming a Physician: A Practical and Creative Guide to Planning a Career in Medicine.* New York: Wiley, 1997.

Iserson, Kenneth, V. *Get into Medical School: A Guide for the Perplexed,* 2d ed. Tuscon, AZ: Galen Press, 1997.

Maier, Thomas. *Dr. Spock: An American Life.*

Konner, Melvin. *Becoming a Doctor: A Journey of Initiation in Medical School.*

Medical Records and Health Information

McMiller, Kathryn. *Being a Medical Records/Health Information Clerk.* Old Tappan, NJ: Pearson Education, 2003.

McMiller, Kathryn. *Being a Medical Records/Health Information Clerk.* Upper Saddle River, NJ: Pearson, 2006.

Peavler Bull, Cynthia. *How to Be A Medical Transcriptionist: A Beginner's Guide to Real Facts and Inside Secrets That Lead to A Successful Career.* Townsend, VA: Cynthia Peavler Bull, 2005.

Nursing

Bozell, Jeanna. *Anatomy of a Job Search: A Nurse's Guide to Finding and Landing the Job You Want.* Philadelphia: Lippincott Williams & Wilkins, 1999.

Ettinger, Laura Ellizabeth. *Nurse-Midwifery: The Birth of a New American Profession.* Columbus, OH: Ohio State University Press, 2006.

Kimble, Melissal. *Nursing Careers: Over 50 Specialties.* Sandy, UT: Aardvark Publishing Company, 2006.

Vallano, Annette. *Your Career In Nursing.* New York: Kaplan Books, 2006.

Nursing Assistants

McGraw-Hill Staff. *The Effective Nursing Assistant,* Student Edition. New York: McGraw-Hill, 2006.

Van Rhee, James. *Physician Assistant Board Review: Certification and Recertification with Online Exam*

Simulation. Philadelphia: Elsevier Health Sciences Division, 2006.

Paramedics and Emergency Medical Technicians

Hancock, Cheryl. *EMT Career Starter.* New York: LearningExpress, 2001.

LearningExpress Staff. *Paramedic Exam.* New York: LearningExpress, 2006.

Pharmacology

Martin, Hyacinth C. *Pharmacology.* Albany, NY: Thomson Delmar Learning, 2006.

Moh, Mary E. *Pharmacy Technician.* Philadelphia: Lippincott Williams & Wilkins, 2005.

Rudin, Markus. *Imaging in Drug Discovery and Early Clinical Trials.* Cambridge, MA: Birkhauser Boston, 2006.

Thurston, David E. *Pharmacological and Chemical Aspects of Chemotherapeutic Drugs.* Philadelphia: Taylor & Francis Group, 2006.

Woodrow, Ruth. *Essentials of Pharmacology for Health Occupations.* Albany, NY: Thomson Delmar Learning, 2006.

Physician Assistants

Blessing, Dennis, J. *Physician Assistant's Guide To Research and Medical Literature.* Philadelphia: F. A. Davis Company, 2005.

Emblad, Gillian Lewke. *Physician Assistant Exam Review.* New York: McGraw-Hill Professional Publishing, 2005.

Heinrich, J. Jeffrey. *Physician Assistants: Who Are They?* Sudbury, MA: Jones & Bartlett Publishers, 2006.

Sacks, Terence J. *Opportunities in Physician Assistant Careers.* New York: McGraw-Hill Companies, 2002.

Radiology and Biotechnology

Buck, Stacie. *Radiology Technologist's Coding Compliance Training Handbook.* Opus Communications: 2005.

Callaway, William J. *Mosby's Comprehensive Review of Radiography: The Complete Study Guide and Career Planner.* Philadelphia: Elsevier, 2005.

Risk Management

Kavaler, Florence and Spiegel, Allen. *Risk Management in Health Care Institutions: A Strategic Approach.* Boston: Jones and Bartlett Publishers, 2003.

B. Periodicals, Publications and Webzines

Magazines, newspapers, membership bulletins and newsletters help keep you up to date with industry happenings and abreast of new trends. There are various periodicals and trade magazines geared towards different parts of the health care industry. Use this listing as a beginning. Space limitations make it impossible to list all periodicals.

Check out your local library, bookstore or newsstand for additional titles of interest. You might also want to contact hospitals, health care facilities, physicians offices, and other medical group offices to see if they would be willing to let you borrow and read trade magazines they might get. College libraries may also be a good source to locate trade magazines that you might not otherwise be able to find easily. Don't forget to look for Web versions of periodicals. While they may require paid subscriptions, most at least provide some free content that you may find useful.

ALTERNATIVE MEDICINE

Alternative Medicine Alert
http://www.altmednet.com/

ART THERAPY

American Journal of Art Therapy
36 College Street
Montpelier, VT 05602
(802) 828-8540

Art Therapy: Journal of the American Art Therapy Association
American Art Therapy Association, Inc.
5999 Stevenson Avenue
Alexandria, VA 22304
(847) 949-6064
info@arttherapy.org
http://www.arttherapy.org

AUDIOLOGY

American Academy of Audiology
11730 Plaza America Drive
Reston, VA 20190
(703) 790-8466
jwilson@audiology.org
http://www.audiology.org

American Journal of Audiology
10801 Rockville Pike
Rockville, MD 20852
(301) 897-5700
subscribe@asha.org
http://www.asha.org

CHIROPRACTIC

ACA News
American Chiropractic Association
1701 Clarendon Boulevard
Arlington, VA 22209
(703) 276-8800
memberinfo@amerchiro.org
http://www.amerchiro.org

Journal of Sports Chiropractic and Rehabilitation (Online Edition)
Atwood Publishing, LLC
380 Wright Road
PO Box 400
Norwalk, IA 50211

(515) 981-9340
http://www.atwood.com

CONSULTING

Consultants News
One Phoenix Mill Lane
Peterborough, NH 03458
(603) 924-0900
dyard@kennedyinfo.com
http://www.kennedyinfo.com

COUNSELING/MENTAL HEALTH

International Journal of Mental Health and Addiction
233 Spring Street
New York, NY 10013
(212) 460-1500
service-ny@springer.com
http://www.springer.com

Journal of Mental Health and Aging
11 W 42nd Street
New York, NY 10036
(212) 431-4370
contactus@springerpub.com
http://www.springerpub.com

Journal of Substance Abuse and Therapy
360 Park Avenue South
New York, NY 10010
(212) 633-3990
usinfo-f@elsevier.com
http://www.elsevier.com

DANCE THERAPY

American Journal of Dance Therapy
233 Spring Street
New York, NY 10013
(212) 460-1500

service-ny@springer.com
http://www.springer.com

DENTISTRY

Journal of American College of Dentists
839 Quince Orchard Boulevard
Gaithersburg, MD 20878
(301) 977-3223
lisa@facd.org

The Dental Assistant
American Dental Assistant Association
35 E Wacker Drive
Chicago, IL 60601
(312) 541-1550

DIET AND NUTRITION

International Journal of Sports Nutrition and Exercise Metabolism
1607 N Market Street
PO Box 5076
Champaign, IL 61825
(217) 351-5076
orders@hkusa.com
http://www.humankinetics.com

Sports Nutrition News
PO Box 986
Evanston, IL 60204
(708) 251-5950

Tufts University Health & Nutrition Letter
Tufts University
School of Nutrition
Medford, MA 02155
(212) 668-0411

FUND-RAISING

Advancing Philanthropy
1101 King Street
Alexandria, VA 22314
(800) 666-3863
http://www.afpnet.org

Chronicle of Philanthropy
PO Box 1989
Marion, OH 43306
(202) 466-1080
orders@allenpress.com;
subscriptions@chronicle.com
http://chronicle.com

GERIATRICS

Geriatric Nursing
11830 Westline Industrial Drive
St Louis, MO 63146
(407) 345-4299
elspcs@elsevier.com
http://www.us.elsevierhealth.com

Geriatrics
Advanstar Communications, Inc.
7500 Old Oak Road
Cleveland, OH 44130
(440) 243-8100
info@advanstar.com
http://www.advanstar.com

Journal of Aging and Ethnicity
11 W 42nd Street
New York, NY 10036
(212) 431-4370
contactus@springerpub.com
http://www.springerpub.com

Journal of Women and Aging
10 Alice Street

Binghamton, NY 13904
(607) 722-5857
getinfo@haworthpress.com
http://www.haworthpress.com

GRANTS

Directory of Biomedical and Health Care Grants
Oryx Press
88 Post Road West
Westport, CT 06881
(203) 226-3571
sales@greenwood.com
http://www.greenwood.com

HEALTH CARE ADMINSITRATION

Health Care Management
J A I Press Inc.
360 Park Avenue South
New York, NY 10010
(212) 989-5800
usinfo-f@elsevier.com
http://www.elsevier.com

HEALTH CARE PROMOTION

American Journal of Health Promotion
1120 Chester Avenue
Cleveland, OH 44114
(248) 682-0707
http://www.healthpromotionjournal.com

HOMEOPATHIC MEDICINE

American Homeopathy
5305 Lee Highway
Springfield, VA 22207

American Journal of Homeopathic Medicine
801 N Fairfax Street
Alexandria, VA 22314
(303) 898-5477
http://www.homeopathyusa.org

Homeotherapy: Journal of Classical Homeopathy
Hahneman Foundation
PO Box 9008
San Diego, CA 92109
(714) 270-3064

HOSPITALS

American Hospital Association News
American Hospital Association
http://www.hospitalconnect.com/ahanews_app/jsp/ahanews.jsp

LABORATORIES

Advance for Medical Laboratory Professionals
Merion Publications, Inc.
2900 Horizon Drive
King of Prussia, PA 19406
(610) 278-1400
advance@merion.com
http://www.advanceweb.com

MARKETING, ADVERTISING, AND PUBLIC RELATIONS

Advertising Age
Crain Communications, Inc.
711 Third Avenue
New York, NY 10017
(212) 210-0280
info@crain.com
http://www.crain.com

Contacts: The Media Pipeline for PR People

Mercomm, Inc.
550 Executive Boulevard
Ossining, NY 10562
(914)923-9400

Creativity

Crain Communications, Inc.
711 Third Avenue
New York, NY 10017
(212) 210-0280
info@crain.com
http://www.crain.com

Journal of Advertising Research

Advertising Research Foundation, Inc.
432 Park Avenue South
New York, NY 10016
(212) 751-5656
(212) 319-5265 (fax)
subscriptions@warc.com
http://www.warc.com

Healthcare P R & Marketing News

1201 Seven Locks Road
Potomac, MD 20854

Health Marketing Quarterly

Haworth Press, Inc.
10 Alice Street
Binghamton, NY 13904
(607) 722-5857
getinfo@haworthpress.com
http://www.haworthpress.com

Journal of Hospital Marketing & Public Relations

Haworth Press, Inc.
10 Alice Street
Binghamton, NY 13904
(607) 722-5857
getinfo@haworthpress.com
http://www.haworthpress.com

Journal of Hospital Marketing & Public Relations

Haworth Press, Inc.
10 Alice Street
Binghamton, NY 13904
(607) 722-5857
getinfo@haworthpress.com
http://www.haworthpress.com

Journal of Marketing

311 South Wacker Driver
Chicago, IL 60606
(312) 542-9000
info@ama.org
http://www.ama.org

Journal of Marketing Research

311 South Wacker Driver
Chicago, IL 60606
(312) 542-9000
info@ama.org
http://www.ama.org

Marketing News

311 South Wacker Driver
Chicago, IL 60606
(312) 542-9000
info@ama.org
http://www.ama.org/pubs/mn/pub2.html

Med Ad News

820 Bear Tavern Road
Trenton, NJ 08628
(609) 530-0044

Public Relations Journal

PRSA
33 Maiden Lane
New York, NY 10038

(212) 460-1400
http://www.prsa.org

Public Relations Quarterly
Hudson Associates
44 W Market Street
Box 311
Rhinebeck, NY 12572
(845) 876-2081
hphudson@aol.com
http://www.newsletter-clearinghse.com

Public Relations Strategist
Public Relations Strategist
33 Maiden Lane
New York, NY 10038
(212) 460-1400
http://www.prsa.org

MEDICINE

American Medical News
American Medical Association
515 N. State Street
Chicago, IL 60610
(800) 621-8335
http://www.ama-assn.org

MUSIC THERAPY

Journal of Music Therapy
American Music Therapy Association
8455 Colesville Road
Silver Springs, MD 20910
(301) 589-3300
http://www.musictherapy.org

NURSING

AANA Journal
222 S Prospect Avenue
Park Ridge, IL 60068

(847) 692-7050
info@aana.com
http://www.aana.com

American Journal for Nursing Practitioners
American College of Nurse Practitioners
111 19th Street NW
Washington, DC 20036
(202) 659-2190
http://www.webnp.net

American Journal of Critical Care
PO Box 626
Holmes, PA 19043
ajcc@aacn.org
http://ajcc.aacnjournals.org

American Journal of Critical Care
101 Columbia
Aliso Viejo, CA 92656
(949) 362-2000
http://www.aacn.org

Clinical Nurse Specialist
PO Box 1620
Hagerstown, MD 21741
(800) 638-3030
http://www.cns-journal.com

Critical Care Nurse
American Association of Critical Care Nurses
101 Columbia
Aliso Viejo, CA 92656
(946) 362-2000
ajcc@aol.com
http://ccn.aacnjournals.org/

Journal of Emergency Nursing
11830 Westline Industrial Drive
St Louis, MO 63146
(407) 345-4299

elspcs@elsevier.com
http://www.us.elsevierhealth.com

Journal of Gerontological Nursing
6900 Grove Road
Thorofare, NJ 08086
(856) 848-1000
http://www.slackinc.com

Journal of Nursing Administration
Lippincott Williams & Wilkins
530 Walnut Street
Philadelphia, PA 19106
(215) 521-8300
custserv@lww.com
http://www.lww.com

Journal of Nursing Care Quality
Lippincott Williams & Wilkins
530 Walnut Street
Philadelphia, PA 19106
(215) 521-8300
custserv@lww.com
http://www.lww.com

Nursing Education Perspectives
National League for Nursing
61 Broadway
New York, NY 10006
(212) 363-5555
nlnweb@nln.org
http://www.nln.org

OCCUPATIONAL THERAPY

Occupational Therapy In Mental Health
10 Alice Street
Binghamton, NY 13904
(607) 722-5857
getinfo@haworthpress.com
http://www.haworthpress.com

PHARMACY

Advances in Pharmacy
Aspen Publishers, Inc.
111 Eighth Avenue
New York, NY 10011
(212) 771-0600
customer.service@aspenpubl.com
http://www.aspenpublishers.com

American Pharmacists Association. Journal
American Pharmacists Association
2215 Constitution Avenue N W
Washington, DC 20037
(202) 628-4410
japha@aphanet.org
http://www.japha.org

American Journal of Pharmaceutical Education
American Association of Colleges of Pharmacy
1426 Prince Street
Alexandria, VA 22314
(703) 739-2330
mail@aacp.org
http://www.aacp.org

Consultant Pharmacist
American Society of Consultant Pharmacists
1321 Duke Street
Alexandria, VA 22314
(703) 739-1300
http://www.ascp.com/public/pubs/tcp

Journal of the American Pharmaceutical Association
John Wiley & Sons, Inc.
111 River Street
Hoboken, NJ 07030
(800) 825-7550

uscs-wis@wiley.com
http://www.wiley.com

PHYSICAL THERAPY

Advance for Physical Therapists and PT Assistants

Merion Publications, Inc.
2900 Horizon Drive
King of Prussia, PA 19406
(610) 278-1400
advance@merion.com
http://www.advanceweb.com

Physical Therapy

American Physical Therapy Association
1111 N Fairfax Street
Alexandria, VA 22314
(703) 684-2782
ptunderscorejournal@apta.org
http://www.apta.org

Physical Therapy Products

Novicom, Inc.
6100 Center Drive
Los Angeles, CA 90045
http://www.novicom.com

PHYSICIANS AND PHYSICIAN ASSISTANTS

American Academy of Family Physicians

11400 Tomahawk Creek Parkway
Leawood, KS 66211
(913) 906-6000
http://www.aafp.org

American Academy of Physician Assistants News

950 N Washington Street
Alexandria, VA 22314
(703) 836-2272
http://www.aapa.org

Association of American Physicians & Surgeons News

Association of American Physicians & Surgeons, Inc.
1601 N Tucson Boulevard
Tucson, AZ 85716
(800) 635-1196
aaps@aapsonline.org
http://www.aapsonline.org

PREVENTIVE MEDICINE

American Journal of Preventive Medicine

Elsevier Inc.
360 Park Avenue South
New York, NY 10010
(212) 633-3730
usinfo-f@elsevier.com
http://www.elsevier.com

RADIOLOGY

Advance for Imaging and Radiation Therapy Professionals

Merion Publications, Inc.
2900 Horizon Drive
King of Prussia, PA 19406
(800) 355-5627
http://www.advanceweb.com

RESPIRATORY CARE

Advance for Respiratory Care Practitioners

Merion Publications, Inc.
2900 Horizon Drive
King of Prussia, PA 19406
(610) 278-1400
advance@merion.com
http://www.advanceweb.com

Journal of Nuclear Medicine
Society of Nuclear Medicine
1850 Samuel Morse Drive
Reston, VA 20190
(703) 708-9000
salexand@snm.org
http://www.snm.org

SOCIAL SERVICES

Clinical Supervisor
10 Alice Street
Binghamton, NY 13904
(607) 722-5857
getinfo@haworthpress.com
http://www.haworthpress.com

The New Social Worker
White Hat Communications
PO Box 5390
Harrisburg, PA 17110
(717) 238-3787
linda.grobman@paonline.com
http://www.socialworker.com/

Social Work in Mental Health
10 Alice Street
Binghamton, NY 13904
(607) 722-5857
getinfo@haworthpress.com
http://www.haworthpress.com

Social Work With Groups
10 Alice Street
Binghamton, NY 13904
(607) 722-5857
getinfo@haworthpress.com
http://www.haworthpress.com

VISION CARE

Optometry Journal of the American Optometric Association
243 N Lindbergh Boulevard
St. Louis, MO 63141
(314) 991-4100
http://www.aoa.org

INDEX

W